# FOR THE LOVE OF THE COUNTRY

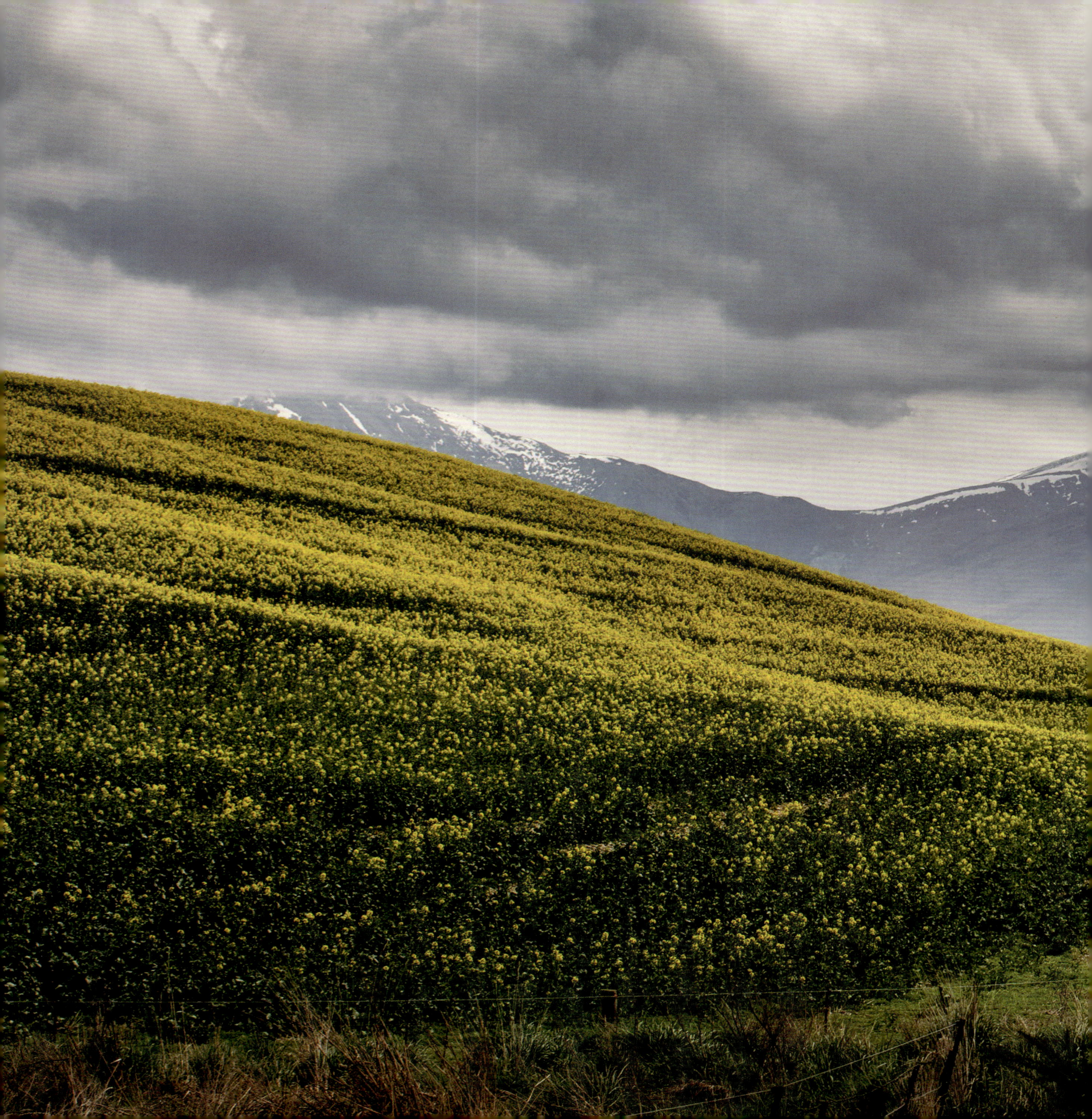

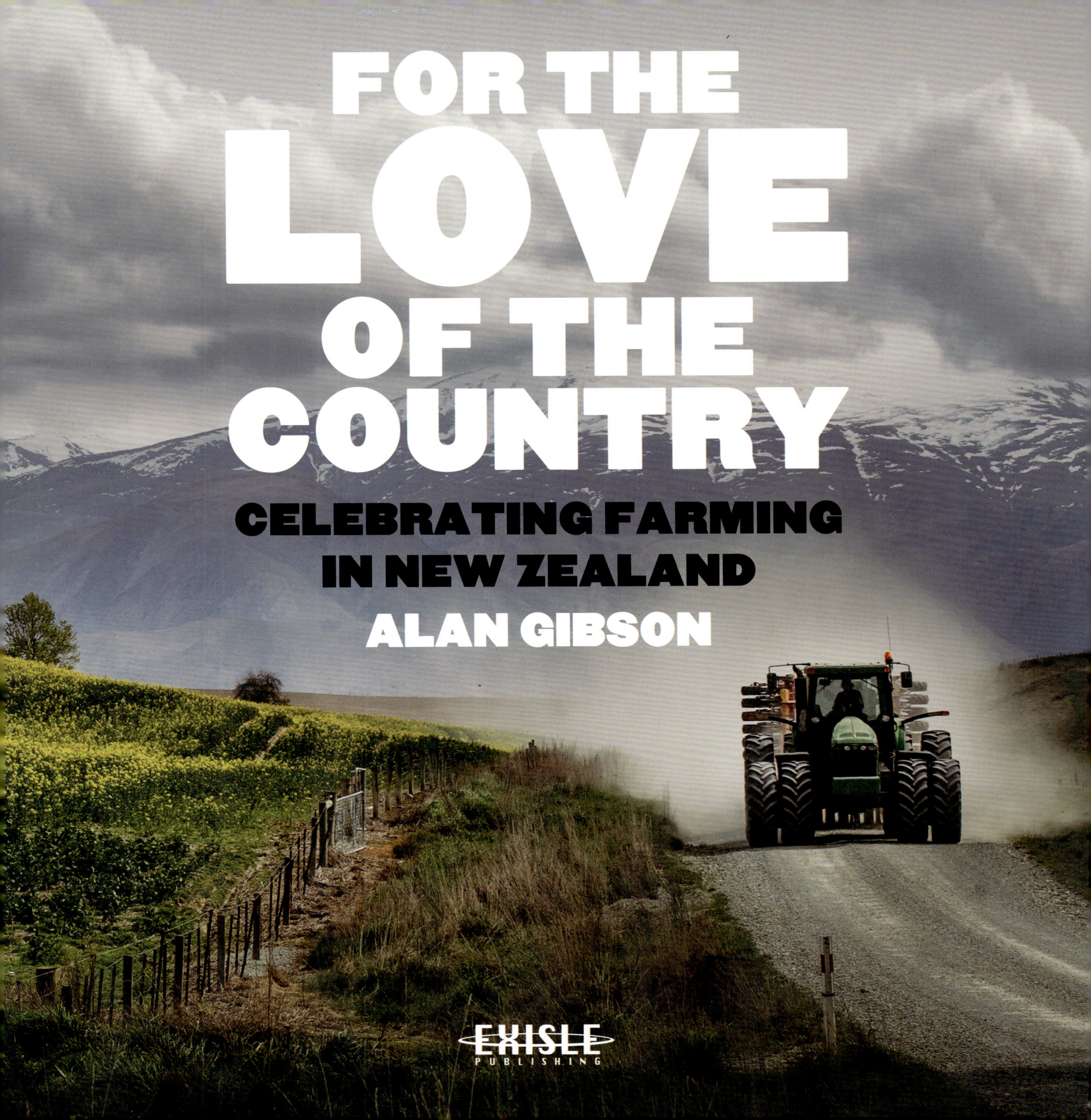

# FOR THE LOVE OF THE COUNTRY

## CELEBRATING FARMING IN NEW ZEALAND

ALAN GIBSON

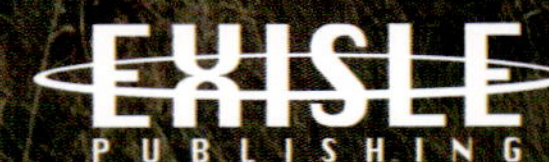

First published 2022

Exisle Publishing Pty Ltd
226 High Street, Dunedin, 9016, New Zealand
PO Box 864, Chatswood, NSW 2057, Australia
www.exislepublishing.com



A CiP record for this book is available from the National Library of New Zealand.

ISBN: 978-1-99-100121-4

Designed by Nick Turzynski, redinc. Book Design, www.redinc.co.nz
Typeset in Inter Light 10/12
Printed in China
This book uses paper sourced under ISO 14001 guidelines from well-managed forests and other controlled sources.

10 9 8 7 6 5 4 3 2 1

To my father and all the other great photographers who paved the way for me,
and to my beautiful wife and family who have supported me
all the way down that road.

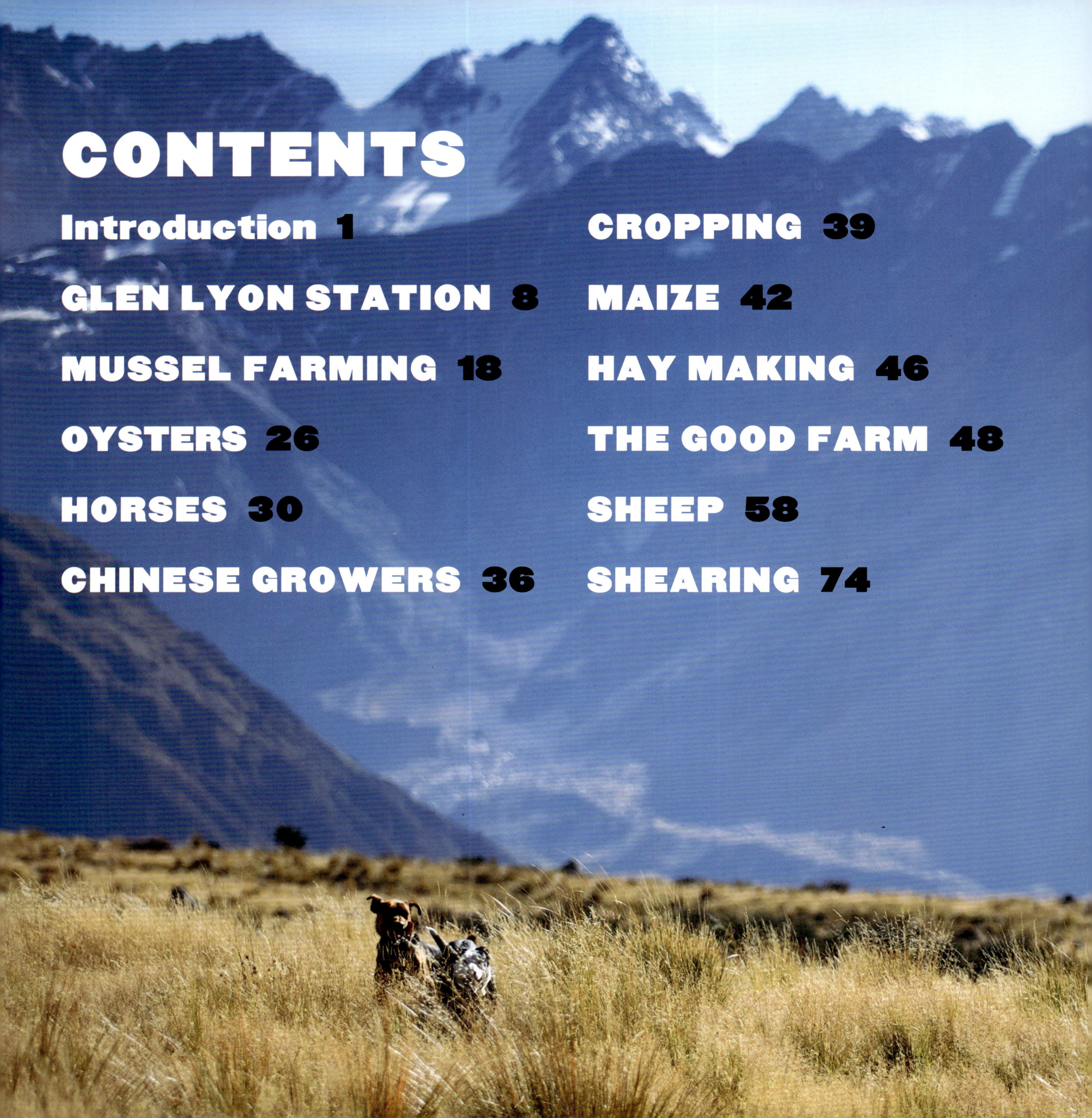

# CONTENTS


Introduction 1

GLEN LYON STATION 8

MUSSEL FARMING 18

OYSTERS 26

HORSES 30

CHINESE GROWERS 36

CROPPING 39

MAIZE 42

HAY MAKING 46

THE GOOD FARM 48

SHEEP 58

SHEARING 74

LOGAN WILLIAMS 84
WINE 86
DAIRYING 94
FARM DOGS 104
DEER FARMING 111
CRATER LAKE 116
KIWIFRUIT 120
APPLES 122
LAMBING 124
CHICKENS 130
CHARACTERS 136
SALEYARDS 140
A&P SHOW 146
BEES 148
Index 151

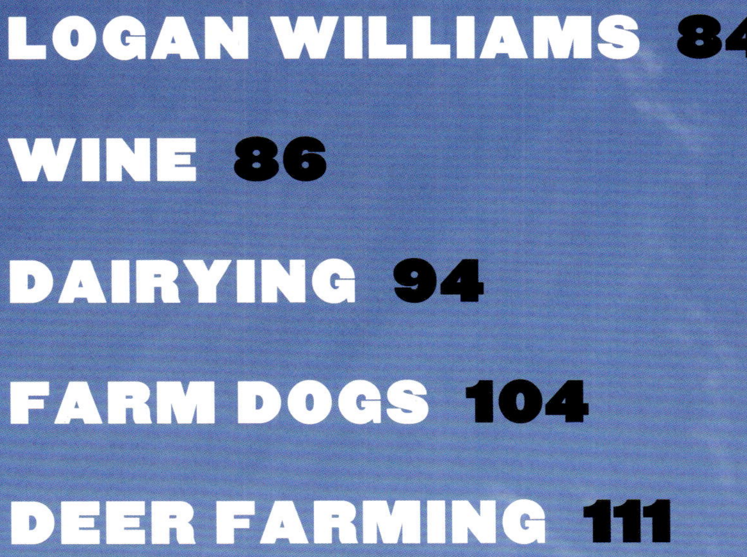

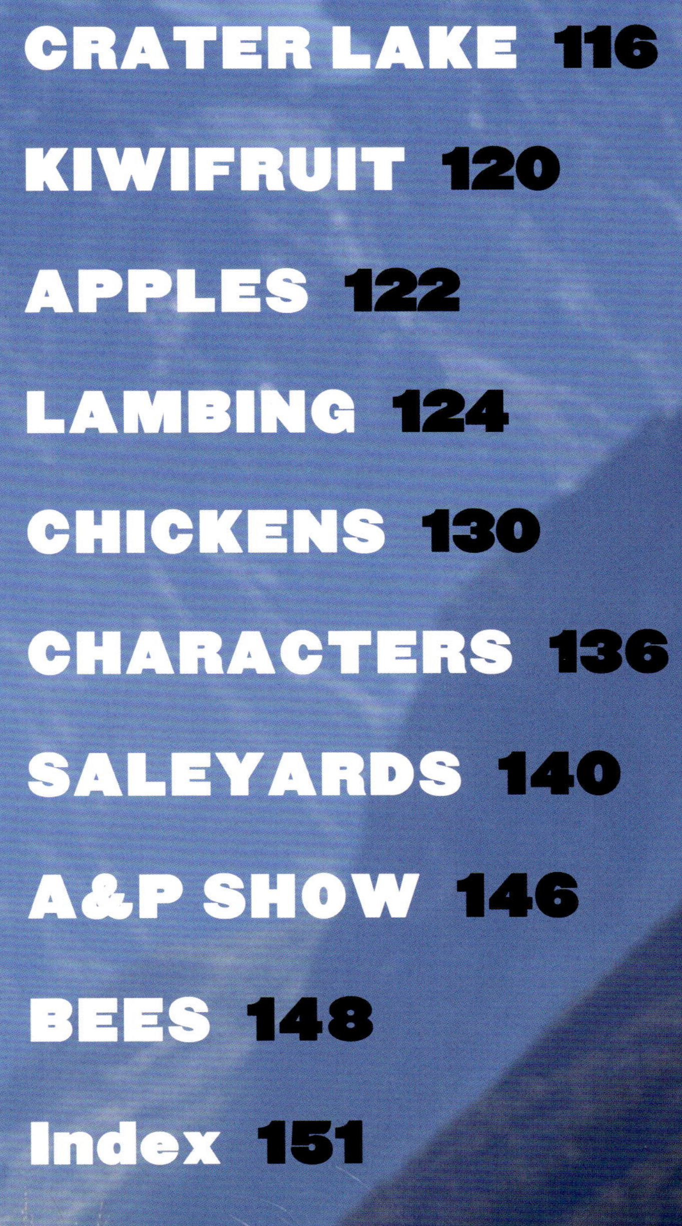

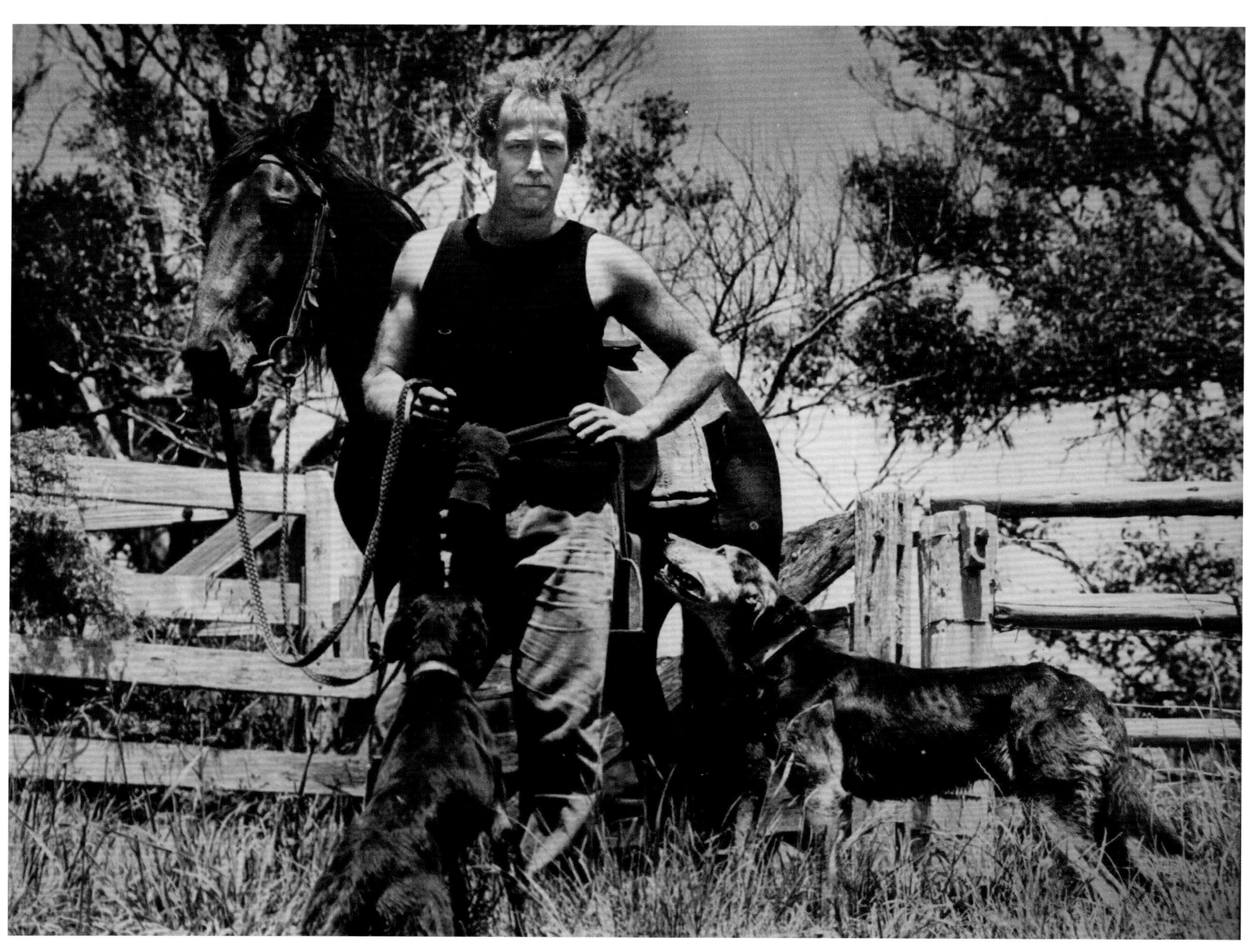

My father Bill Gibson, farmer and photographer, on our family farm, early 1980s. Photo by Ross Land.

# Introduction

**When I received a phone call** inviting me to photograph a book celebrating all aspects of farming, my first thought was 'Awesome, dream come true'. My second thought was 'How the hell am I going to cover everything?'

Farming in New Zealand has grown from the early days of sheep, beef, dairy and a few crops to include everything from alpacas to micro-greens to truffles and now, controversially, even carbon. I quickly realised that it would be foolhardy to attempt to illustrate everything and would result in a once-over-lightly publication of little interest to anyone. I knew what I needed to do was tell the stories of the people behind a few of the mainstays of New Zealand farming — the people who love this land and love what they do with it.

I knew there were great stories to be told. I grew up surrounded by such people on a hill-country farm in a remote corner of coastal Waikato. My family were there for the best part of a century working, living and farming alongside hard but good men and women who all, in their own way, had a deep affection for the country way of life.

My father introduced me to the world of photography, having discovered it himself while at boarding school in Taranaki. I think he must have shocked and horrified my grandfather when he announced he was going to become a press photographer instead of returning to the family farm, which was the more common path in those days. He spent several happy years working in newspapers in New Plymouth alongside some of the best in the business before eventually deciding to return to the land with his young family.

And what a piece of land it was: 500 hectares of beautiful hill country, broken in with the blood, sweat and tears of my grandparents and their parents before them. The farm extended to the coast where we could access a stunning stretch of beach with reefs at both ends. It was a paradise. There was world-class fishing, hunting and surfing to be had, copious shellfish and crayfish to be gathered and for my father endless stunning photographs to be taken.

But after thousands of images of sunsets over rugged reefs had been captured, he came to realise, as I would, that the really interesting images are those of the people living their lives in those landscapes. He continued to document life on our farm and in our district, including the weddings, sports days, school events, funerals and farming. Eventually he was recognised for this work by winning all the major awards in the New Zealand Guild of Agricultural Journalists Primary Light photographic competition. This was a huge achievement for a hill-country farmer.

Through his guidance I also came to see the extraordinary beauty in shafts of light piercing the dust as a mob of sheep

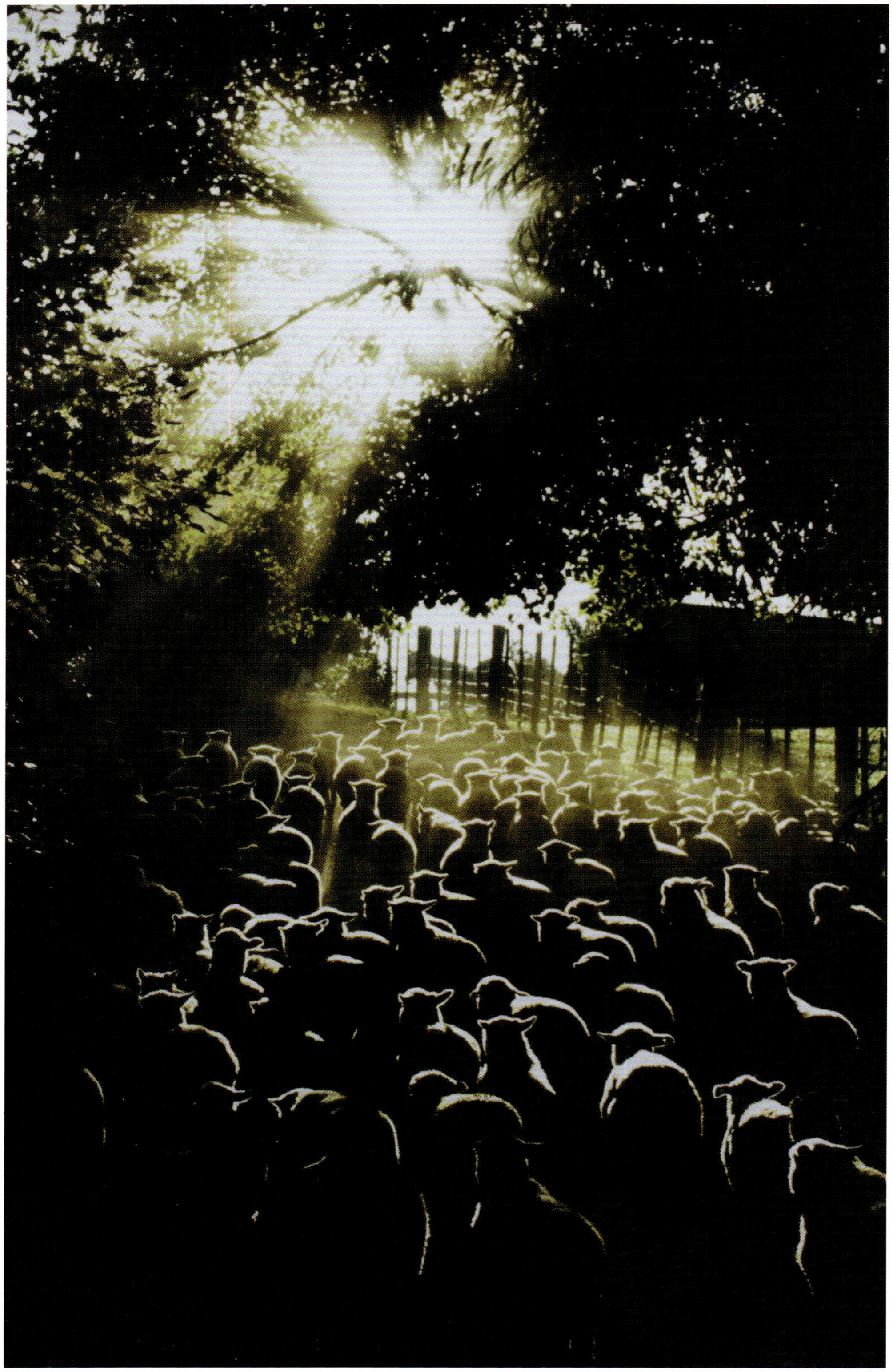

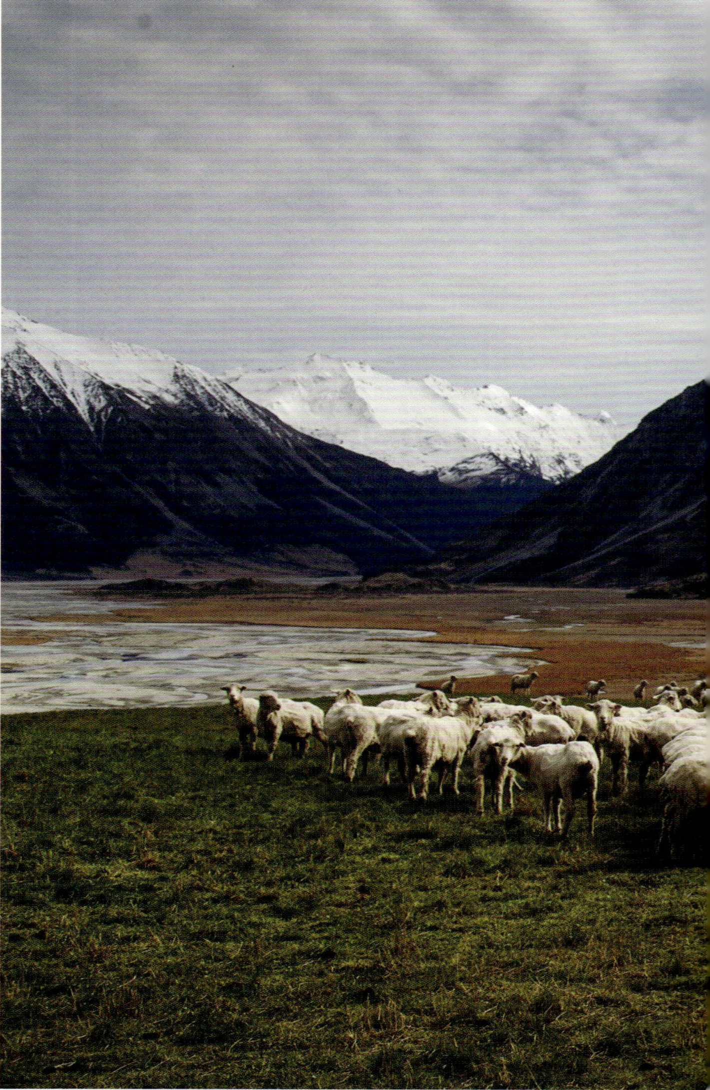

A mob of ewes enjoy a feed of grain on the flats at Glen Lyon Station, Canterbury.

An award-winning image taken by Bill Gibson during a day's work on the family farm at Te Ākau, Waikato.

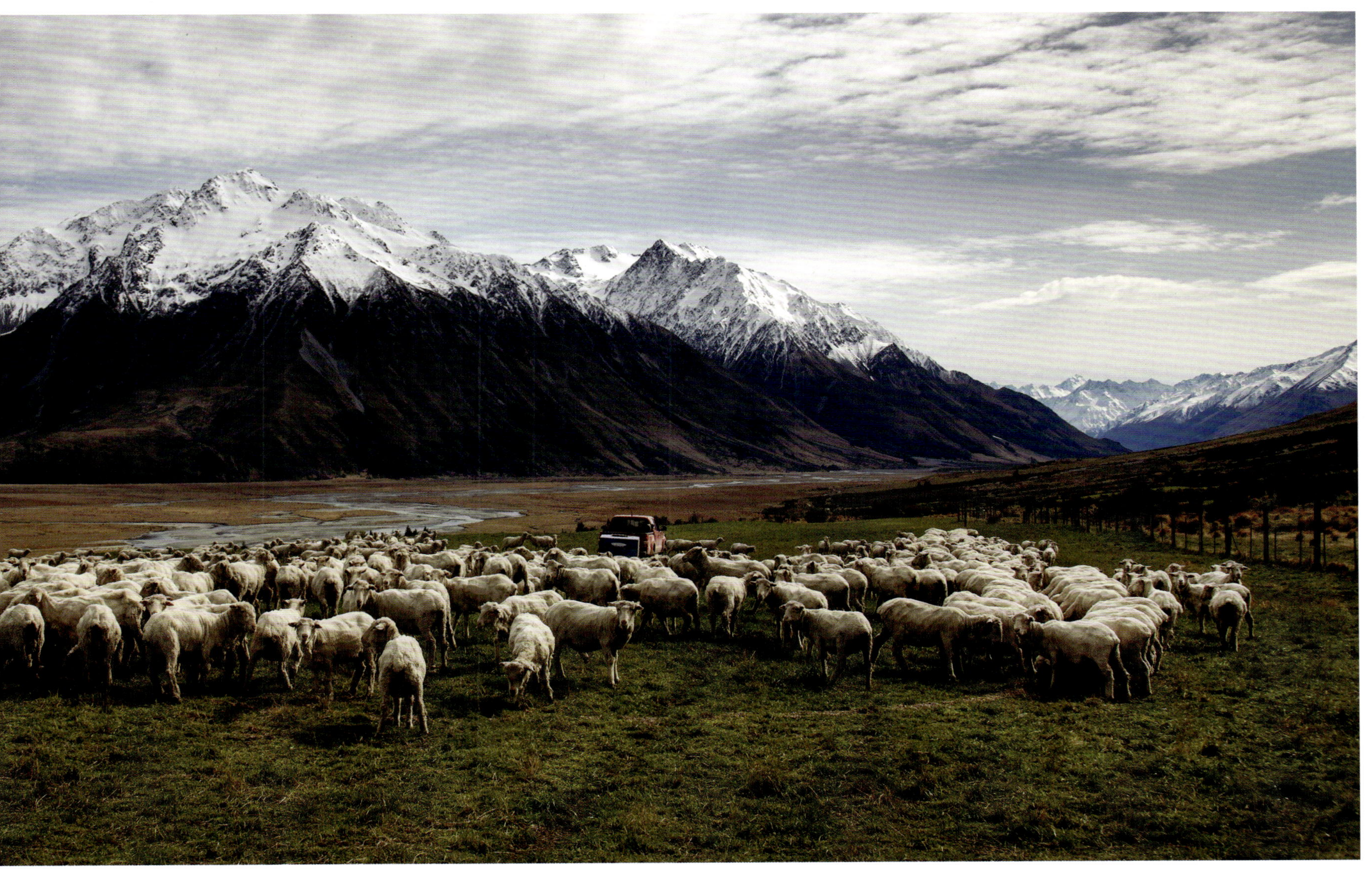

are driven down the lane or in the way a rustic old woolshed produces some of the most amazing modelling light and darkest shadows a photographer could ever hope for. I too went on to a career as a press photographer, first at the *Waikato Times* then the *New Zealand Herald* and for a time in London's Fleet Street, covering all manner of subjects around the world. However, it was always assignments that took me back out into the rural heartland of this country that I loved the most. The landscapes were both rugged and breathtaking, the people were often just as rugged but always had a generosity of spirit as well. We have so many great stories to tell in Aotearoa New Zealand and I intend to spend the rest of my days helping tell them.

To be given an opportunity to get out there and photograph some of the farmers, growers and producers of this country for a book has been an absolute honour. I was continually amazed how open and positive people were when a complete stranger rang and asked if he could come into their farms, businesses and homes and point a camera at them. Having explained that

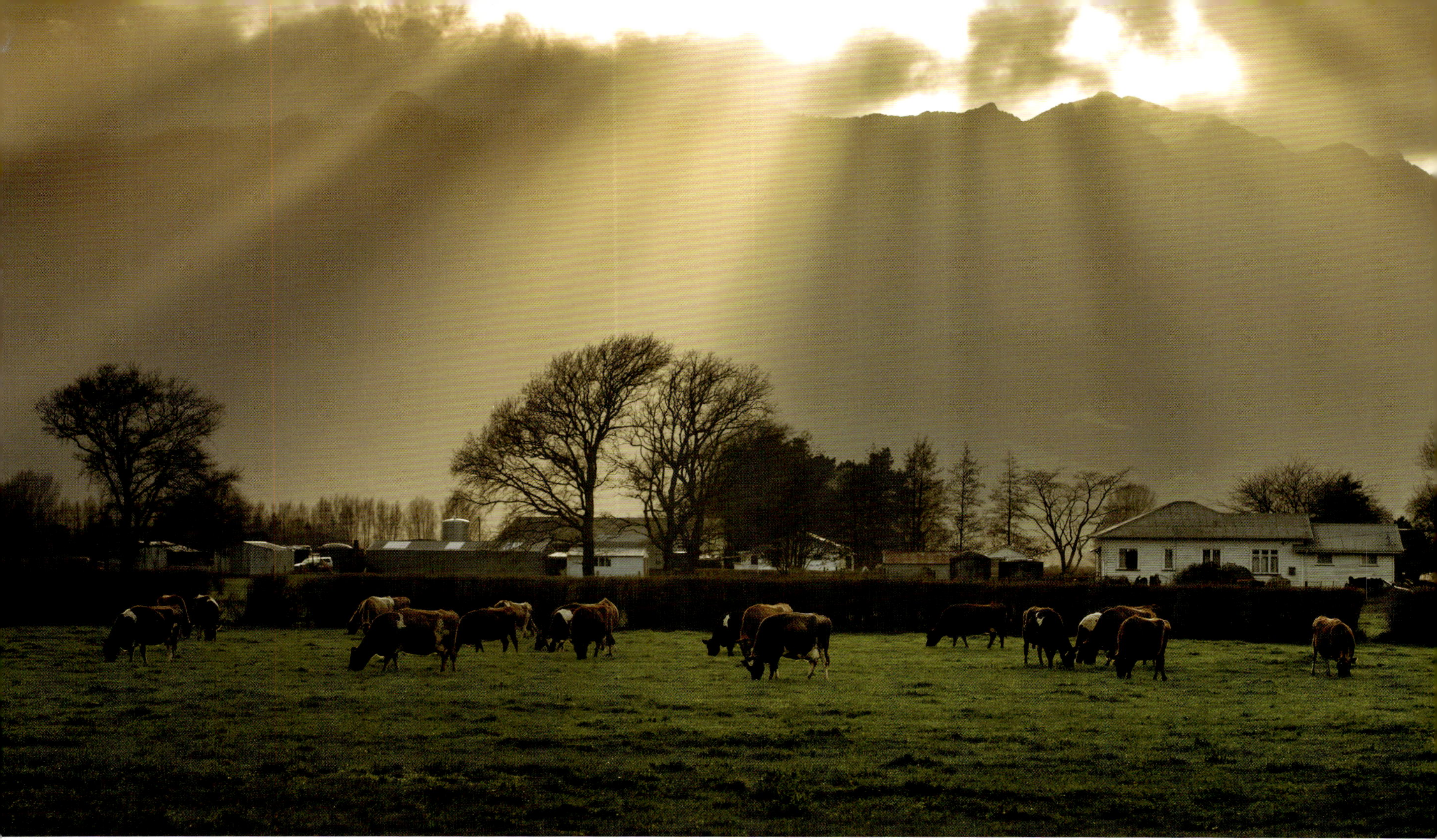

Tania White's Jersey cows amid shafts of sunlight peeking through clouds on the Kaimai Range at Te Aroha, Waikato.

I would like to get some 'nice' pictures of them at work but also hang around and try to record more of the people they are, every single one said 'No worries'.

Having been invited in, I found myself in the most amazing places, whether it was speeding in a boat through the Marlborough Sounds at dawn en route to a mussel farm or gazing with wonder at the most incredible night sky as I drifted off to sleep in the open tussock on a high-country station muster. I was aware these were experiences people the world over would die for, and I never forgot what a privilege it was to be allowed into these farmers' worlds.

Equally impressive with the landscapes were the people themselves. I had the pleasure of riding along on the autumn cattle muster with Johnny Wigley and his crew on Glen Lyon Station near Aoraki Mt Cook. To watch Johnny and his partner Caro, along with family members and musterers, clear those valleys of cattle was an experience that will stay with me forever. Closer to home, I got to make multiple visits to Crater Lake Farm which sits on the edge of a dormant volcano between stunning Rotorua lakes. The small farm is home to

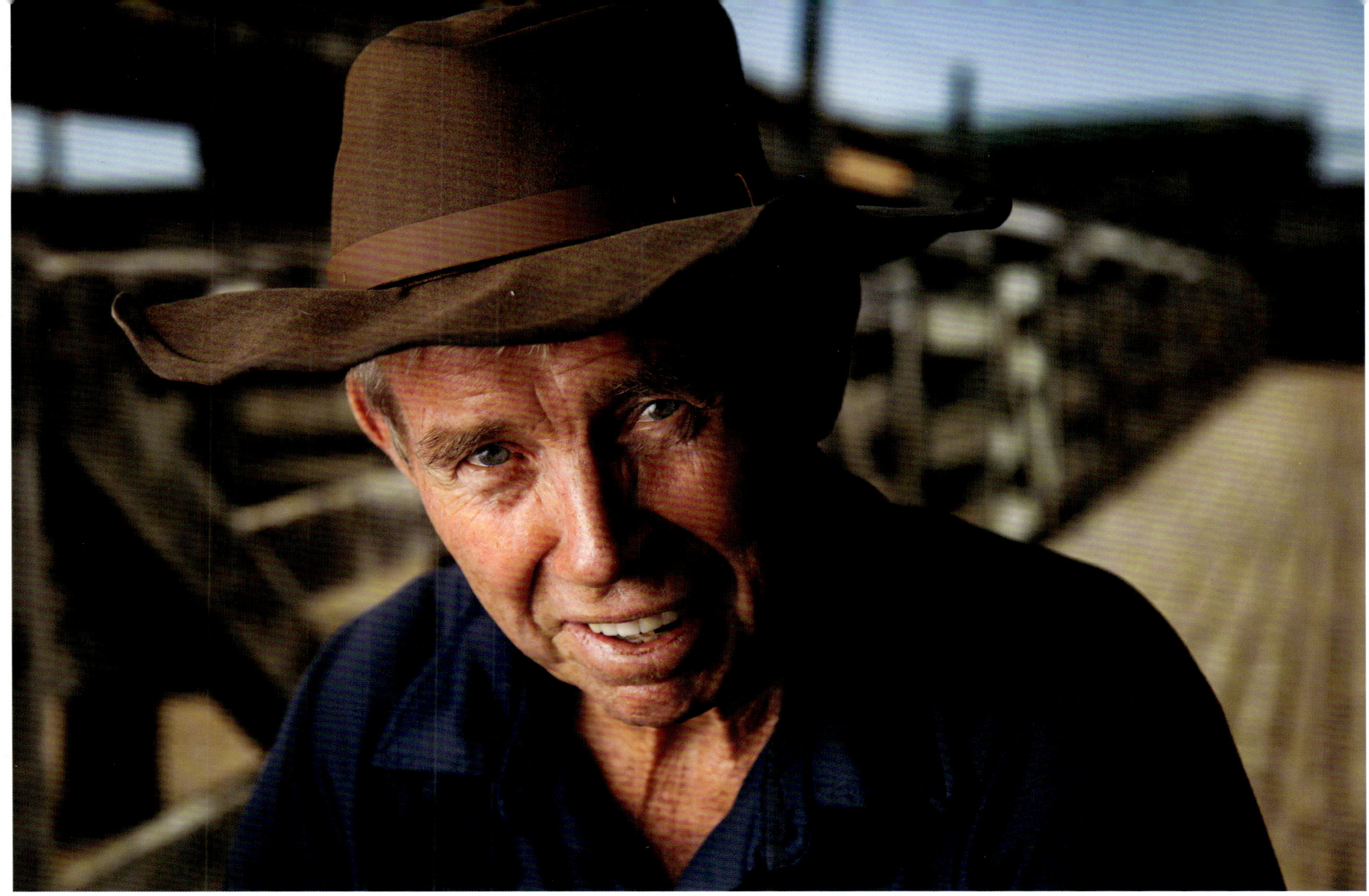

Paddy Sands and his family who all pitch in to help run sheep, beef and deer in the beautiful but challenging location. Being with them at 8.30 on a winter's night as they wrestled with an army of orphaned lambs at feeding time and realising they would be back early the next morning to do the same again really illustrated just how hard our farmers work.

Up in the coastal hill country at Port Waikato I had the privilege of observing Fiona Gower and her family go about their lives in a landscape they all clearly loved. Her young son Anthony's lifestyle reminded me of my own adventure-filled youth spent just a little further down the coast. He also reminded me of how the New Zealand character was formed, by young rural kids finishing a day's schooling then being sent out to help in a workplace that demanded a level of maturity well beyond their years. Whether it was moving a herd of cattle, helping fence a near vertical cliff, using firearms or butchering meat for the table, a tough, hard-working steeliness is imbued into those who live this life, and it is reassuringly comforting to see.

**Saleyards manager and farming veteran Chris D'Arcy in one of the races at the Bay of Plenty site he now oversees.**

The sense of unity and strength in family came through time and again in the farming operations I visited. I had the

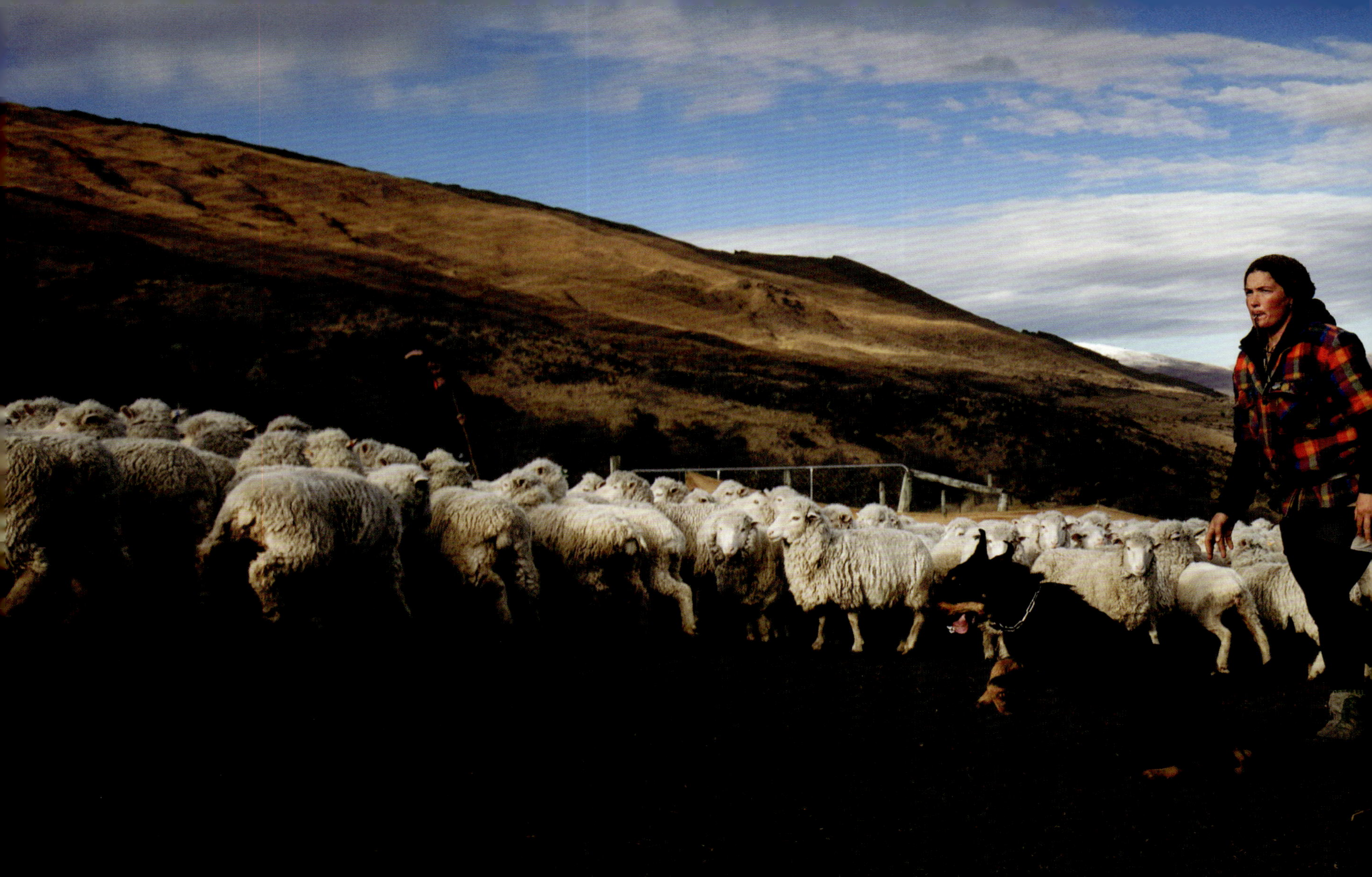

pleasure of spending time with Mark and Catriona White and their children Letisha and Lachlan on their organic kiwifruit orchard near Ōpōtiki. The two kids manage their own small block within the enterprise, taking care of the pruning, thinning and everything else that requires attention during the growing season. Being with them on a frosty Sunday morning planting kiwifruit seedlings, I got a real sense that they knew the hard work was building a better future and that they genuinely enjoyed their time together on that land.

I also got to make multiple visits to the Waikato dairy farm run by Tania White with help from her super-keen 13-year-old daughter Ruby. It was heart-warming to watch Tania lovingly manage her herd through all types of weather and challenges while young Ruby took control of rearing dozens of calves, and to see the animals respond to the care and attention these hard-working women bestowed upon them. They are truly a great example of the best of our farmers.

Having travelled all over this country in pursuit of images

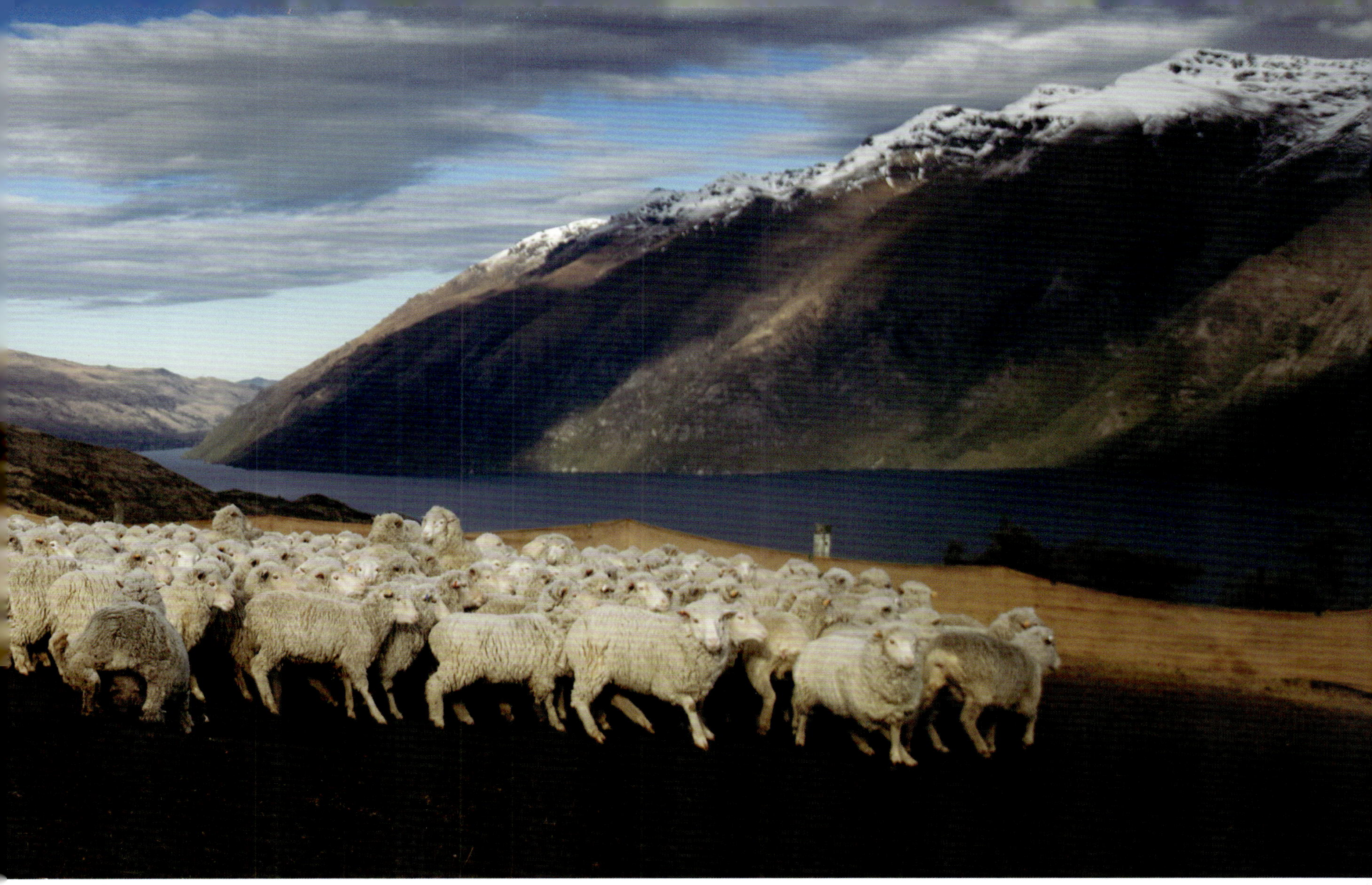

**Shepherd Kelly Smith pushes sheep through the yards on Loch Linnhe Station overlooking Lake Wakatipu near Kingston, Otago.**

for this book I am left with a great sense of optimism for our future. To spend time with thoroughly impressive young women in dairy sheds, to watch as all the members of a shearing gang come together as one, to sit and talk to musterers in a high-country hut or stand in awe as a farmer walks into a herd of antlered stags you come to realise that these are among the best of our people and that everything is going to be alright.

As I mentioned, I could not hope to cover everything that comes under the umbrella term of farming in New Zealand, but what I hope I have achieved is to give readers a glimpse of the lives of those who toil day in, day out on land and sea to provide for their families and our nation. I hope this book is received as a celebration of the New Zealand farmer, people for whom I have the utmost respect and admiration.

# GLEN LYON STATION

Glen Lyon remains an important and dramatic part of New Zealand's farming heritage. The 25,000-hectare high-country station in Upper Waitaki is a sheep and beef farm that has been in the same family for generations. The farm sits at the northern end of Lake Ōhau, where alpine waters from the Hopkins and Dobson rivers meet. Surrounded by majestic mountains, crystal-clear glacial lakes and rivers, the station has its own culture and way of life, with mustering carried out on horseback, shearing done in a rustic shed, and young children home schooled.

***“We can have grunty winters.***

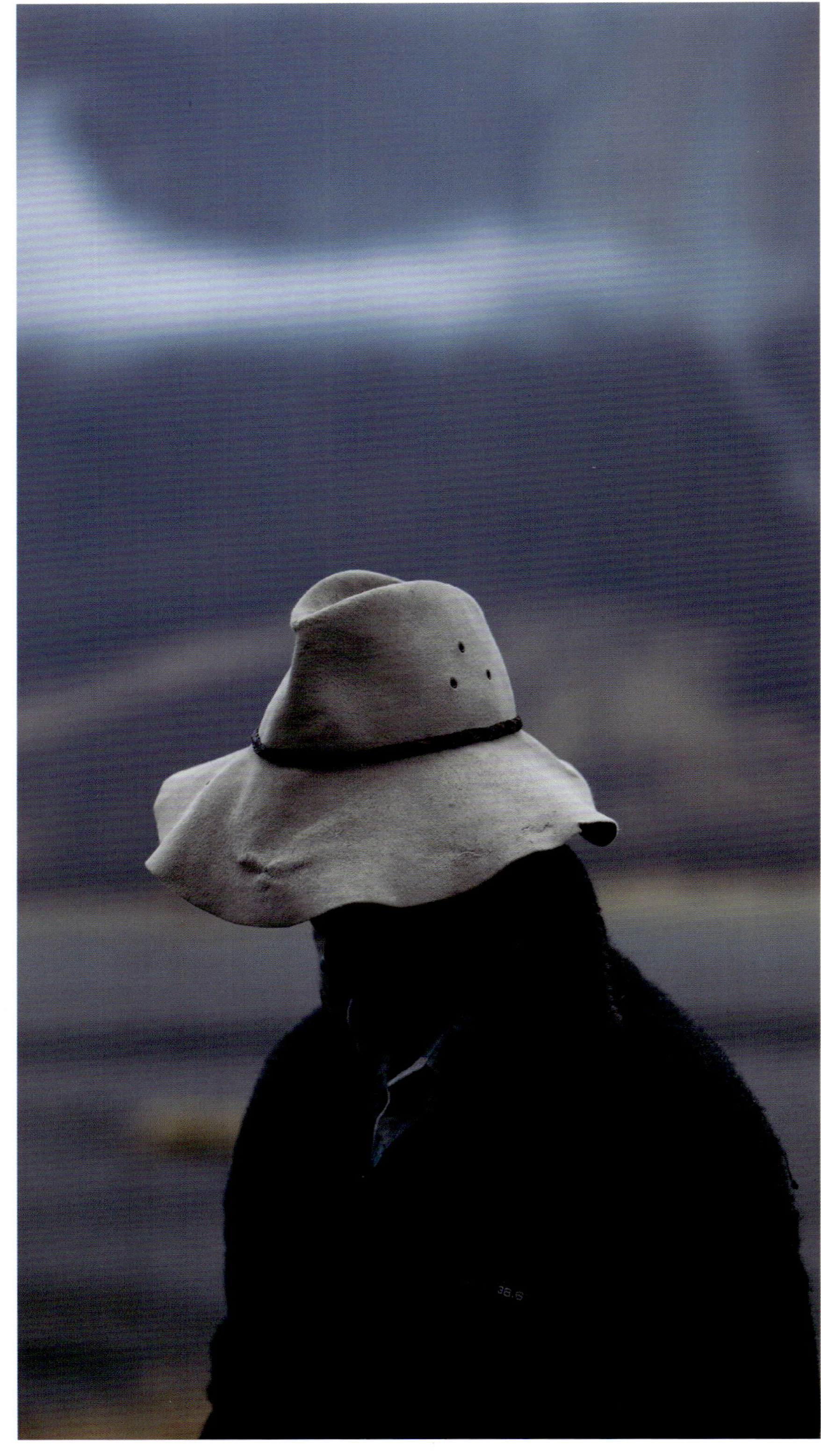

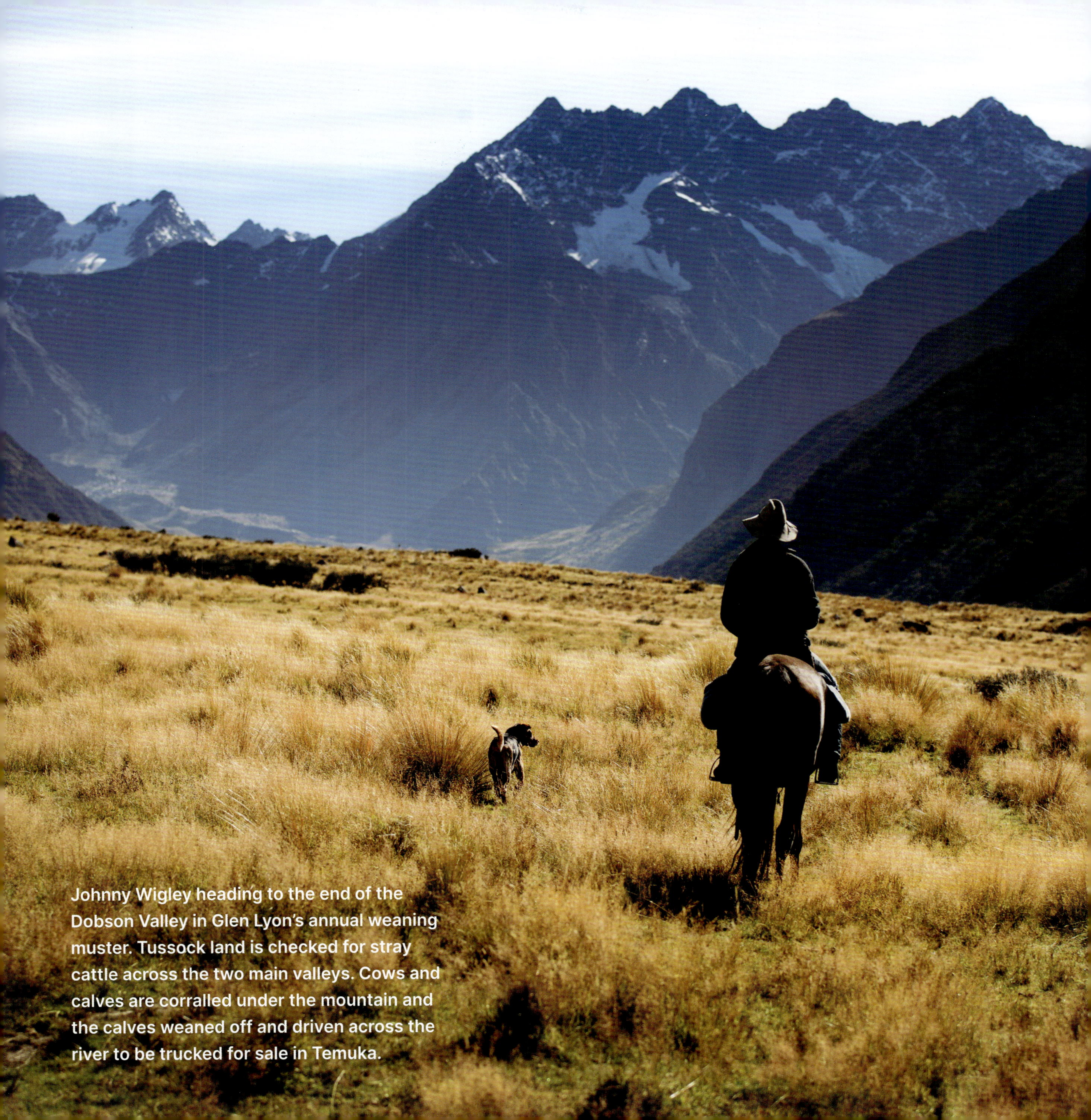

Johnny Wigley heading to the end of the Dobson Valley in Glen Lyon's annual weaning muster. Tussock land is checked for stray cattle across the two main valleys. Cows and calves are corralled under the mountain and the calves weaned off and driven across the river to be trucked for sale in Temuka.

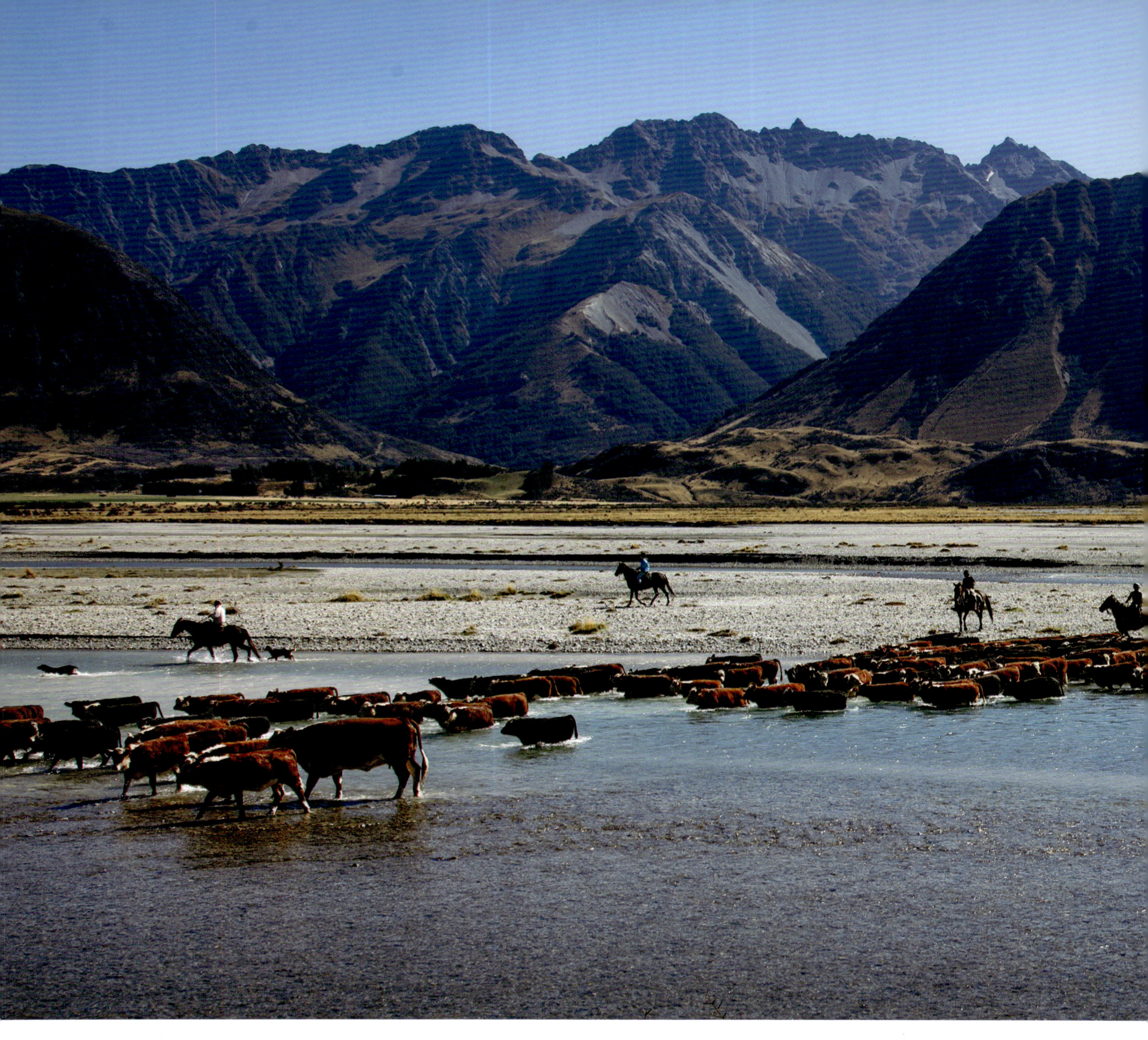

# GLEN LYON STATION

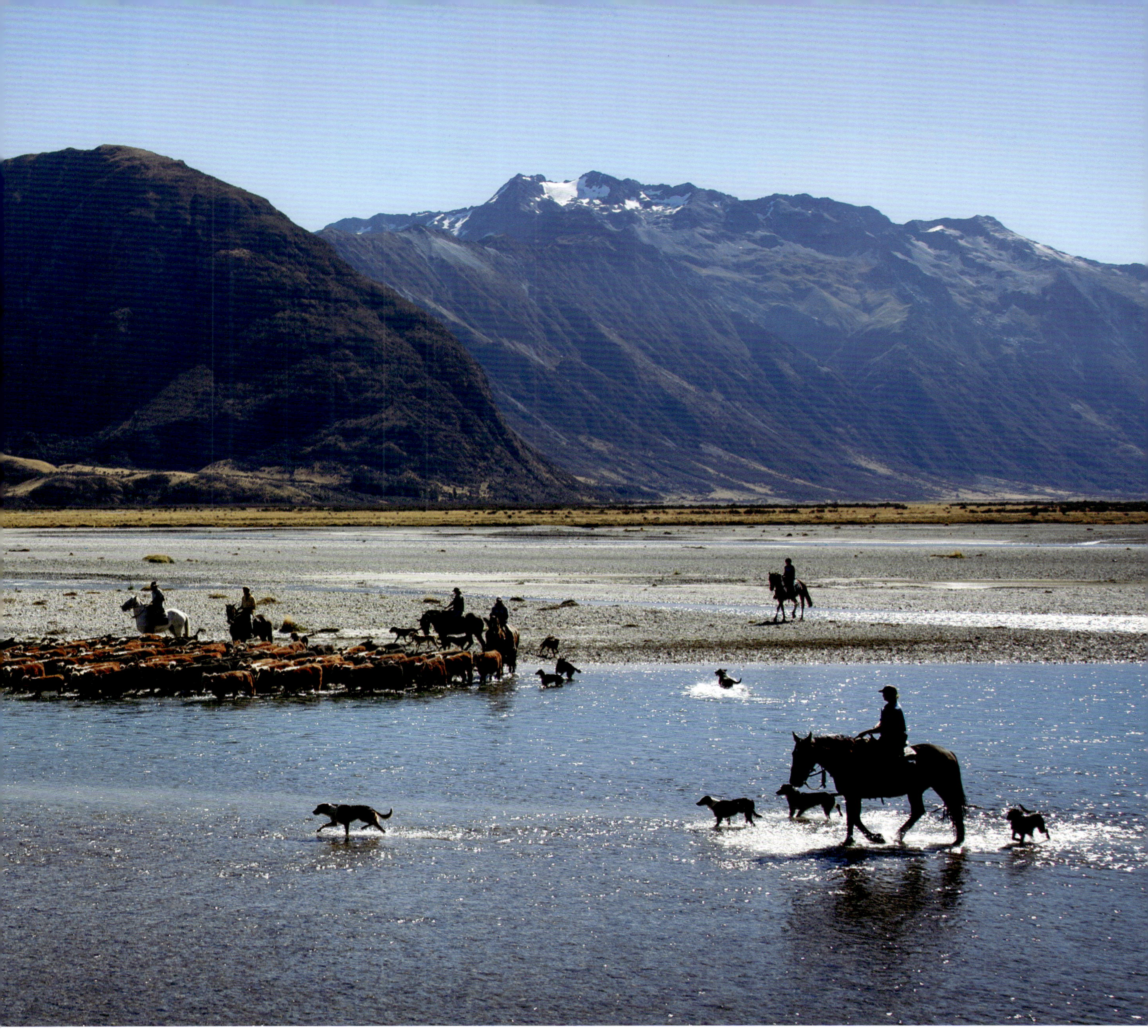

Musterers drive cattle down to the yards at the end of the weaning muster on Glen Lyon Station, Canterbury.

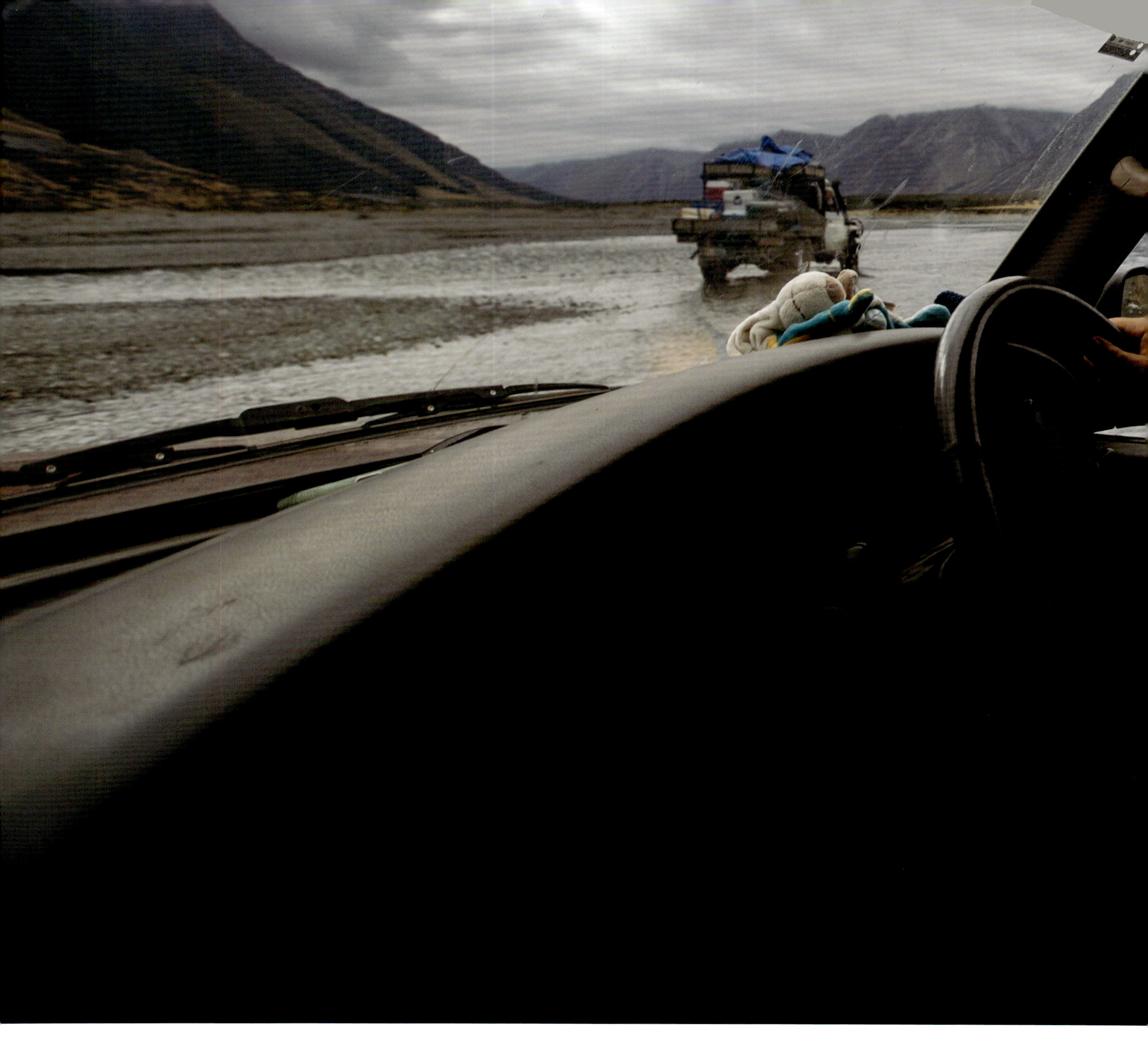

**GLEN LYON STATION**

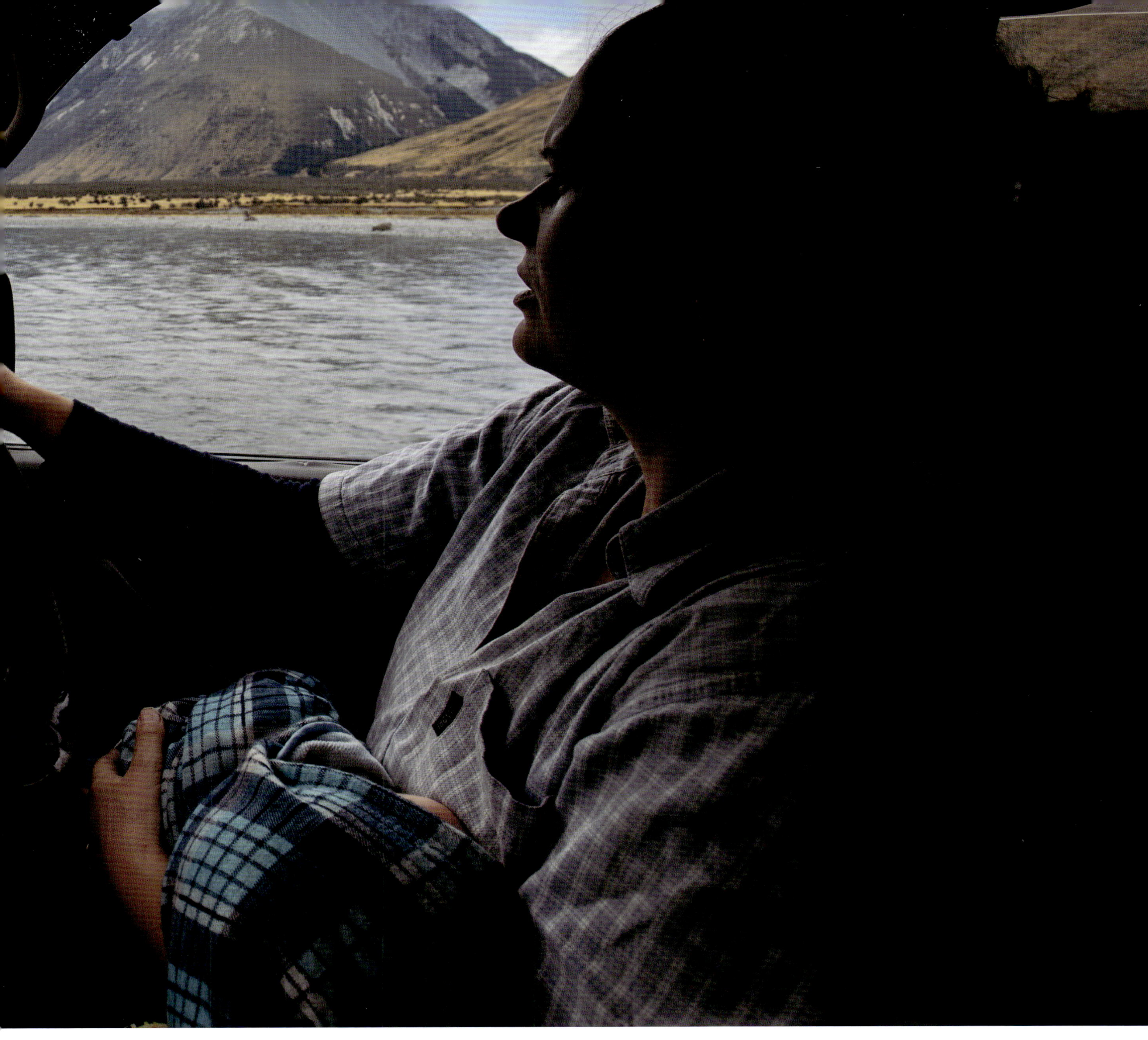

Pippa Rogers feeds her four-month-old baby while navigating up the braided river, which also serves as the road. In the ute ahead her mother is also taking supplies to the mustering team who have ridden further into the valley.

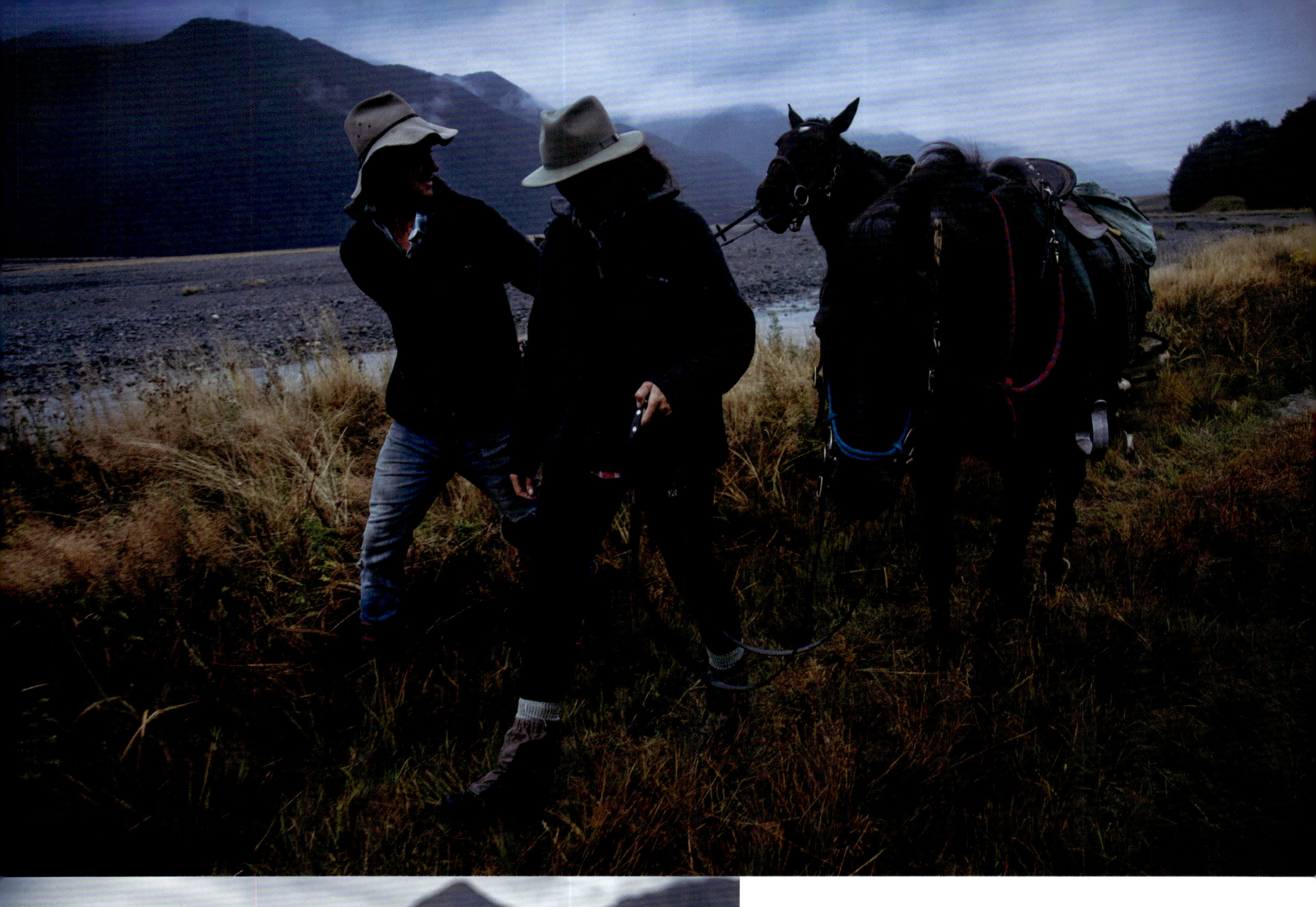

Johnny and Caro Hayes head off into a misty dawn to begin the last day of the weaning muster.

Caro Hayes takes a break from mustering to entertain young Jonty Rogers on his first muster at Glen Lyon Station.

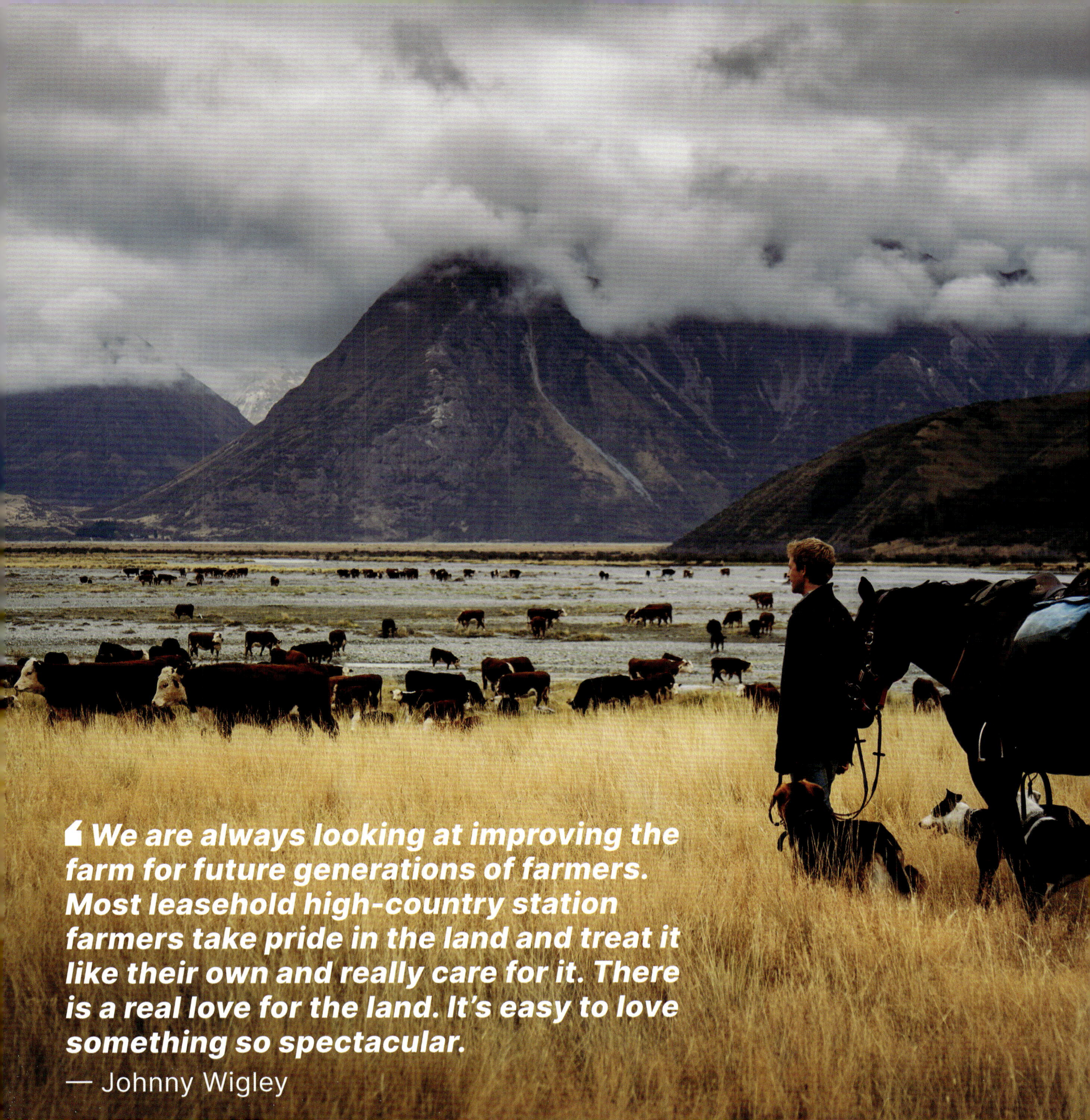

*“We are always looking at improving the farm for future generations of farmers. Most leasehold high-country station farmers take pride in the land and treat it like their own and really care for it. There is a real love for the land. It’s easy to love something so spectacular.*

— Johnny Wigley

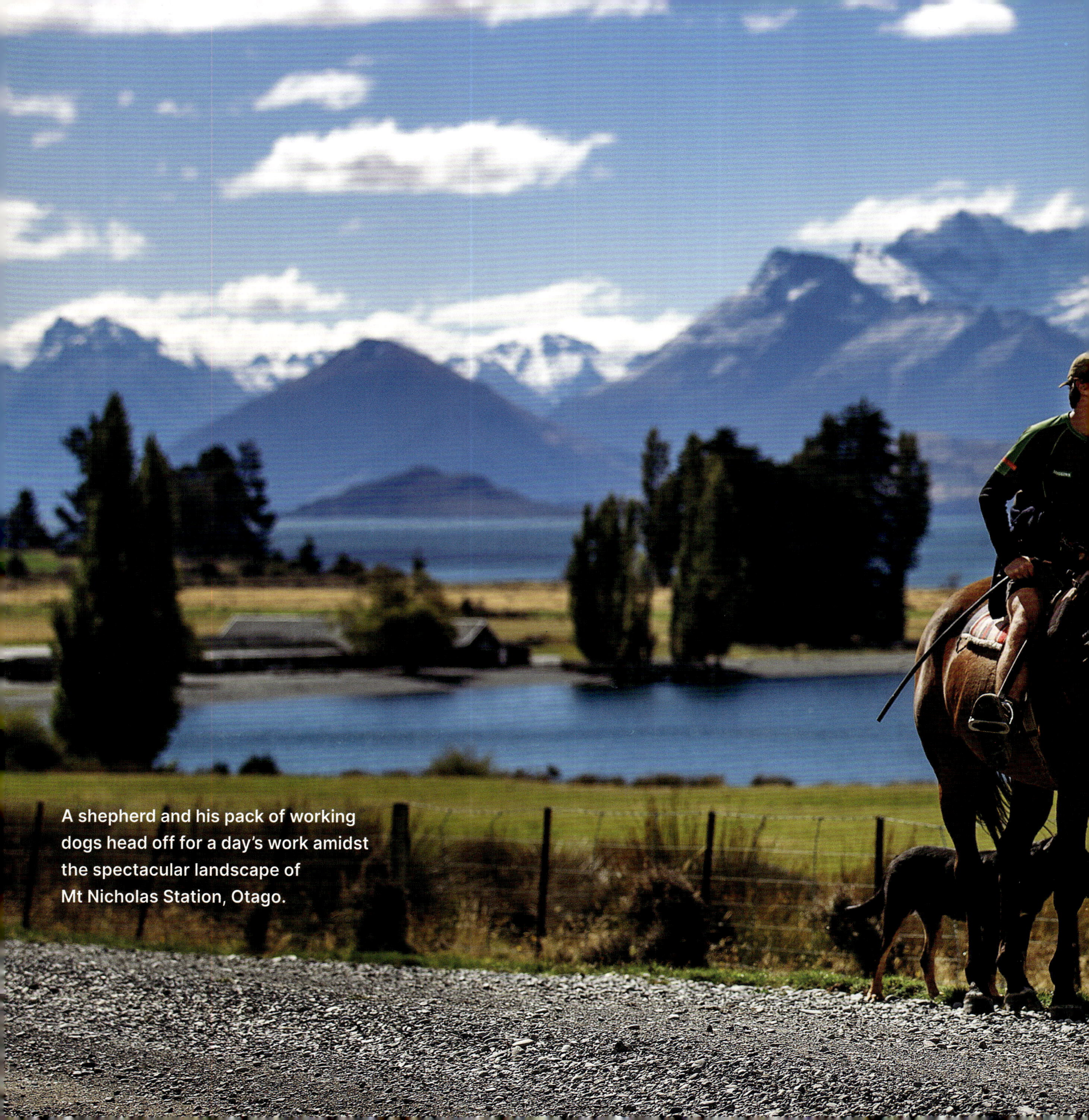

A shepherd and his pack of working dogs head off for a day's work amidst the spectacular landscape of Mt Nicholas Station, Otago.

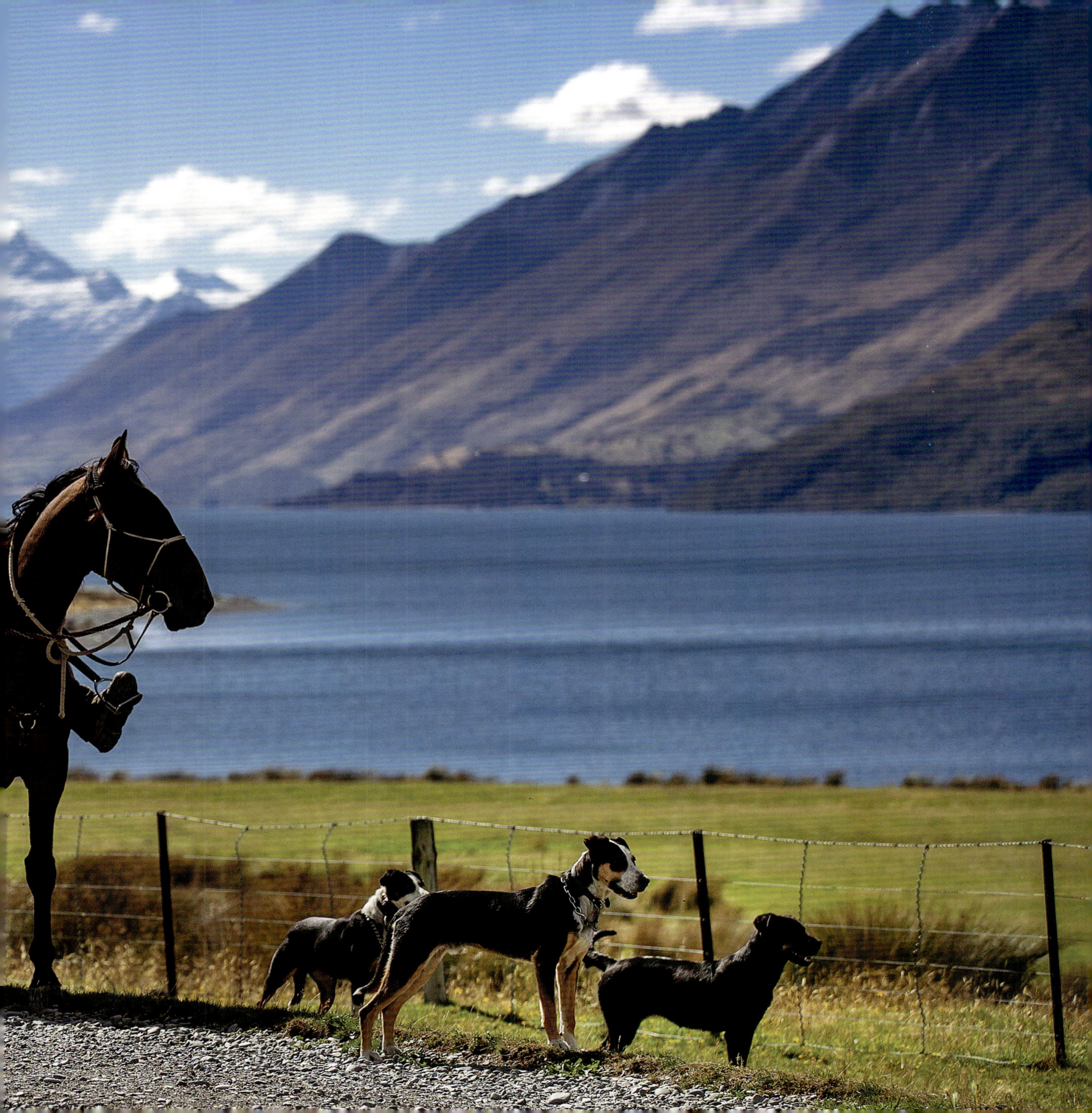

# MUSSEL FARMING

The green-lipped mussel is New Zealand's major aquaculture species, and the mussel industry has grown hugely since its beginnings in the late 1960s. Mussel farms are located in the same areas that wild mussels thrive: in relatively sheltered waters around the coastlines of the North Island, the top of the South and at Rakiura Stewart Island. Key farming areas are the Marlborough Sounds and the Coromandel/Hauraki Gulf. There are over 600 mussel farms in New Zealand, covering thousands of hectares of marine space. Current sales of green-lipped mussels exceed $200 million annually, with most revenue coming from exports. Mussels are also processed to create biopharmaceuticals and health supplements.

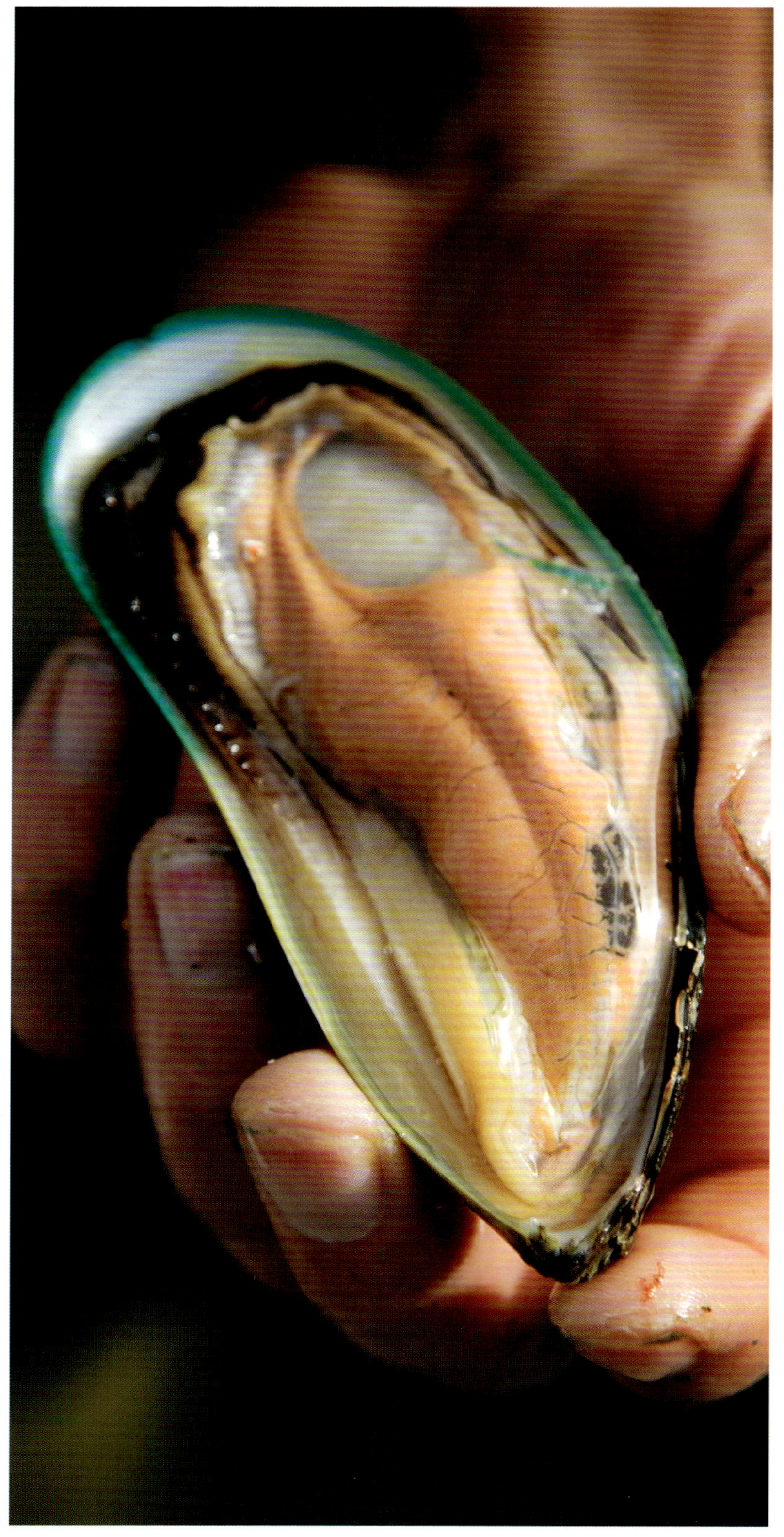

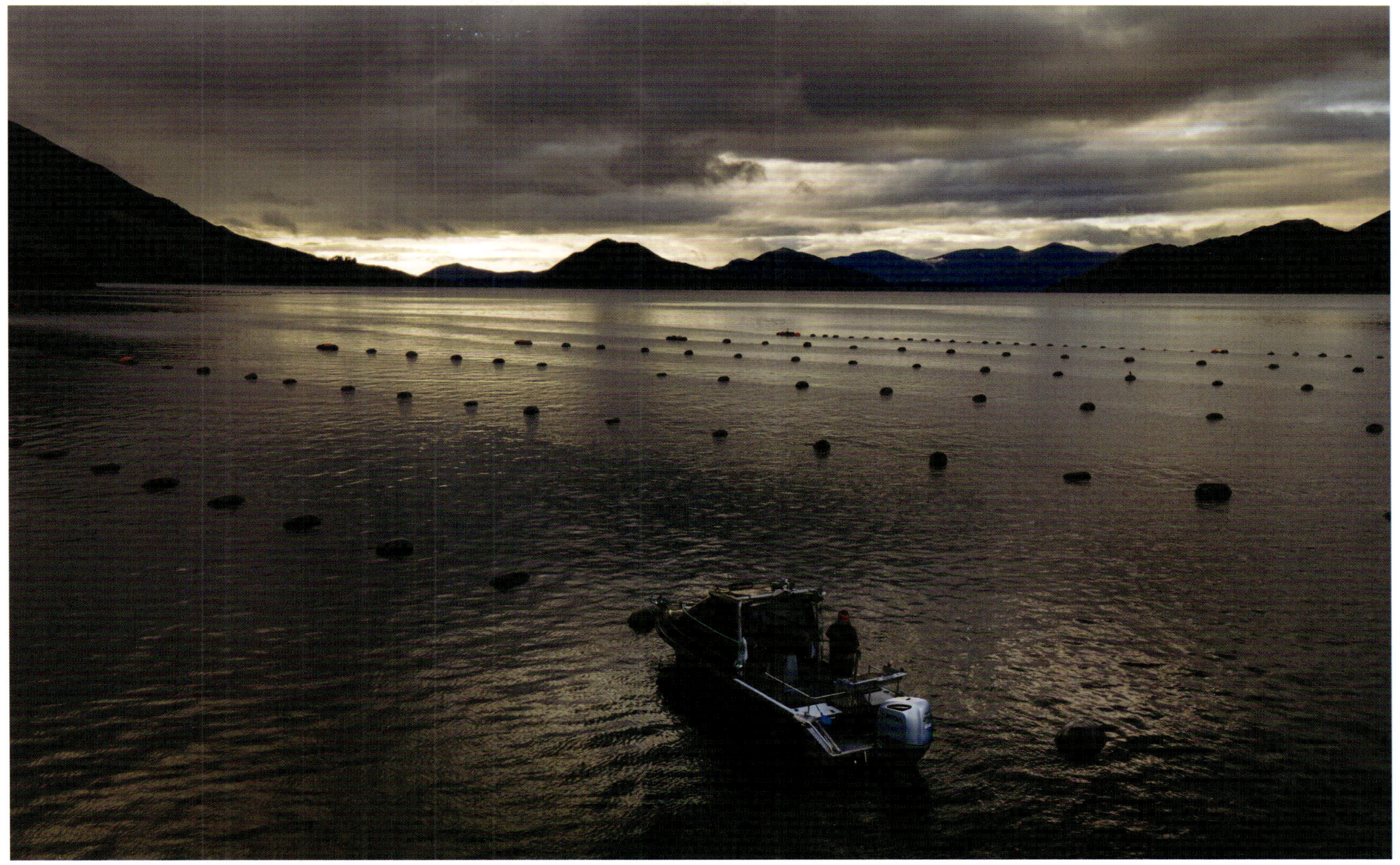

*❛ Aquaculture . . . is here to stay.*

**Simon Pooley inspects his Marlborough Sounds mussel farm in the first light of dawn.**

**Simon Pooley grew up in Elaine Bay in Pelorus Sound, where his family have been mussel farmers for 40 years:**
'I live here with my wife, four daughters and wider whānau. I recently took over the family business. We have 12 staff with 9 full-time on the water. We look after about 25 mussel farms here in the Marlborough Sounds and harvest about 5000 tonnes of mussels a year. There is a huge amount of satisfaction in working through the stages of the farming year and doing things well and working really hard. It's paradise and a beautiful place to work.

The challenges are finding good people that are skilled at their work but who also have good values and ethics and help create that culture. That can be difficult, but we have done it really well.

We love the area and do everything we can to look after this environment. Our carbon footprint is very impressive compared to anything that you can produce on land. But no one talks about that, as our story is not well understood.

Our future is bright and has loads of potential.

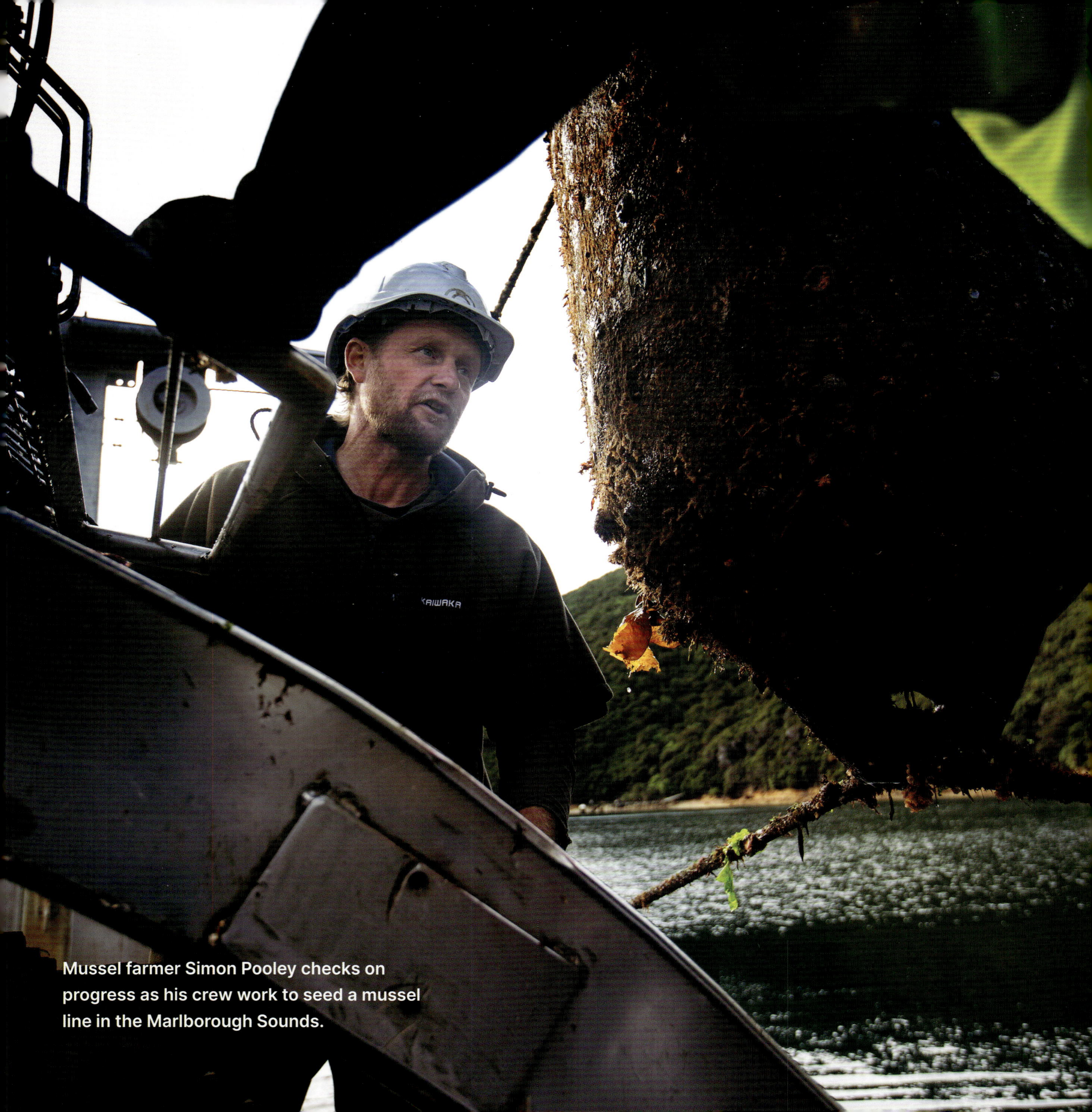


Mussel farmer Simon Pooley checks on progress as his crew work to seed a mussel line in the Marlborough Sounds.

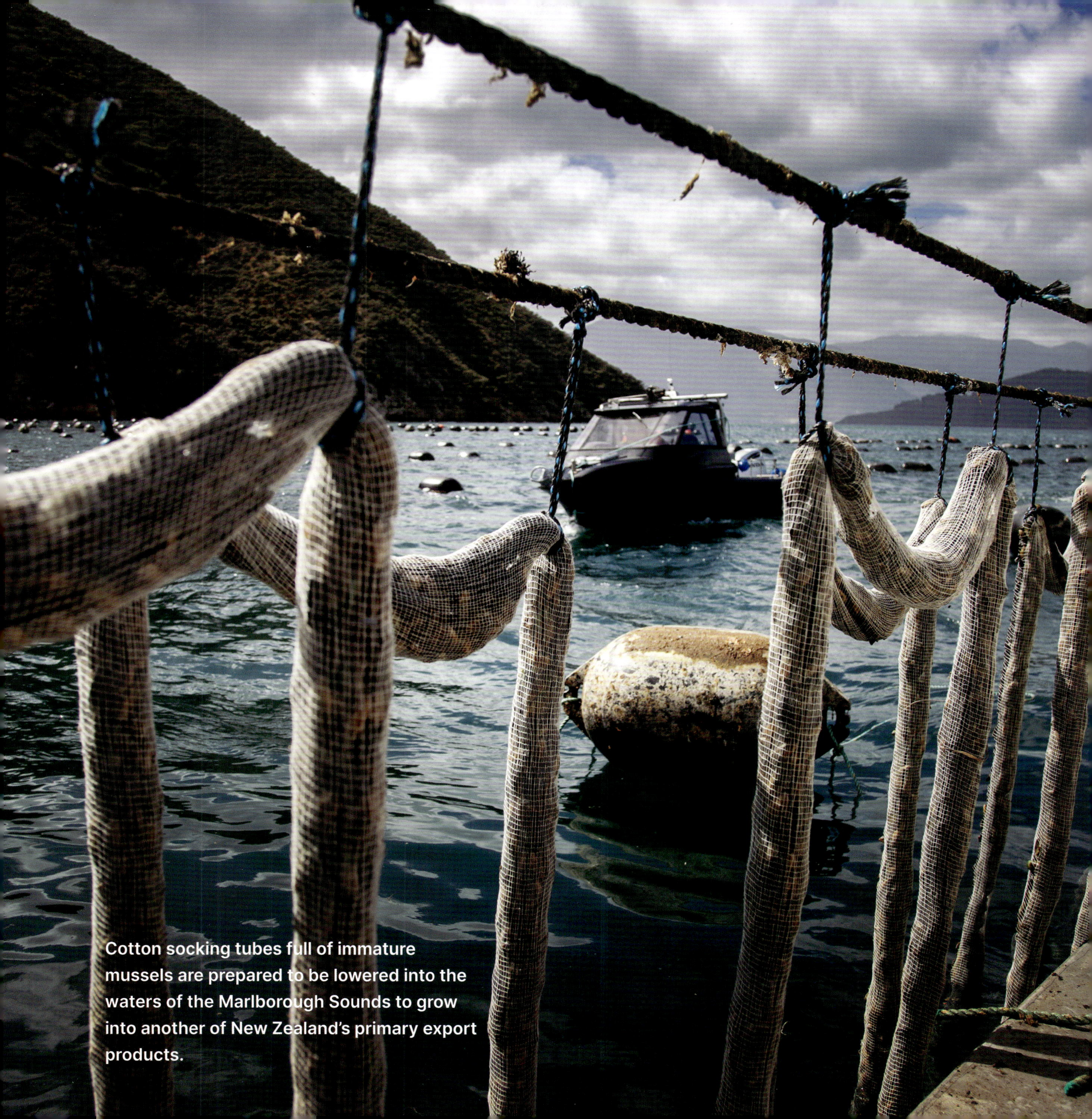

Cotton socking tubes full of immature mussels are prepared to be lowered into the waters of the Marlborough Sounds to grow into another of New Zealand's primary export products.

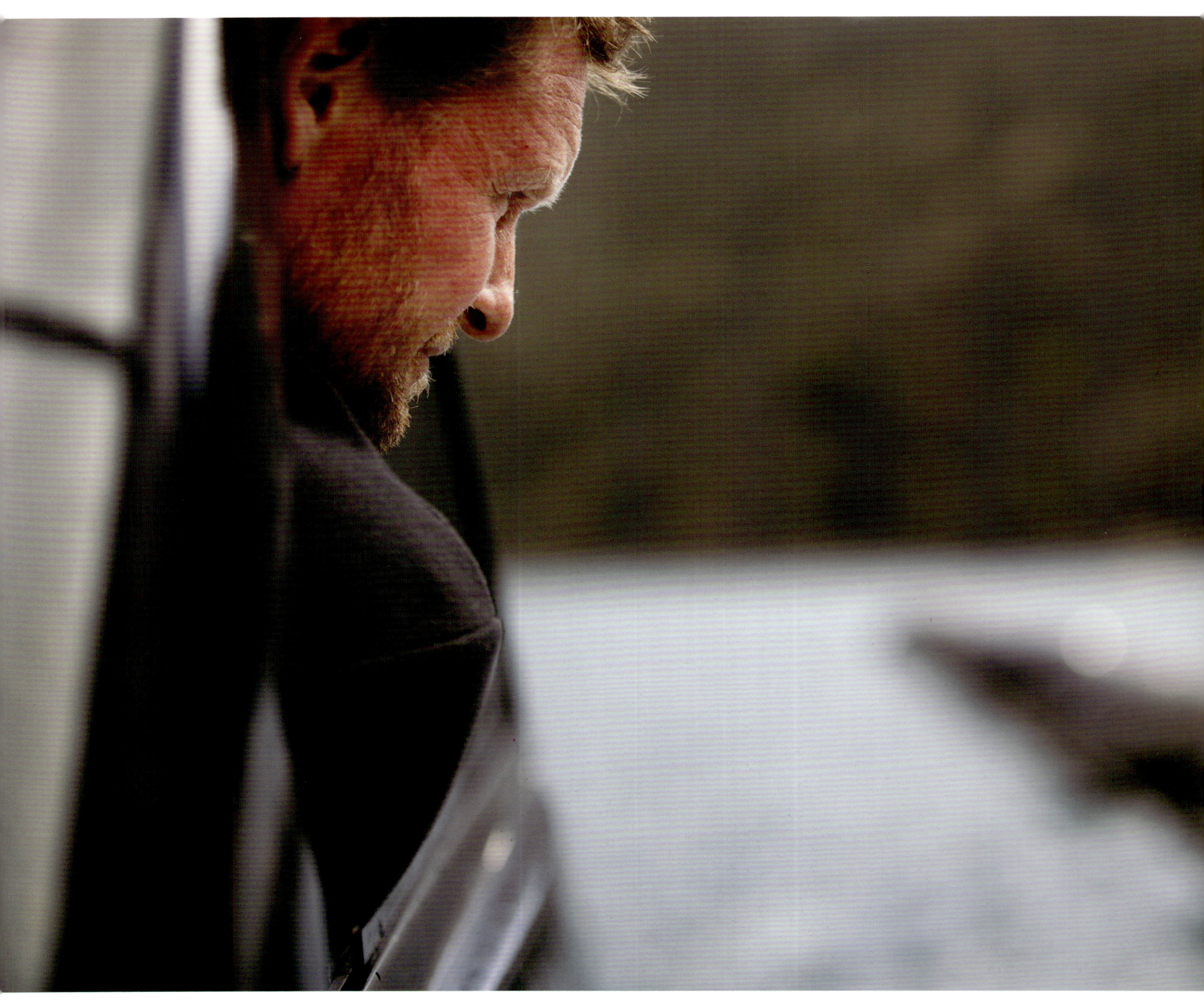

Simon Pooley keeps a close eye on things as he slowly motors down the rows of mussel lines.

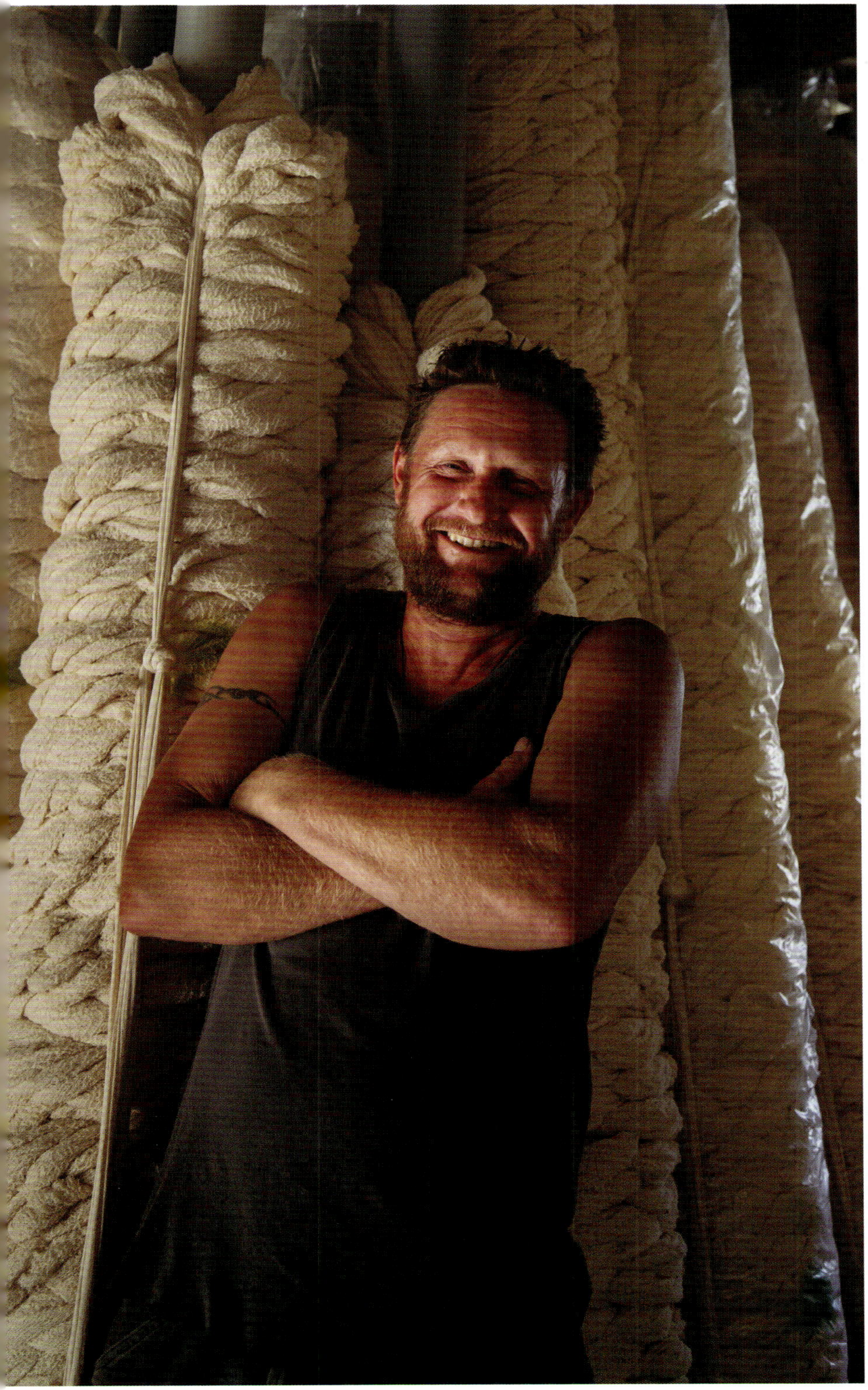

Simon Pooley pictured back at homebase in Elaine Bay with some of the huge quantities of cotton socking he uses on his mussel farming operation in the Marlborough Sounds.

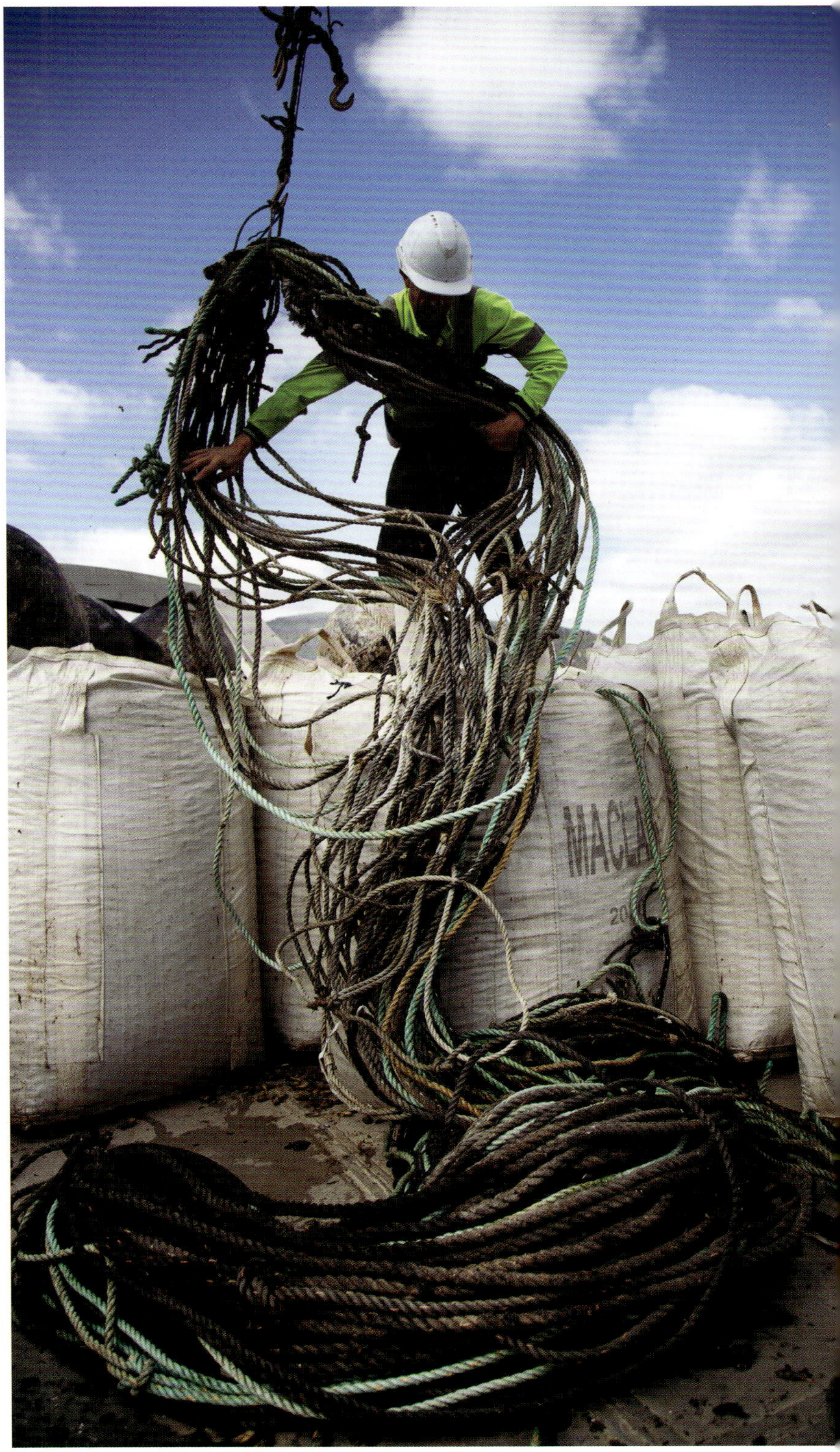

A mussel barge worker tries to organise a tangle of ropes used in the marine farming operation.

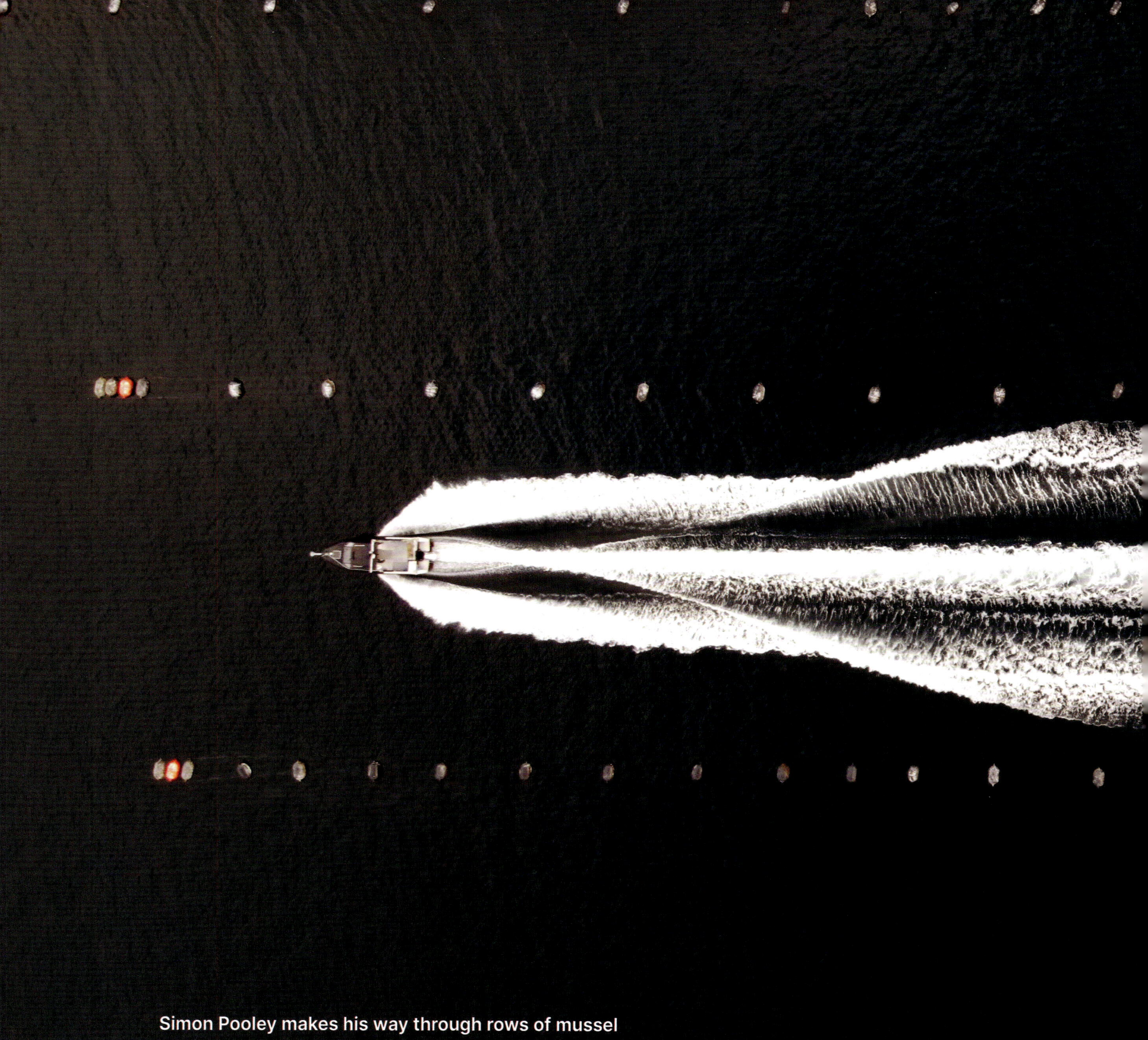

Simon Pooley makes his way through rows of mussel lines on his farm in the Marlborough Sounds.

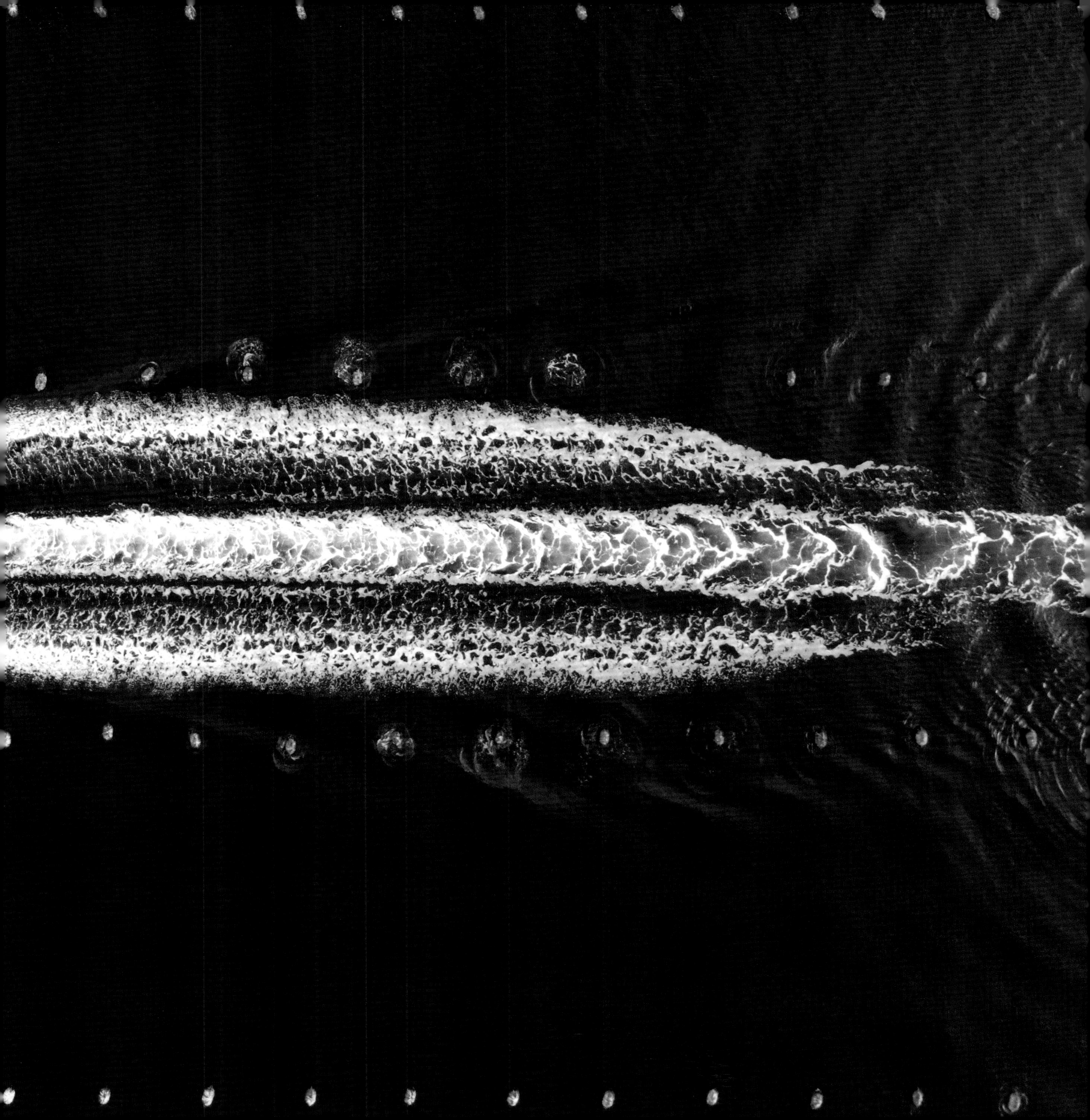

# OYSTERS

Originally accidentally introduced, the Pacific oyster is now the main farm-raised oyster as it is fast-growing and reaches a larger size than native species. It is farmed chiefly in North Island harbours and estuaries as well as in the Marlborough Sounds. Of New Zealand's wild species, the legendary Bluff oyster is dredged from March to August from beds in Foveaux Strait. Oystering in the region began in the 1860s, with shellfish numbers waxing and waning due to harvest pressure and, in recent times, a parasite. The harvest is subject to strict quotas. The rock oyster has also been commercially harvested since the mid-nineteenth century and was the first oyster to be cultivated, beginning in the 1960s. Today there are over 230 oyster farms in New Zealand using over 900 hectares of marine space, and worth about $32 million in annual sales, with over half exported.

***"I can't remember a bad day. But I know I've had them. I remember the good days. I thoroughly enjoy what I do.***

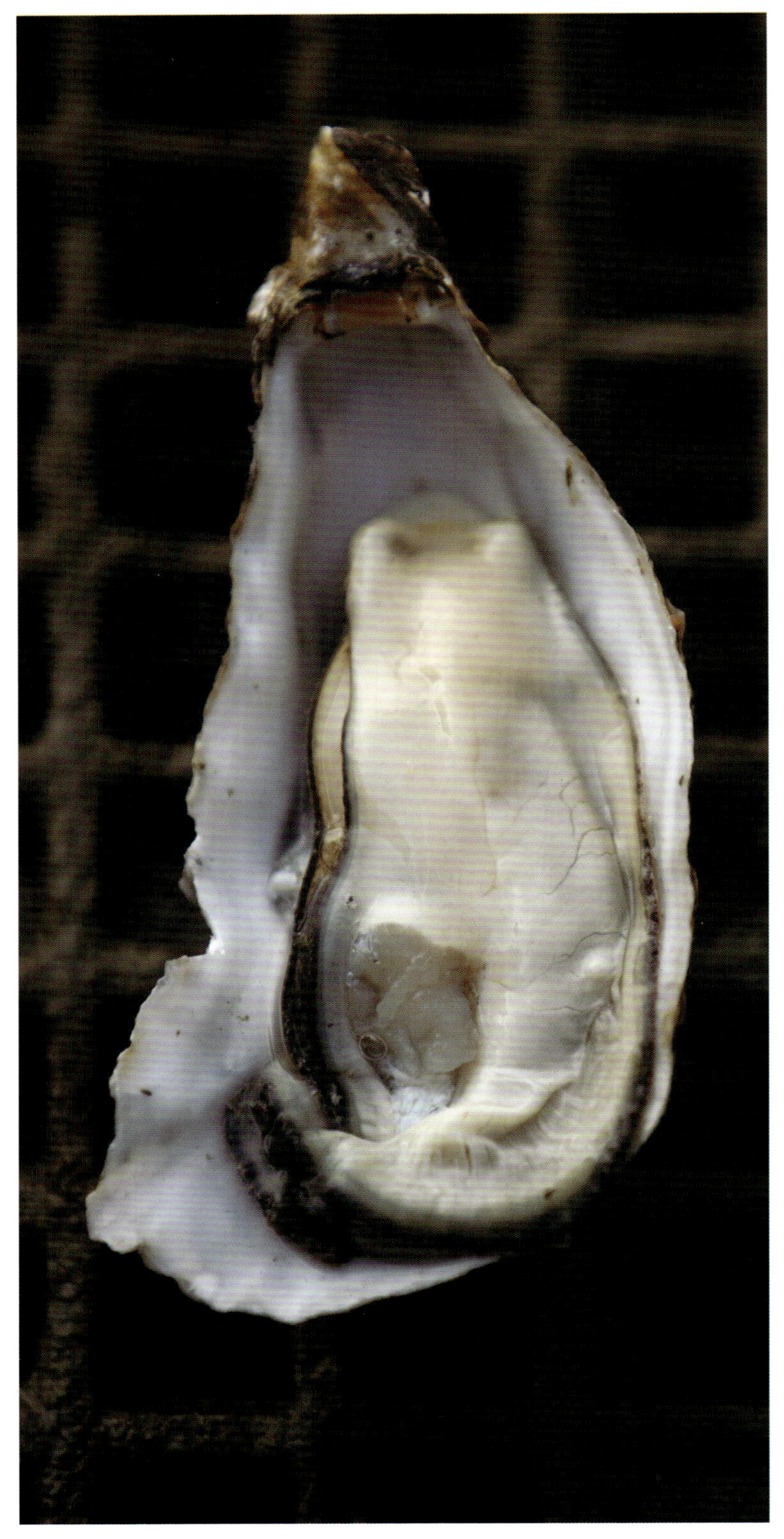

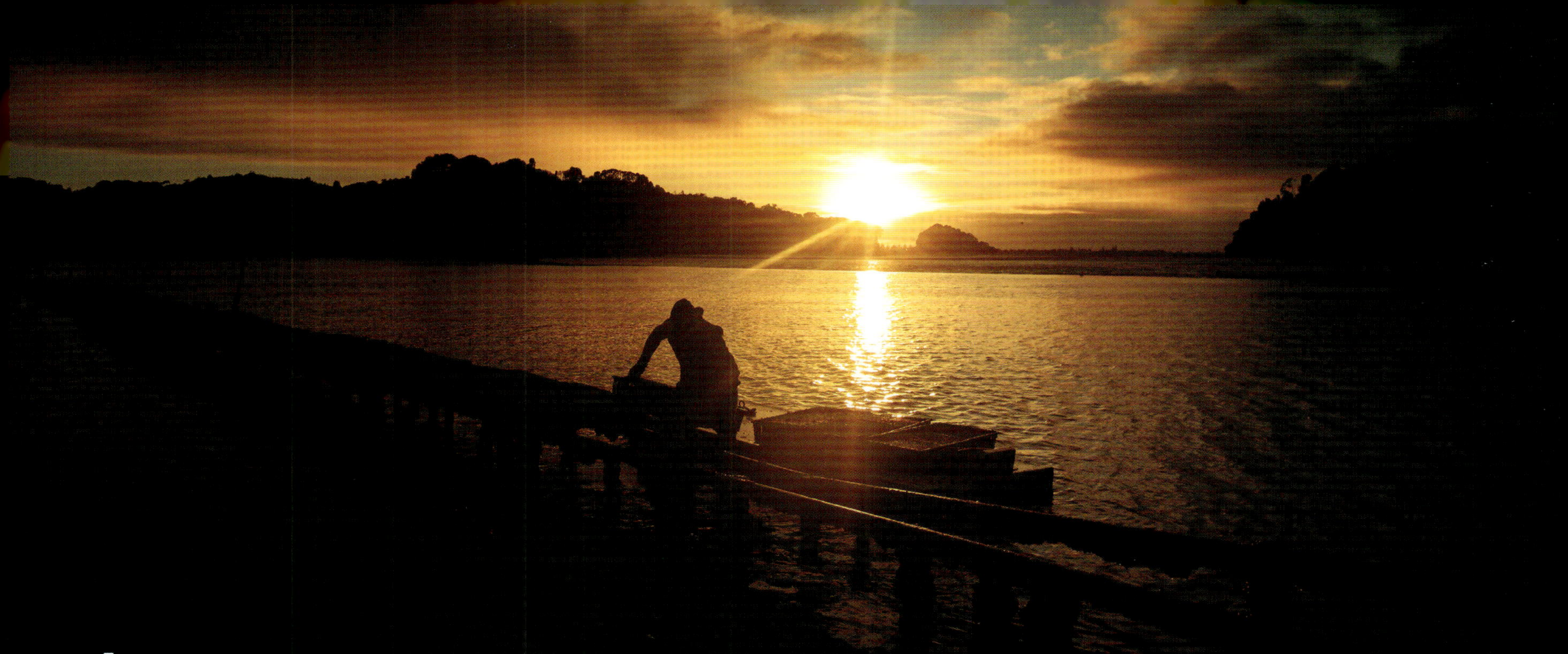

***‘We farm Pacific oysters and the farm has been here since the late 1950s. It’s a way of life, not a get-rich scheme.***

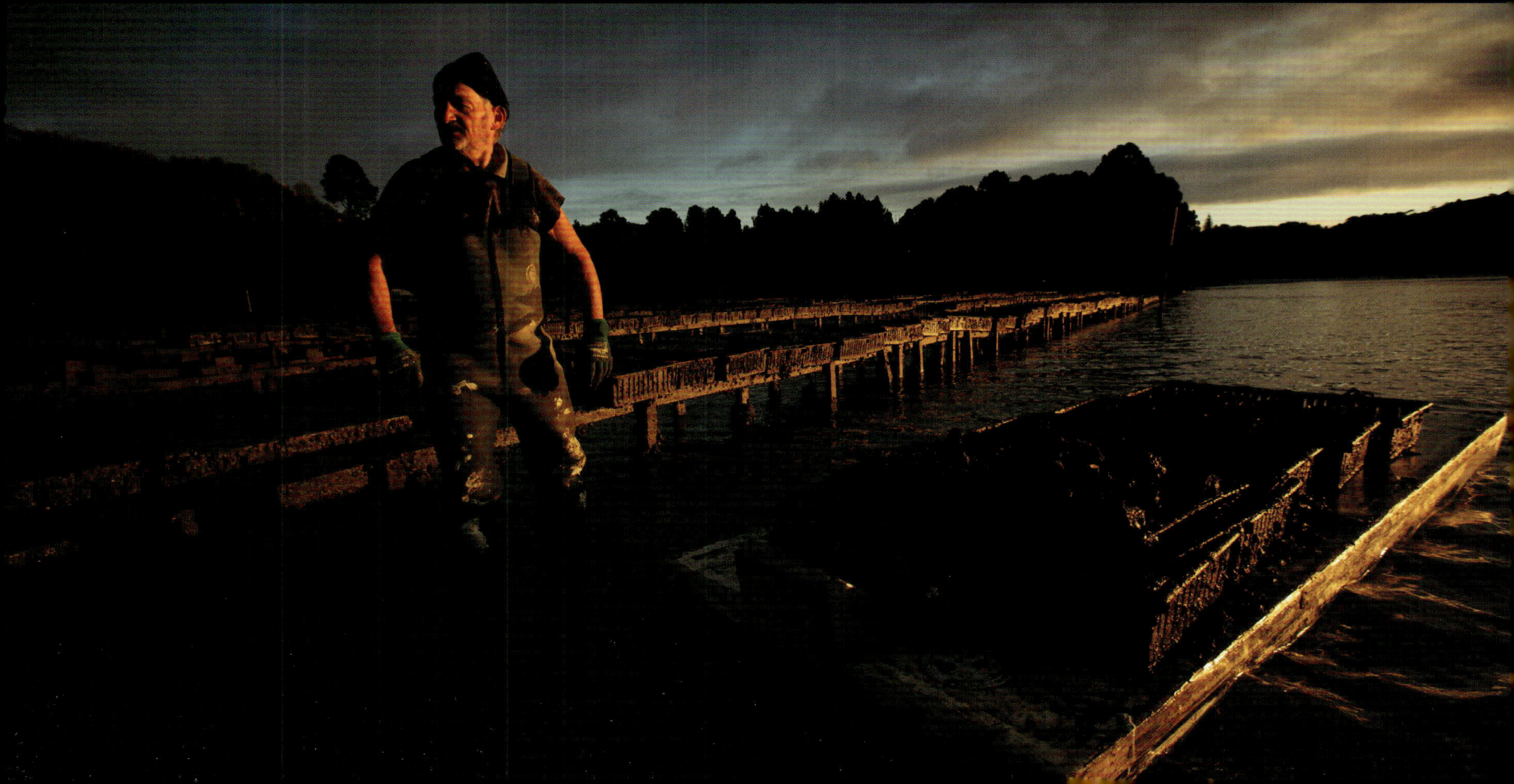

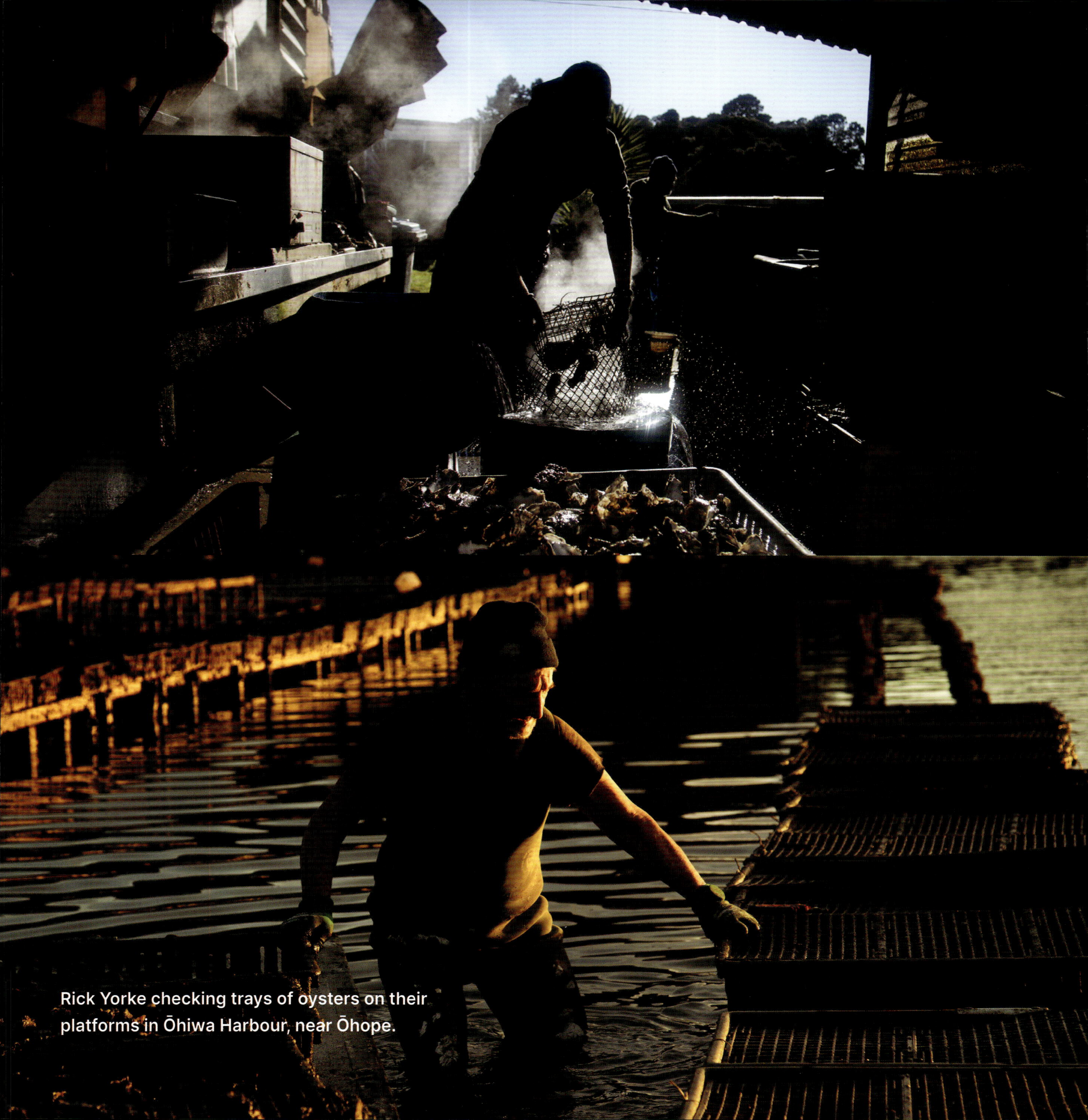

Rick Yorke checking trays of oysters on their platforms in Ōhiwa Harbour, near Ōhope.

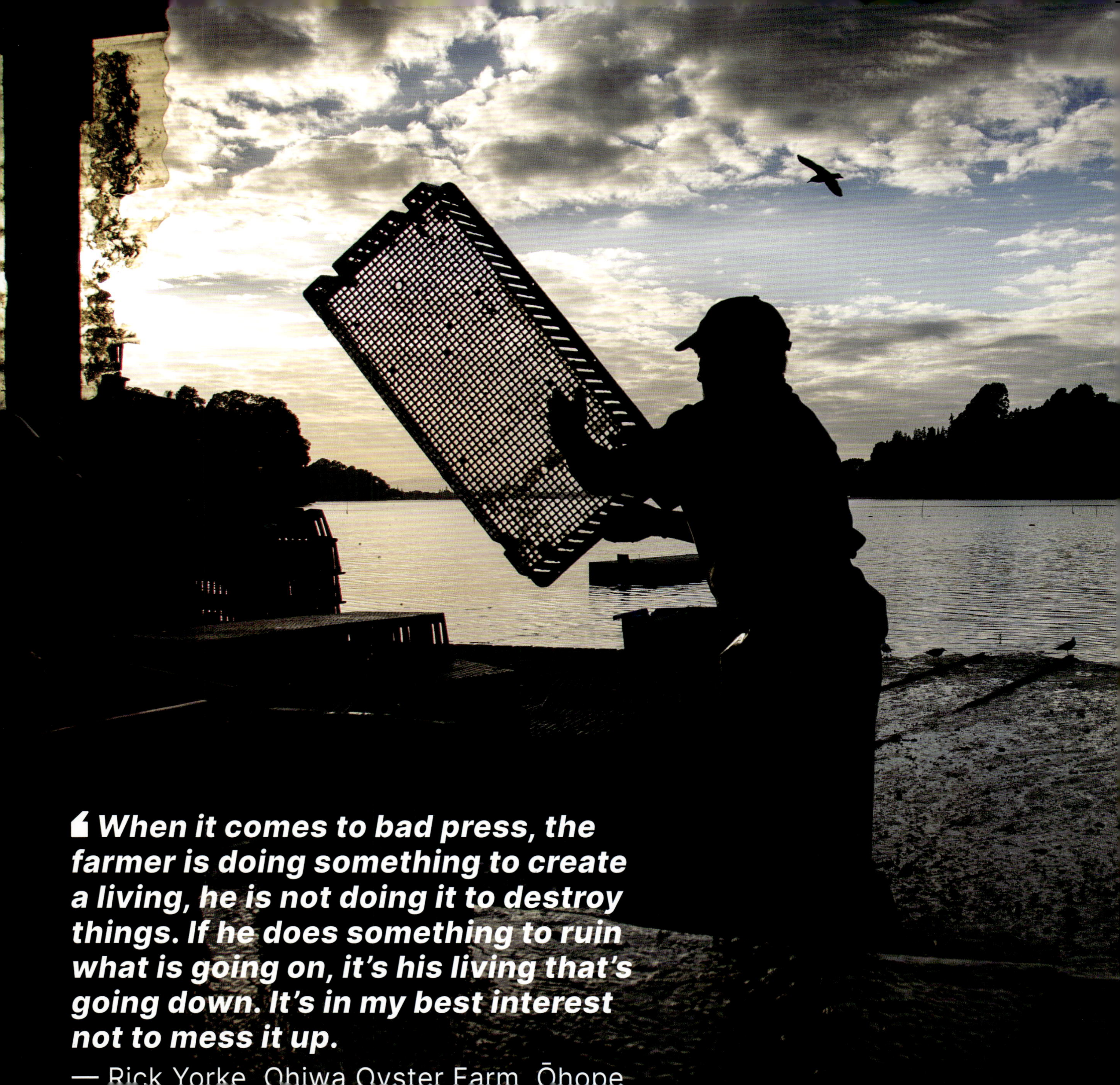

***When it comes to bad press, the farmer is doing something to create a living, he is not doing it to destroy things. If he does something to ruin what is going on, it's his living that's going down. It's in my best interest not to mess it up.***

— Rick Yorke, Ohiwa Oyster Farm, Ōhope

# HORSES

Horses were an integral part of farming life until the mid-1950s, and they are still to found in at work in some districts and especially on hill-country stations where they better suit the terrain. There are plenty of horses to be found, though, with estimates of over 100,000 throughout the country on farms, in the racing industry, in pony clubs and for private use as pets or transport. The local thoroughbred industry incorporates breeding and racing, employing over 14,000 people. New Zealand has an excellent reputation for producing high-quality thoroughbred and harness stock for the domestic market and export, chiefly to Australia, Hong Kong and Singapore. Export values range from $130 to $150 million in most years.

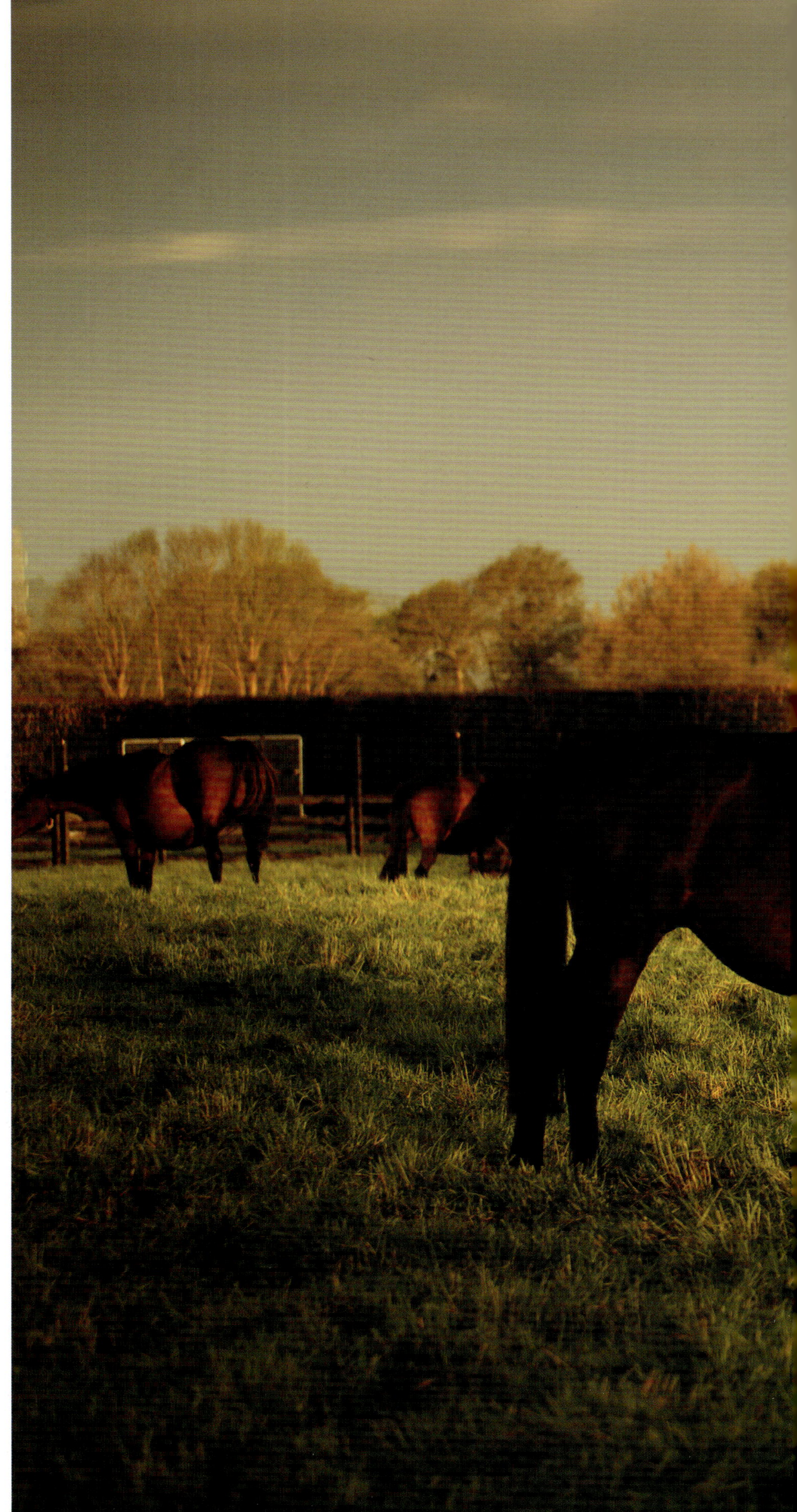

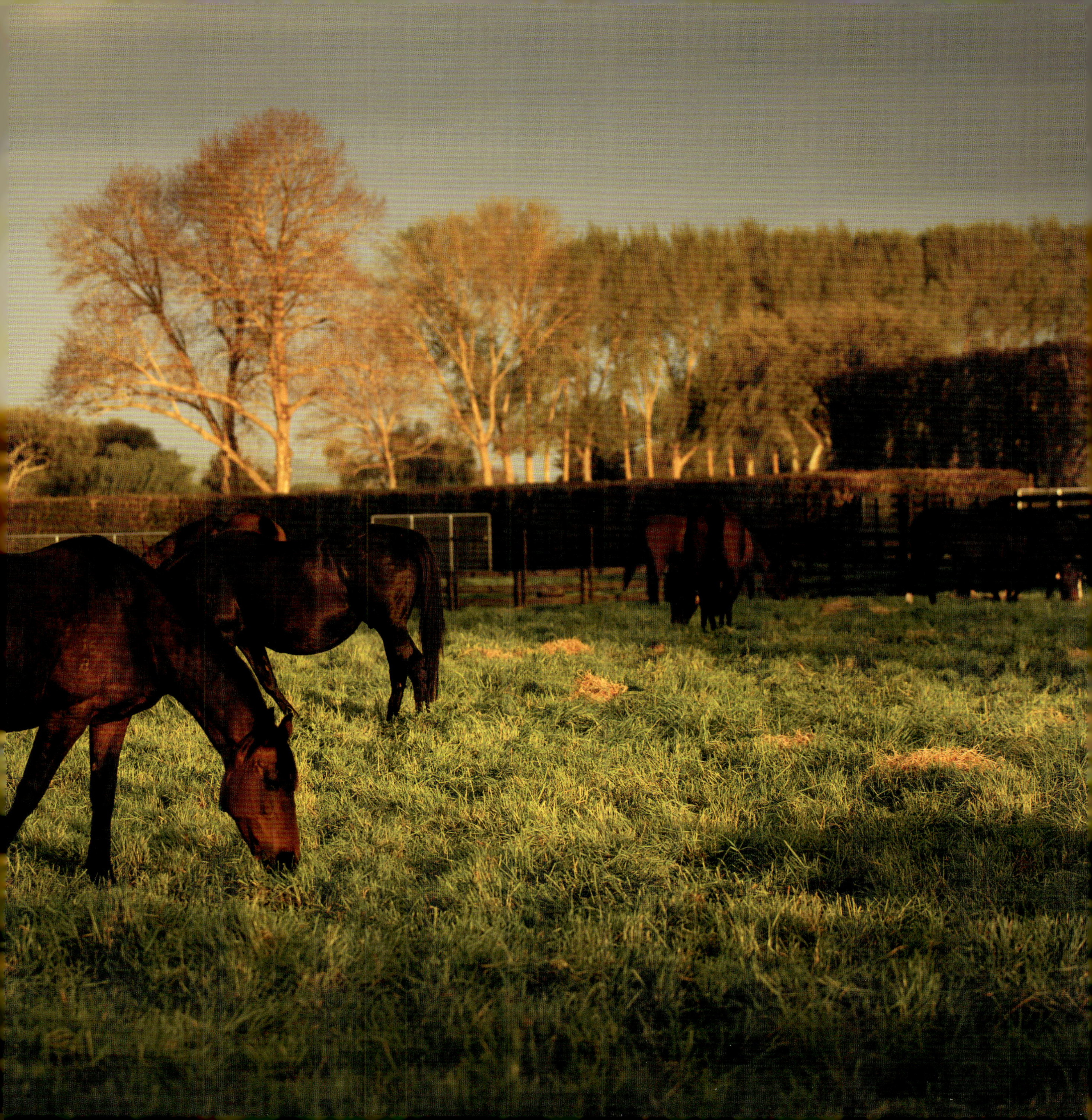

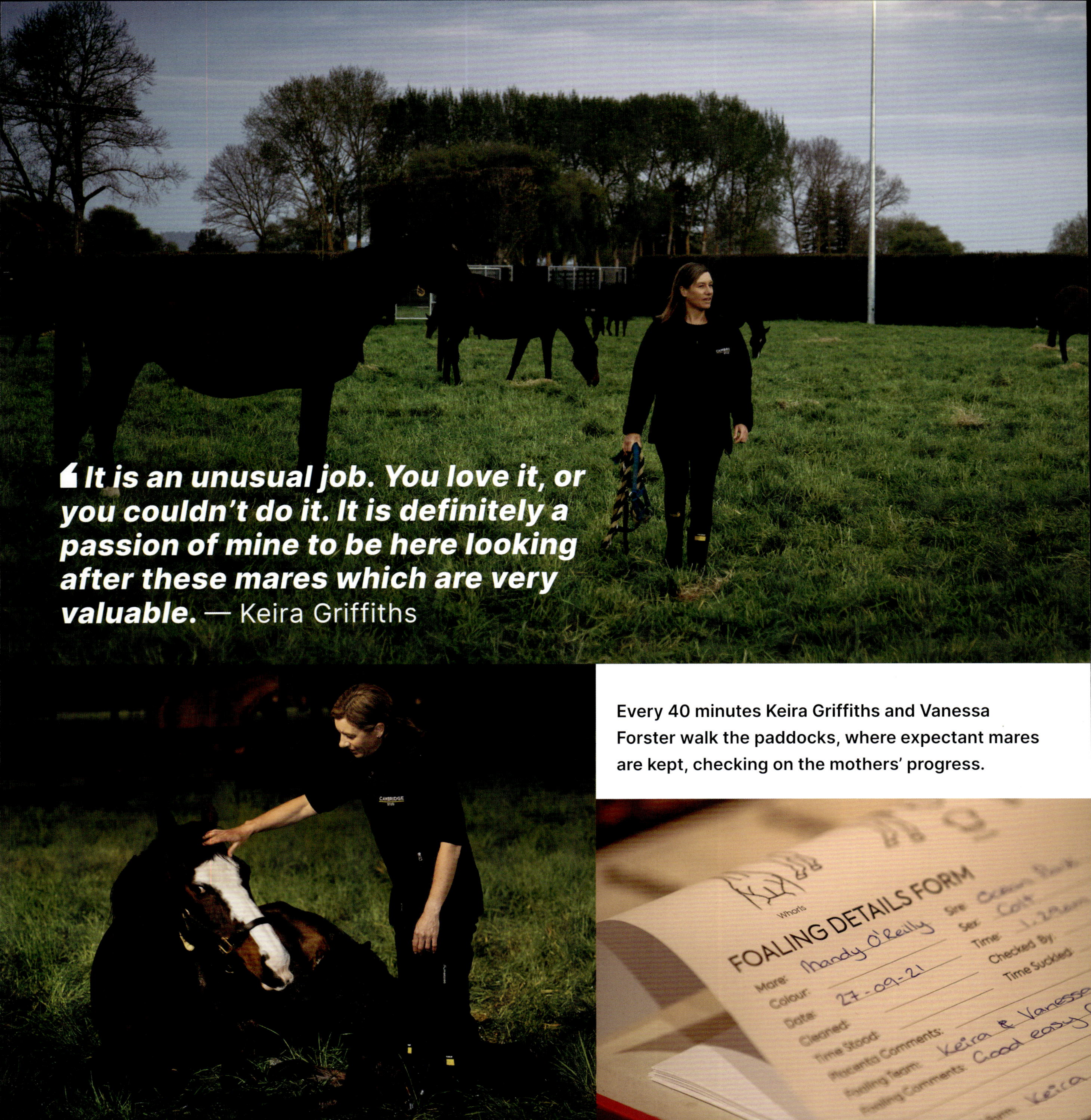


***It is an unusual job. You love it, or you couldn't do it. It is definitely a passion of mine to be here looking after these mares which are very valuable.*** — Keira Griffiths

Every 40 minutes Keira Griffiths and Vanessa Forster walk the paddocks, where expectant mares are kept, checking on the mothers' progress.

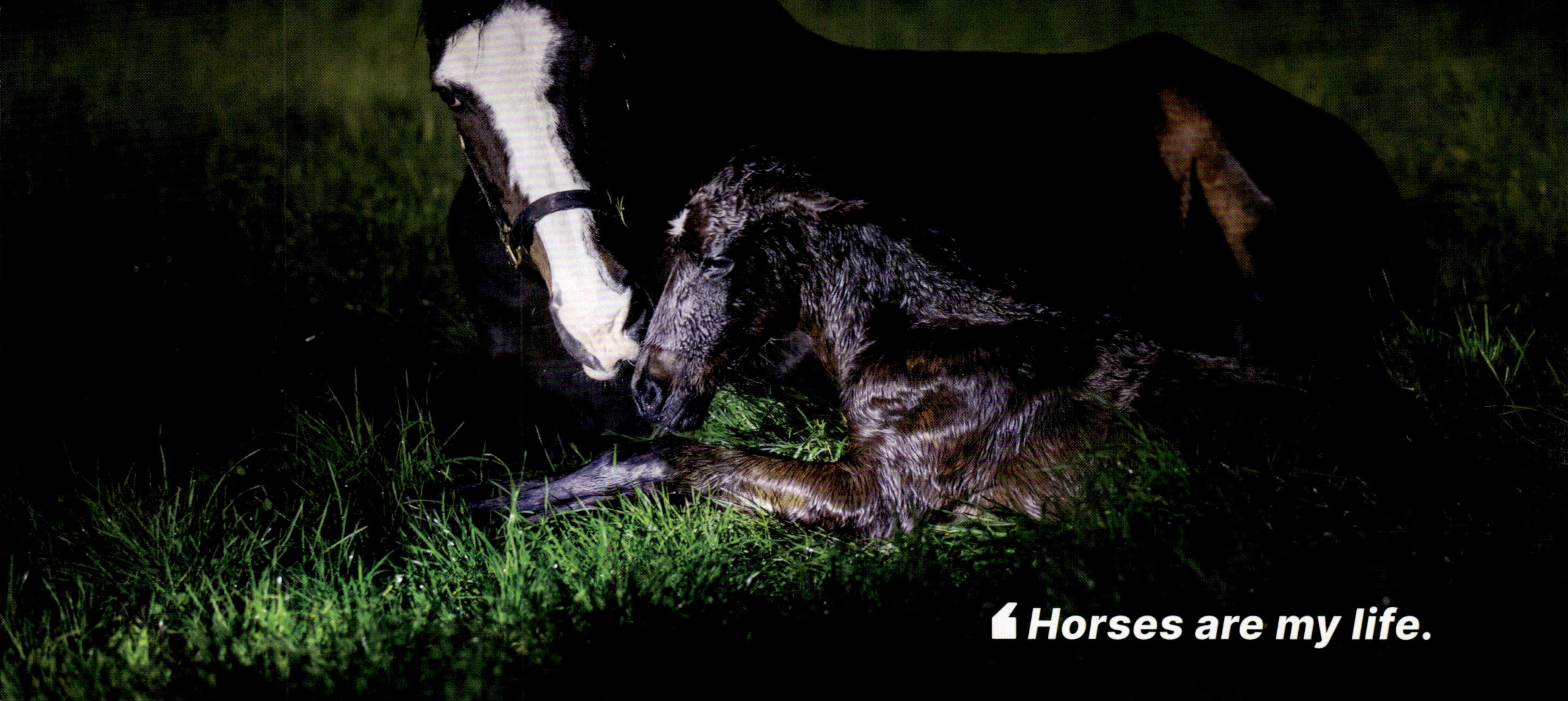


**THE THOROUGHBRED STUDS** around Cambridge have produced many champion horses, which are celebrated in a series of mosaics in the town's pavements. One of the best-known is the legendary Sir Tristram, who produced 45 Group One winners, including Melbourne Cup winner Empire Rose. Other big names in New Zealand horse-racing history include Balmerino, Ethereal, Octagonal, Mainbrace, Might and Power, So You Think, Sunline and Tulloch.

Cambridge is also one of the most successful harness-racing centres in the country.

***My job is foal watch during the night. We are up all night watching a paddock of mares who are due to foal. As soon as they start foaling, we take them from the mob of mares and put them in their own individual paddocks and help deliver a healthy foal, which will be the next superstar.***

— Keira Griffiths

*“The land is home and a place I grew up and where I want to finish.*

— Rachel Beattie

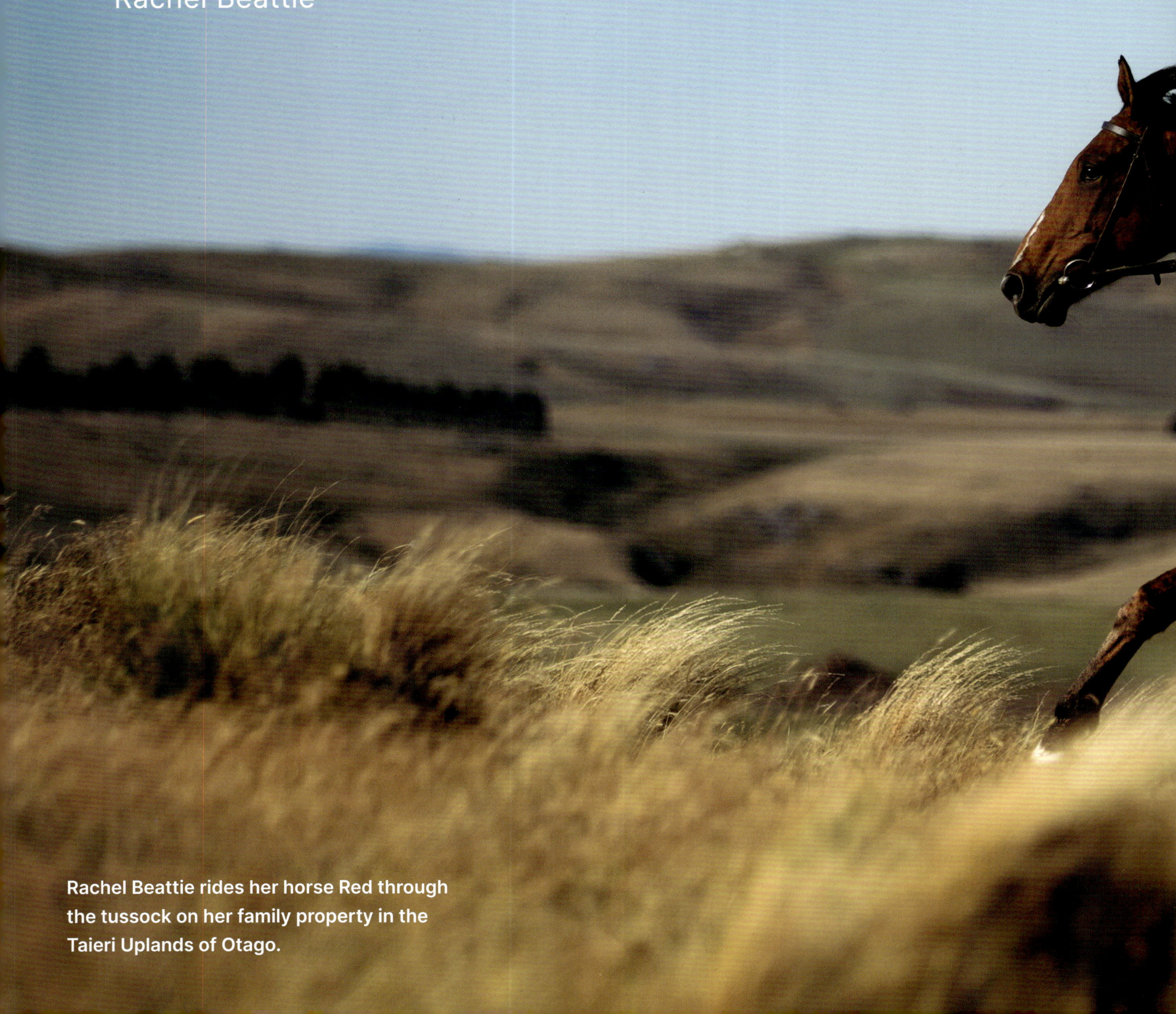

Rachel Beattie rides her horse Red through the tussock on her family property in the Taieri Uplands of Otago.

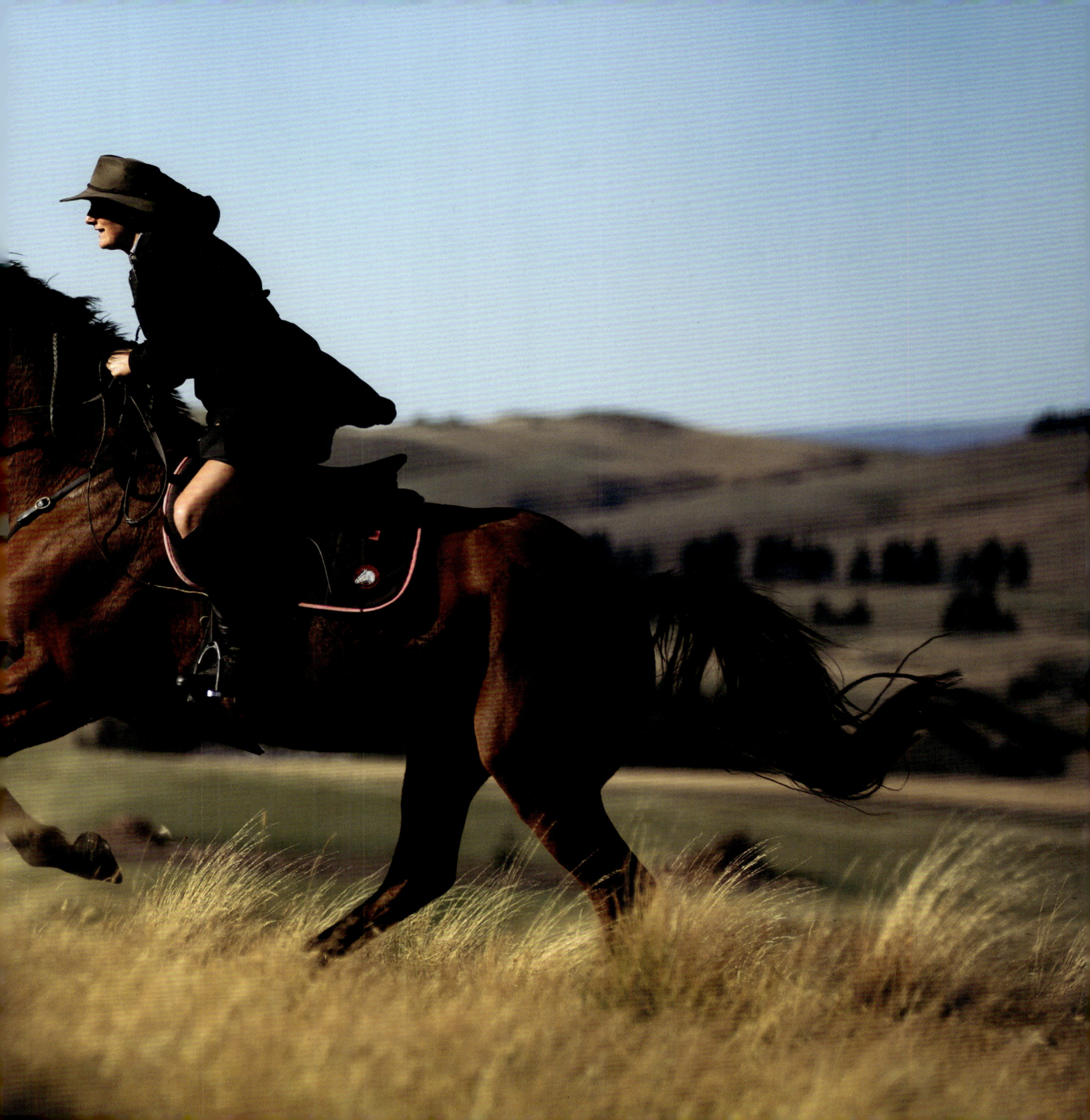

# CHINESE GROWERS

**Some 2000 young Chinese men headed to the Otago goldfields in the 1860s. Like most who joined the rush, they didn't make it rich and, as 'Asiatics', suffered racism and poverty. As the gold ran out, between 1880 and 1913 the sons and young male relatives of the early Chinese prospectors turned to work in fruit shops, laundries and market gardening to make a living. They settled throughout the country, usually leasing land and working together to supply produce to relatives running greengrocery businesses.**

The men who saved enough money to return to China often married there and had a family before returning alone to New Zealand. They were not allowed to bring their wives or young children, although sons who were old enough to work in the market gardens were allowed to come.

After the Second World War, more women and family members were allowed to immigrate, which helped them build their communities and let their businesses prosper. From the 1960s Chinese gardeners produced over 70 per cent of the green vegetables in New Zealand along with a large share of other crops. Today, many family-run market gardens still supply a diverse range of food and the Chinese are an essential part of rural society.

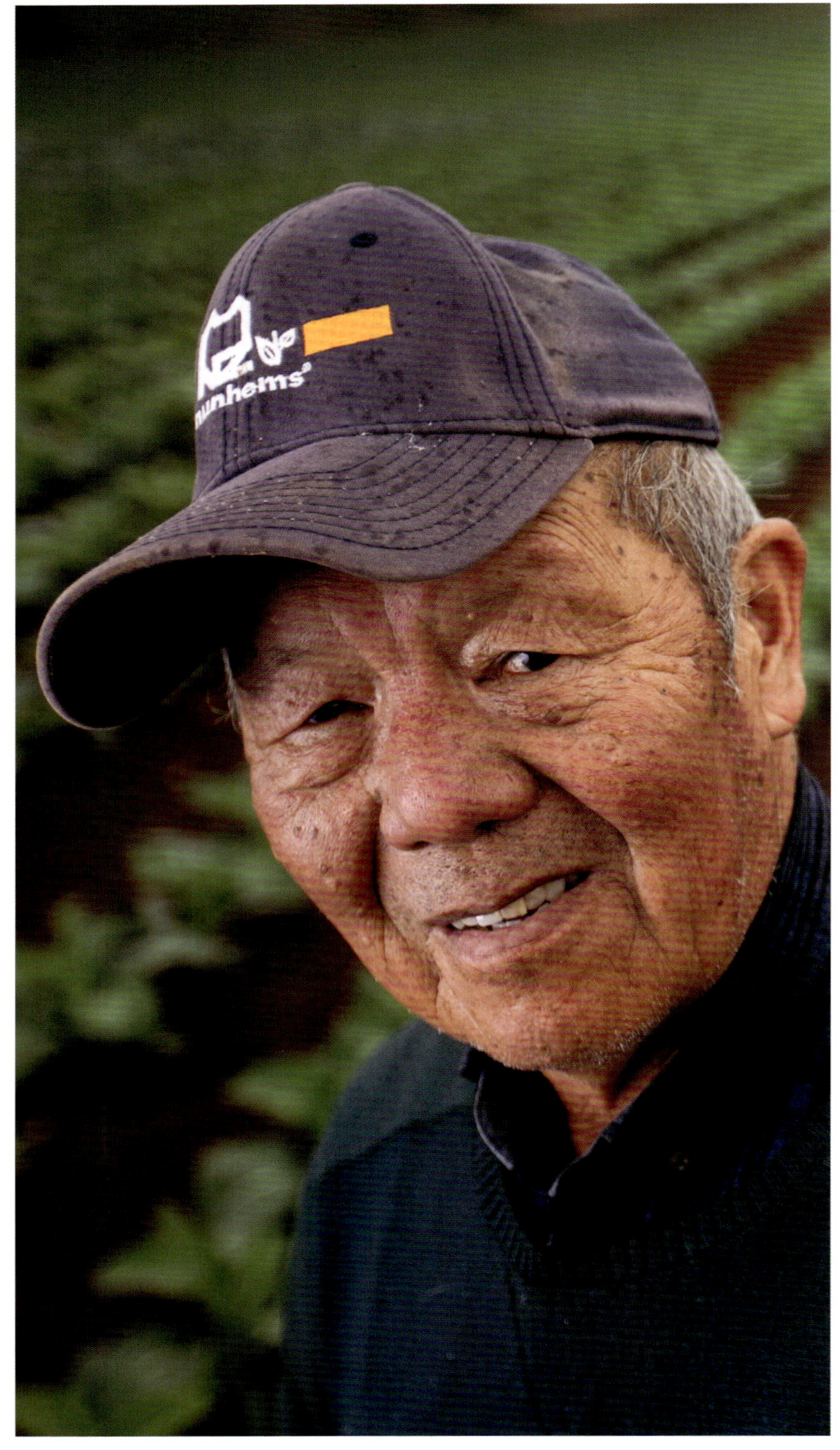

Jackie Young, a third-generation market gardener in Waiuku, Auckland.

Jamie (left) and Jackie Young among boxes of freshly harvested red onions on their multigenerational property.

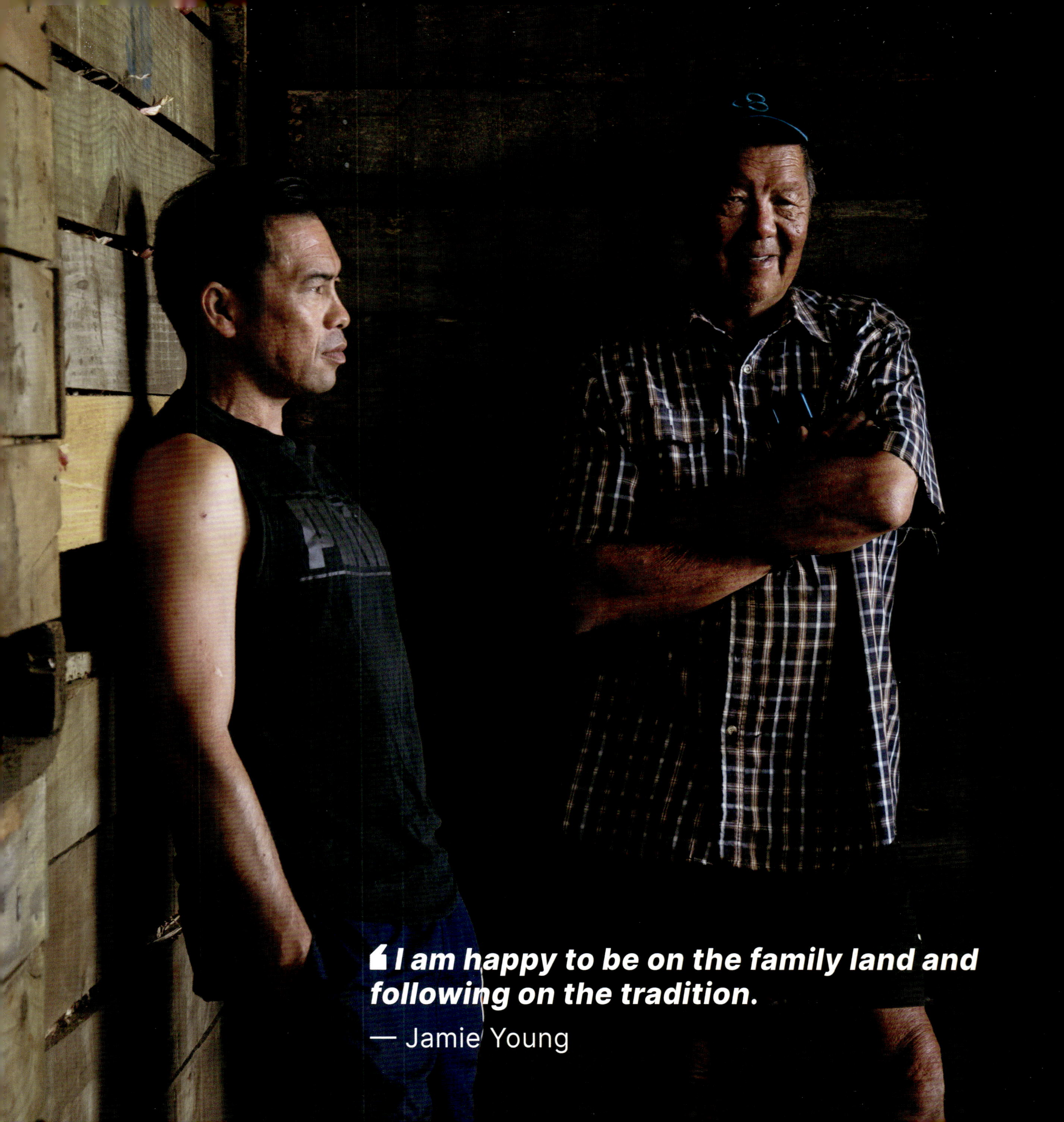

***"I am happy to be on the family land and following on the tradition.***

— Jamie Young

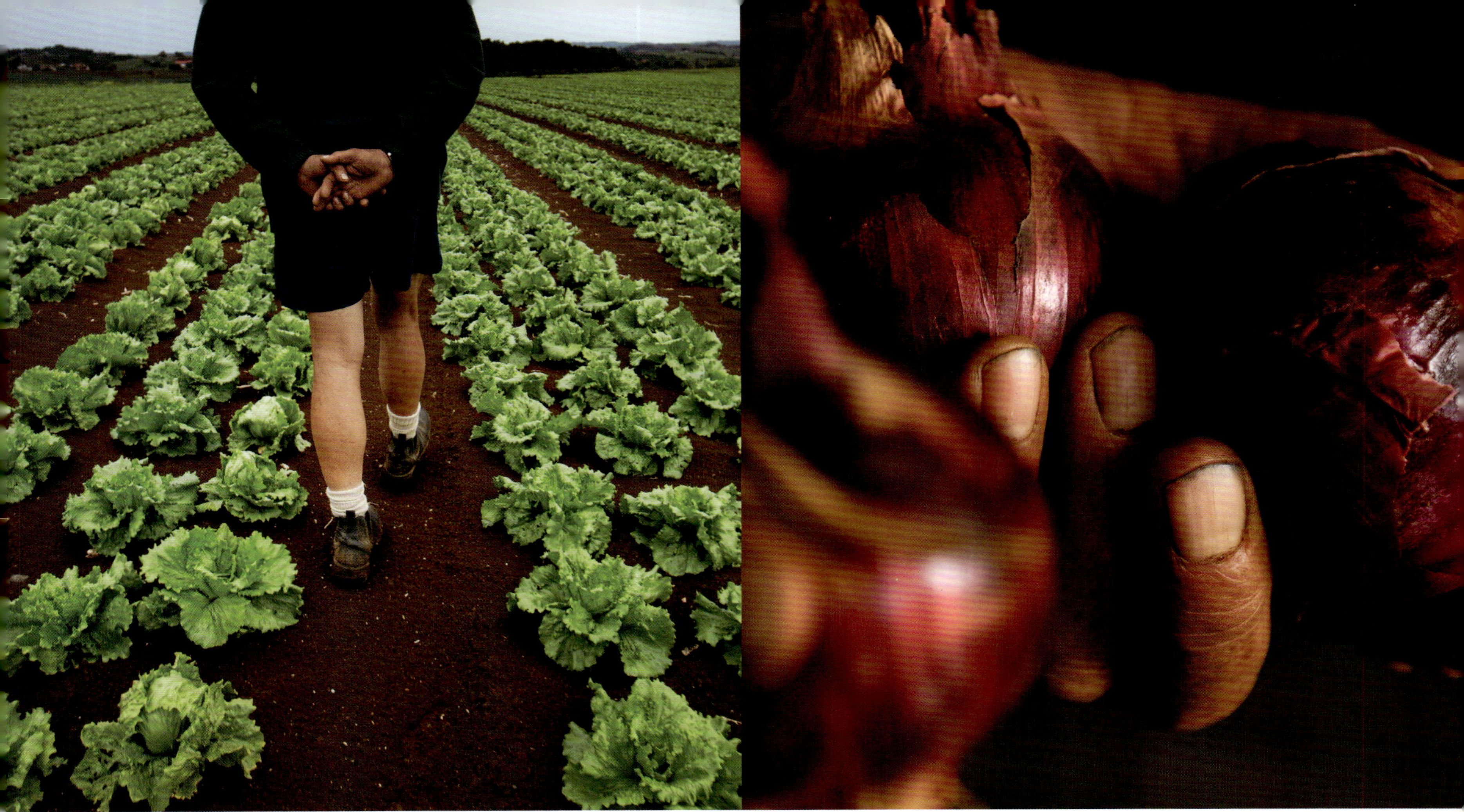

**Third-generation market gardener Jackie Young in one of his fields at Waiuku, South Auckland.**

'My name is Jackie Young and I was born in Wellington. My grandfather came to New Zealand to dig for gold and was at the Shotover River. But by the time he got here all the gold was gone, so he and his shipmates teamed up and started growing some vegetables here and everywhere. He managed to sponsor my grandmother over. Then the Second World War broke out and they were on temporary visas and none of them could go home because of the war. So the government gave us all permanent residence.

I am a third-generation market gardener. It's a pretty good life. You're doing something every day and you never get bored. The challenge is always there, and you are meeting a lot of interesting people all the time. The social life is good.

At the moment we are growing cabbage, cauliflower, broccoli, corn and onions. Prices are determined by supply and demand.

'I am Jamie Young, a fourth-generation market gardener. I love this life. If I didn't, I wouldn't be here. I am looking at future-proofing things and looking at how to make things more efficient. I am happy to be on the family land and following on the tradition. I am hoping in the future that there is another bloodline to follow on here.

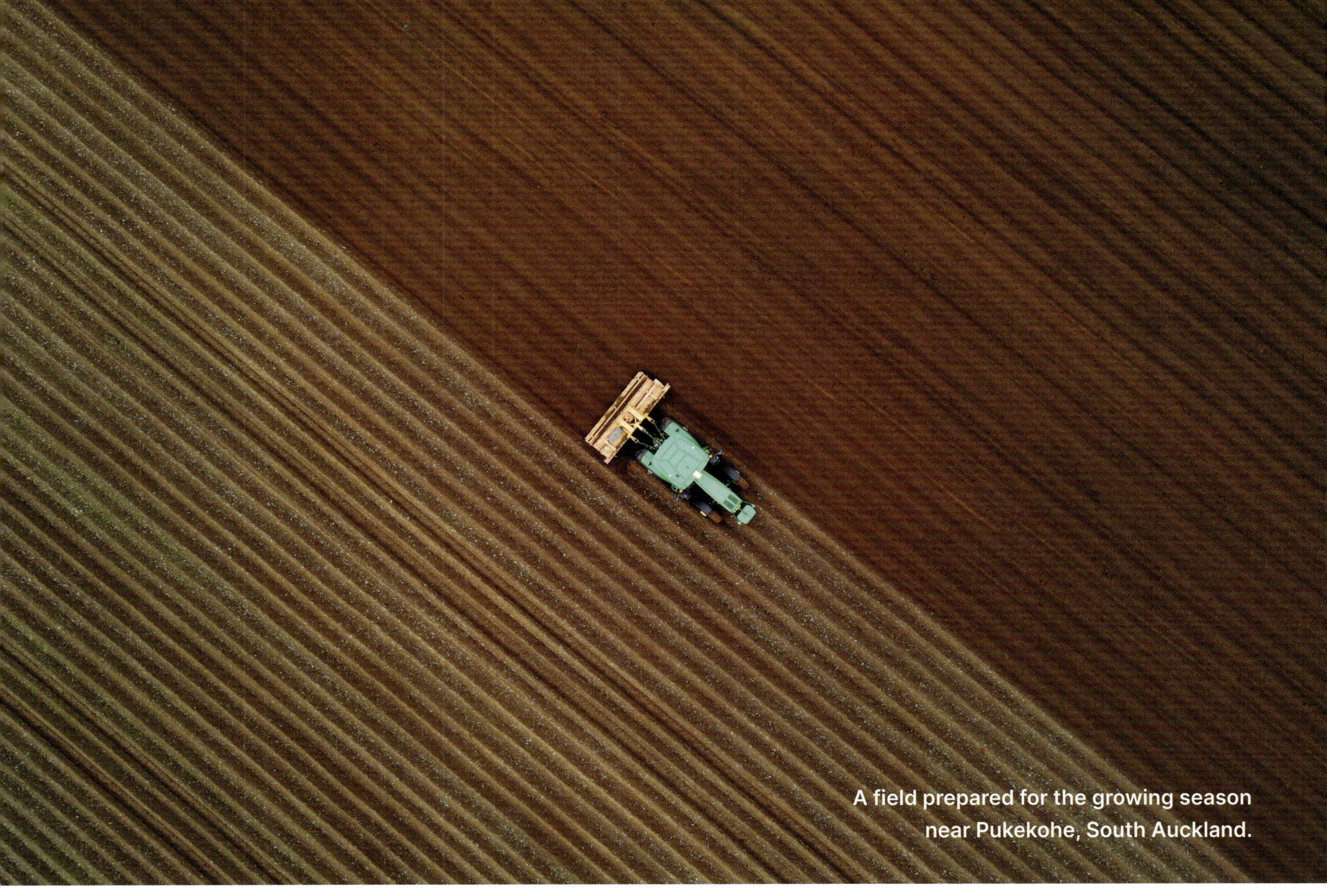

A field prepared for the growing season near Pukekohe, South Auckland.

# CROPPING

When wool prices declined in the 1870s, pastoralists in Canterbury and Otago turned to large-scale cropping, made possible through improvements in ploughs and harvesting machinery. Today, arable farming in New Zealand includes cereal cropping, with barley, wheat and oats the key grains. Animal forage crops include maize, brassicas (swedes, turnips, oil-seed rape, kale) and cereals. Vegetable crops such as peas, lentils, corn, potatoes, beans and carrots are usually sold to companies for freezing or canning. Herbage crops include ryegrass and white clover grown for seed. Overall, cropping provides essential raw materials worth around $5 billion annually to the wider food industry. Around two-thirds of arable production land area is in Canterbury, which grows the bulk of the country's wheat, oats, barley and peas, along with Southland, Otago and Manawatū-Whanganui and Hawke's Bay. Most of the maize grain, however, is grown in the North Island.

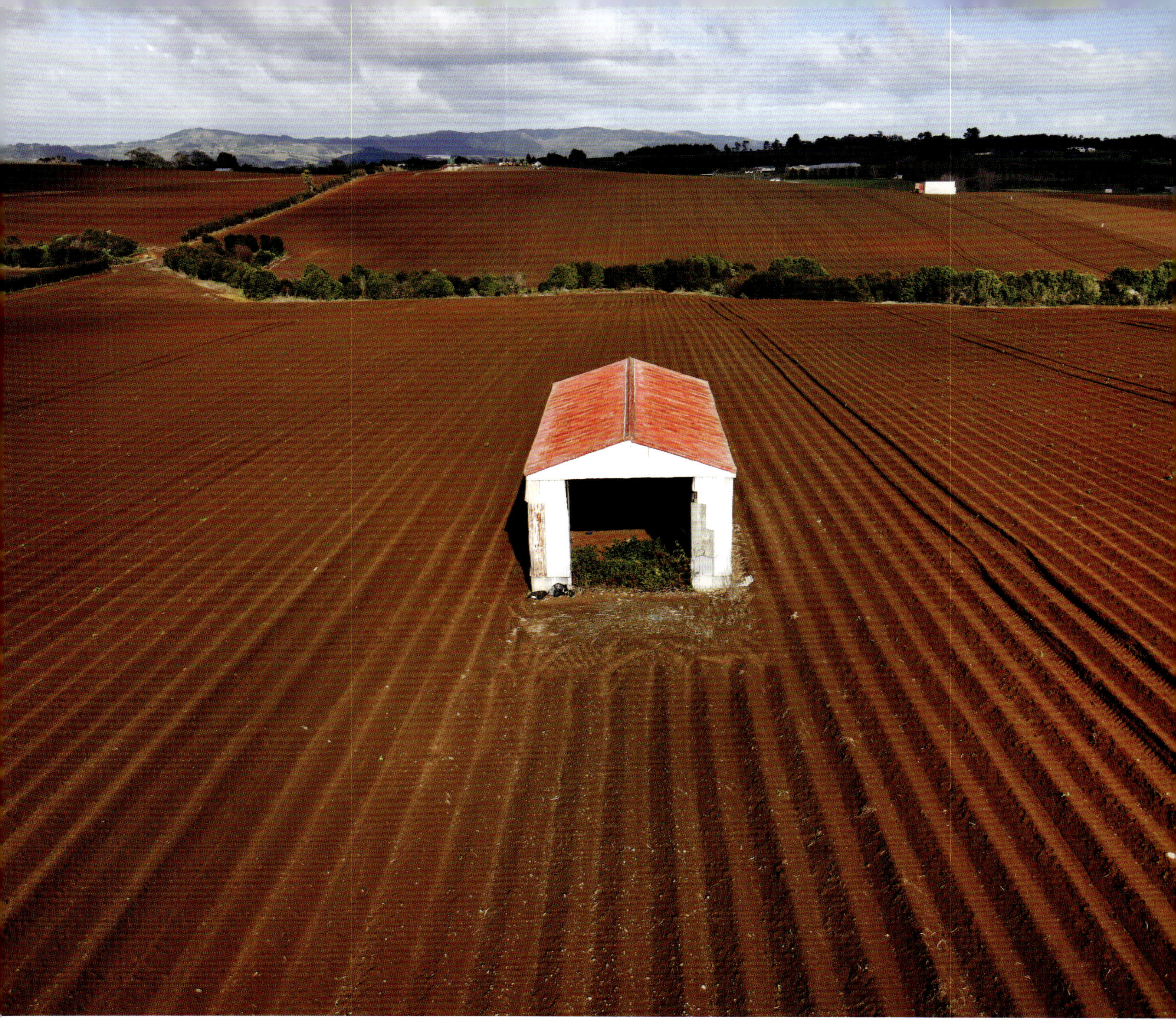

A shed interrupts the perfect lines of rich volcanic soil at Waiuku, South Auckland. The area has kept Auckland and much of New Zealand fed for generations.

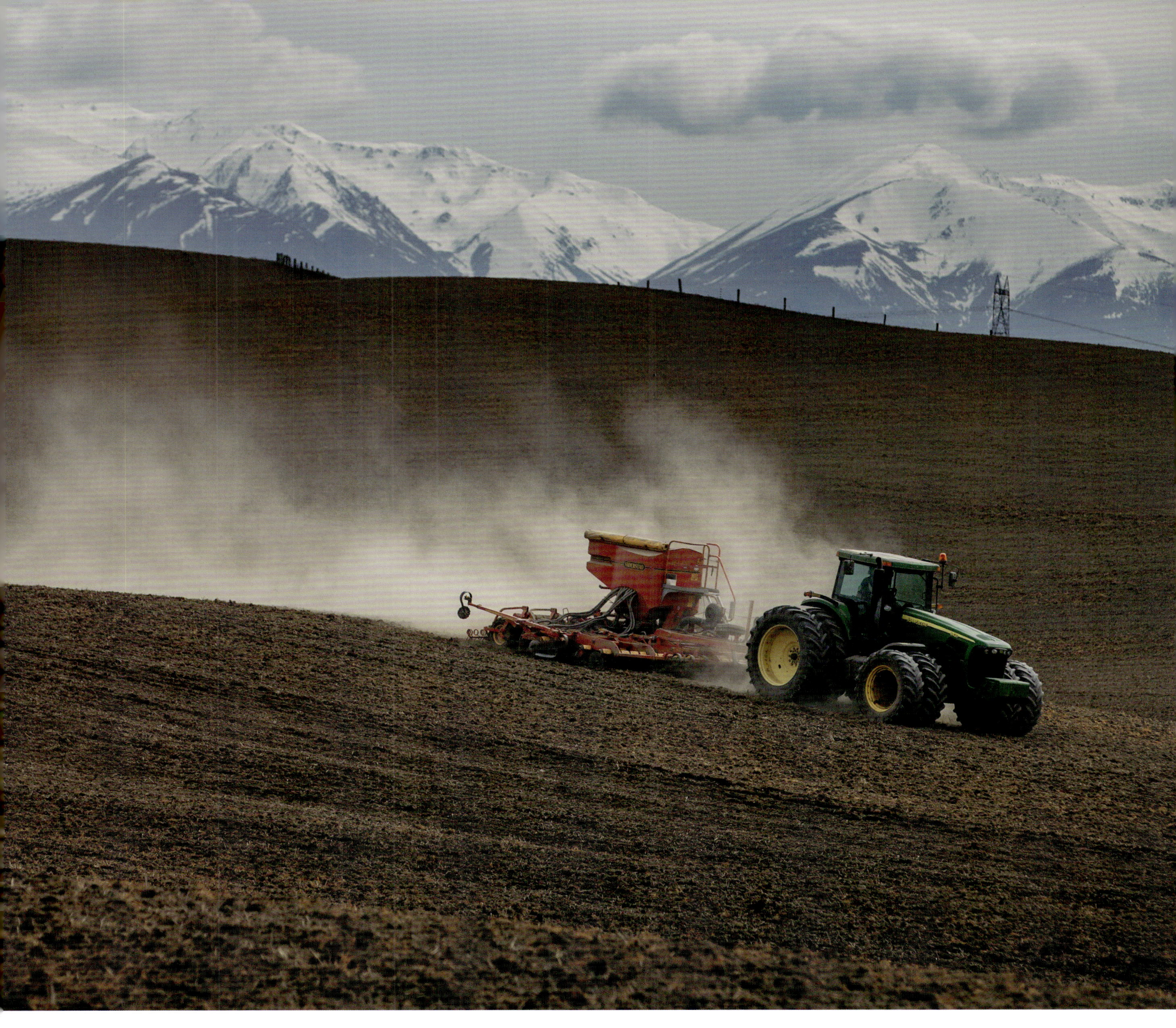

Working arable land on rolling hills under the
Southern Alps, Canterbury.

# MAIZE

Maize is a vital crop for New Zealand dairy farmers, with nearly all of it used for maize silage. The Waikato region is the largest grower of maize, producing nearly half of the national crop. Maize for silage is harvested when the plant is in full leaf, but before it is too dry or mature. When matured, the grain is harvested and sold, mostly for animal feed to dairy farmers, or as seed. New Zealand maize production has increased slowly since the 1970s, with 190,000 tonnes harvested in 2020.

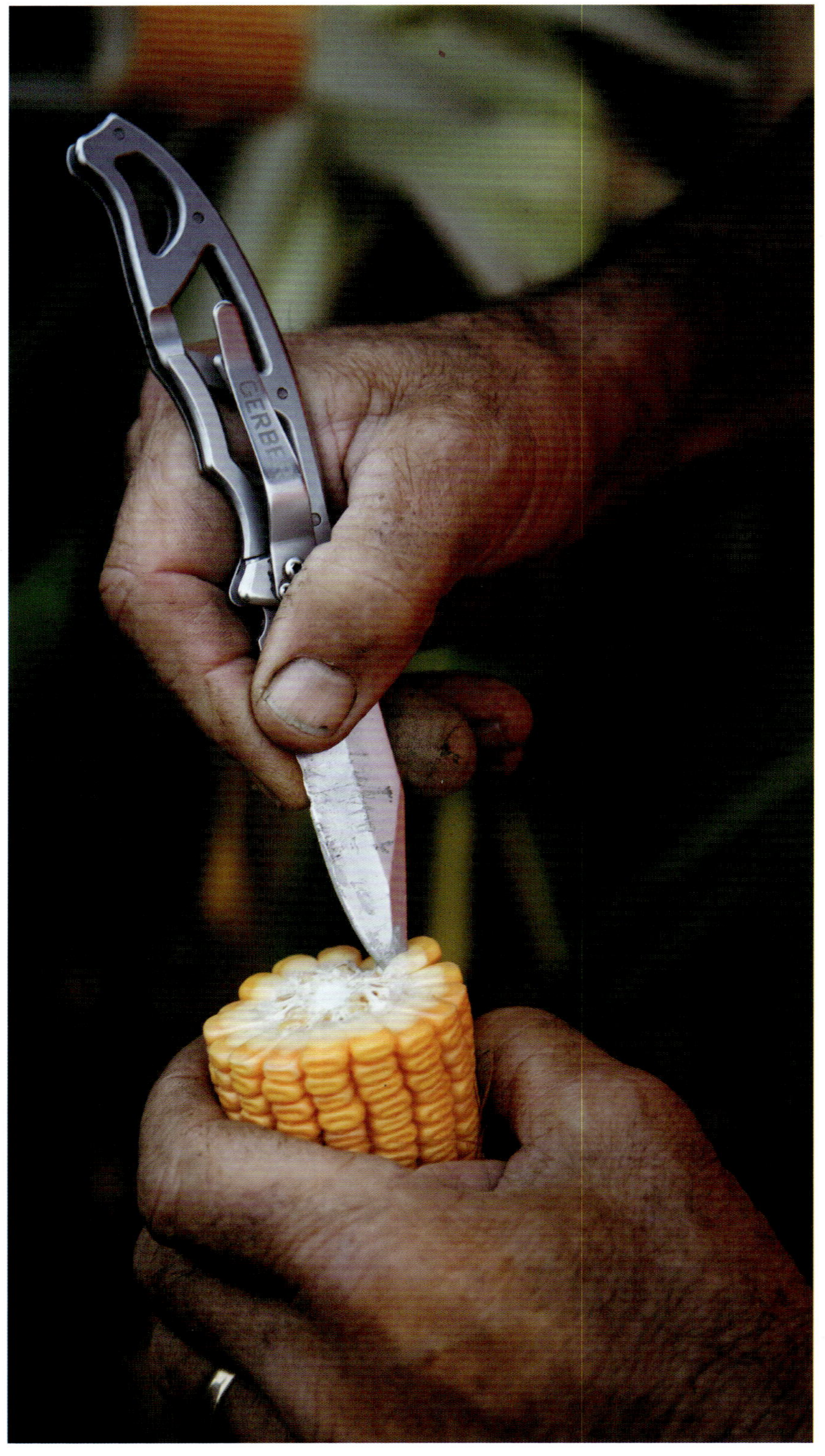

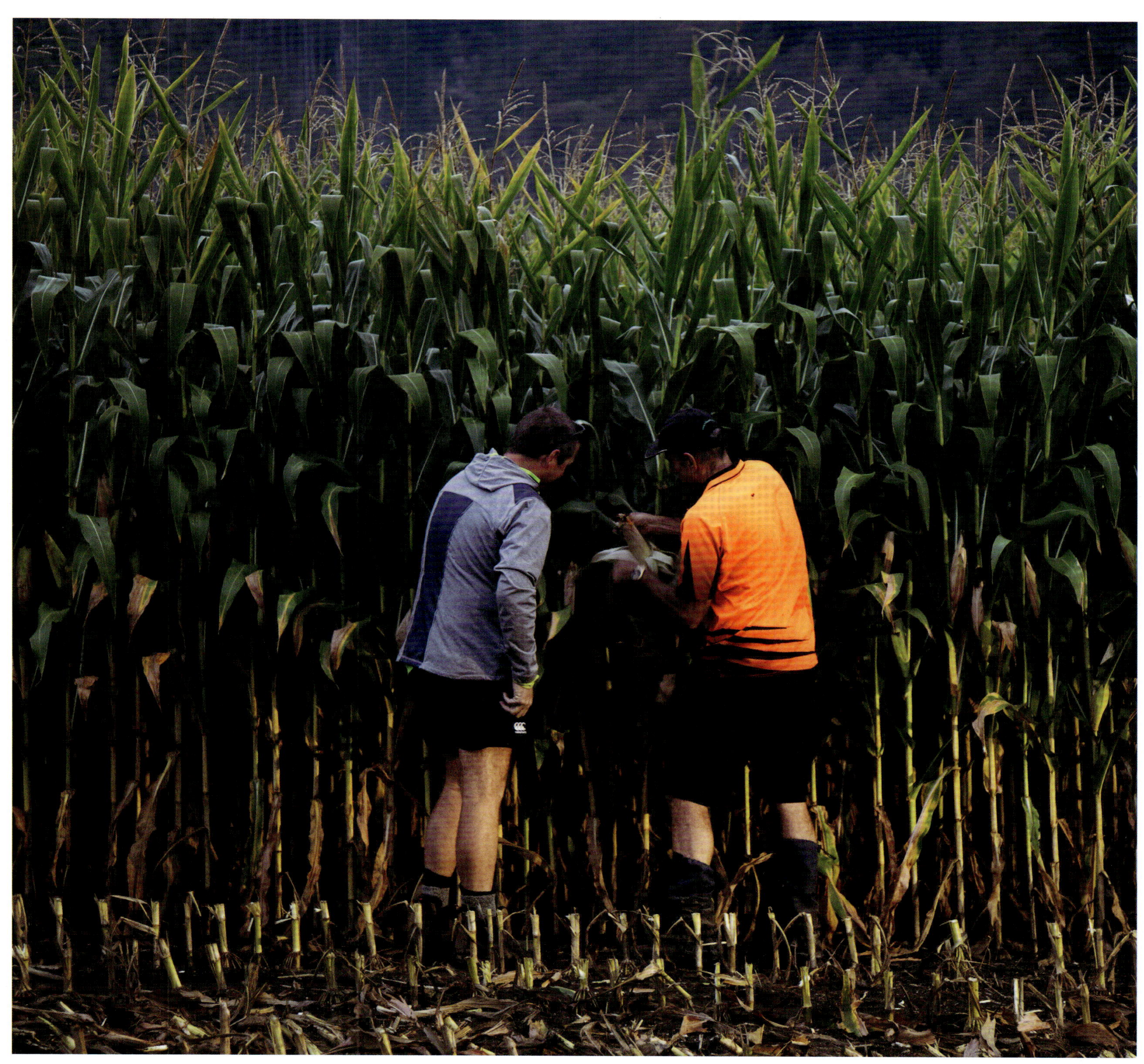

Contractors Craig Harrison (left) and Bill Webb inspect a crop of maize in the Bay of Plenty. Vast areas are planted in the crop annually, harvested as feed for the country's dairy herds.

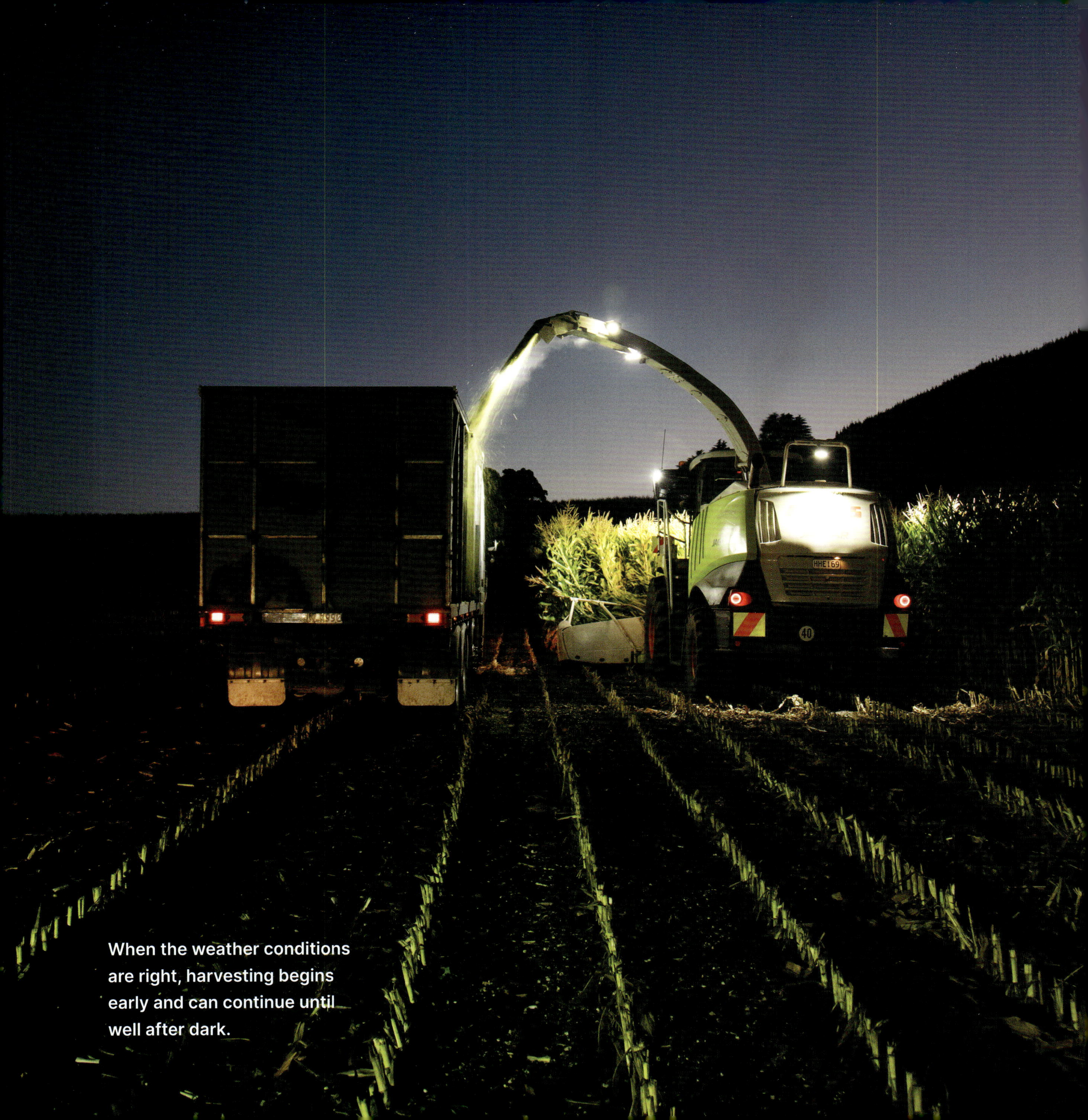


When the weather conditions are right, harvesting begins early and can continue until well after dark.

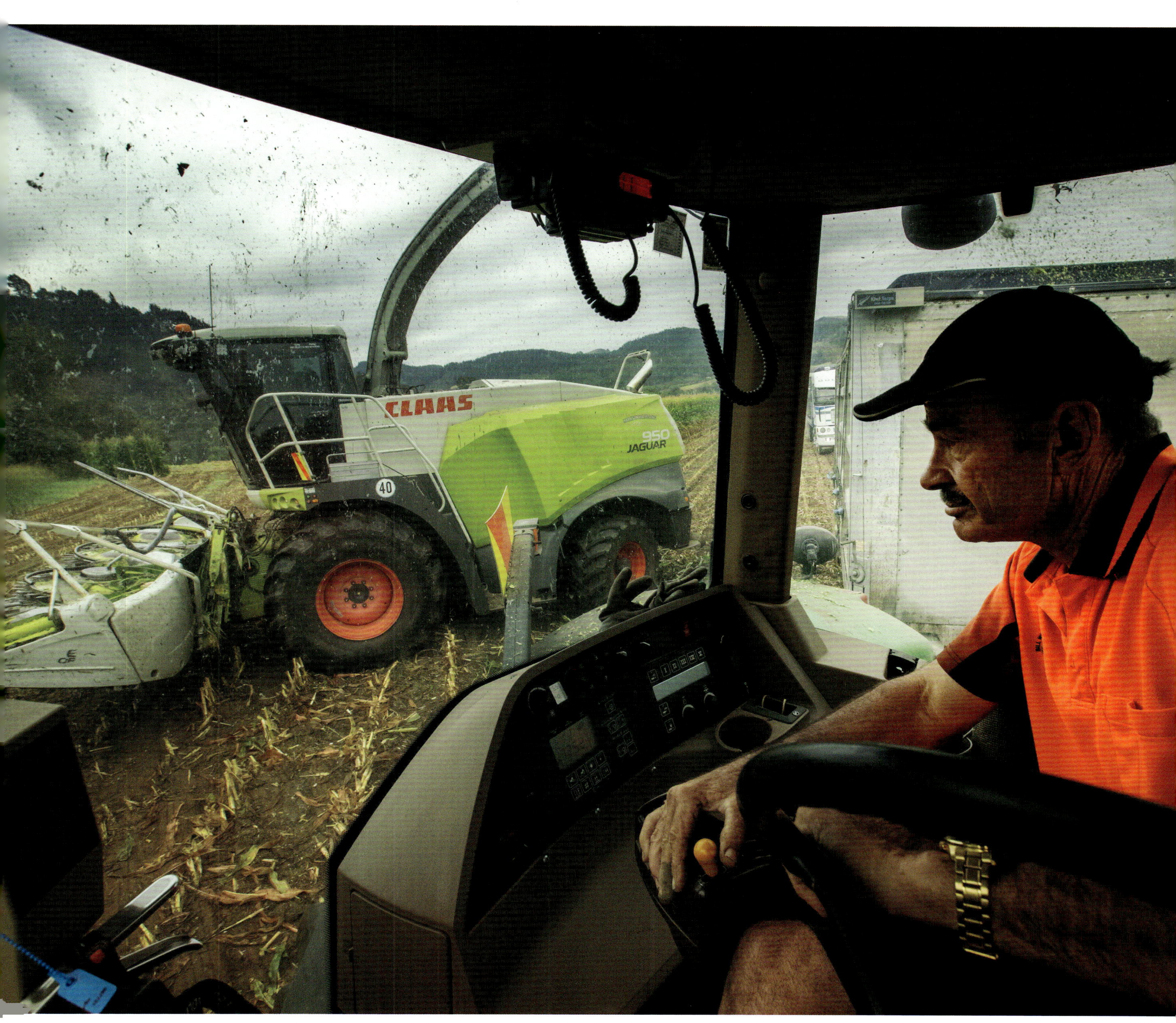


Bill Webb expertly guides his trailer alongside the combine harvester, keeping pace with the huge vehicle.

# HAY MAKING

Hay is not only an important crop but hay making has long been a summer tradition on New Zealand farms. When small conventional bales were the norm, it was often a whole-family affair to pick up and transport bales from paddocks to barn. It was always hot and thirsty work. Hay required more physical labour and is more vulnerable to the weather than silage. Consequently, a lot of effort and innovation has gone in to reducing field losses and physical work, with technology and mechanisation replacing a lot of the sweat and muscle. Not all hay is consumed locally, with exports going chiefly to Japan and Australia worth several million dollars annually.

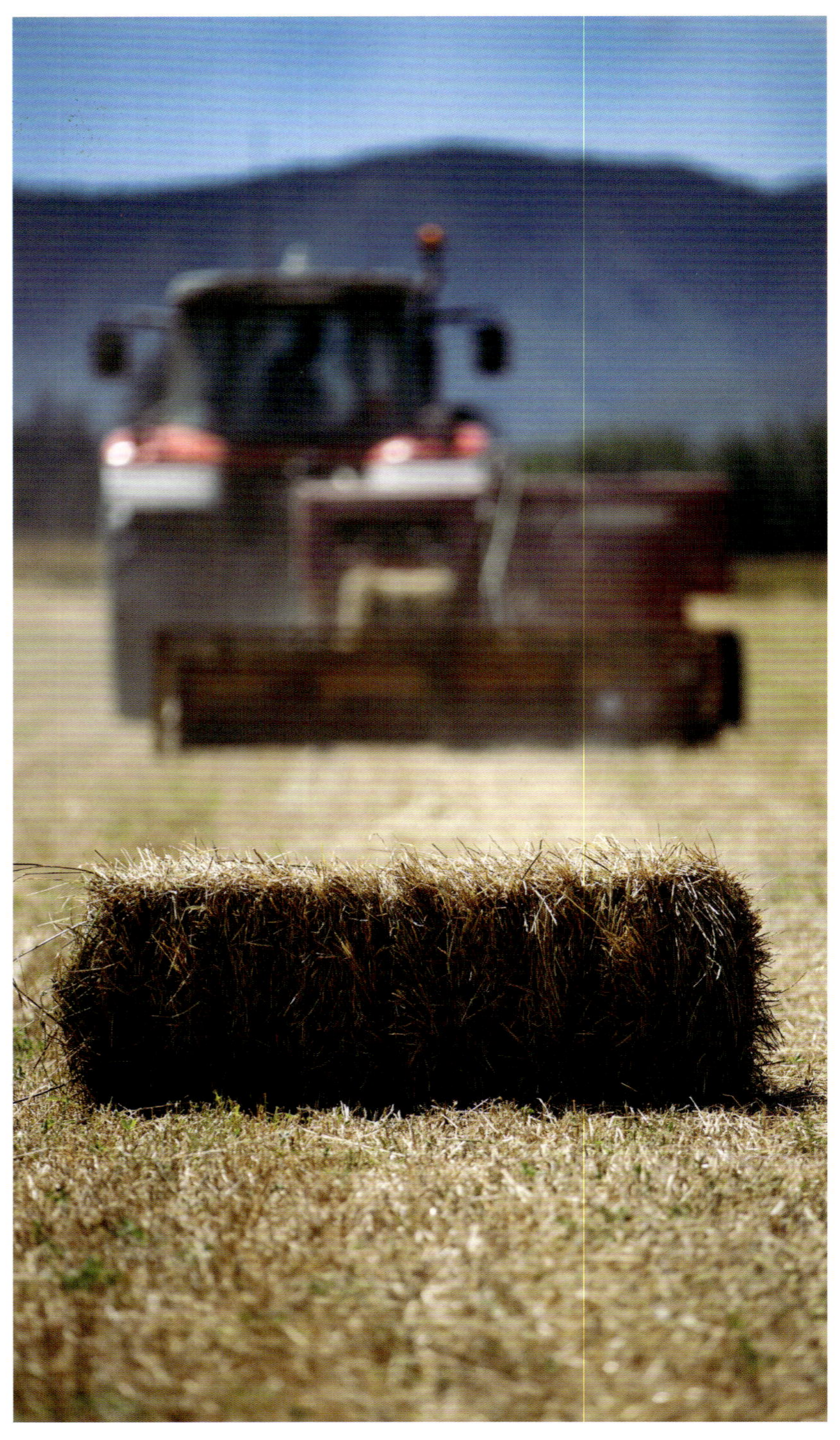

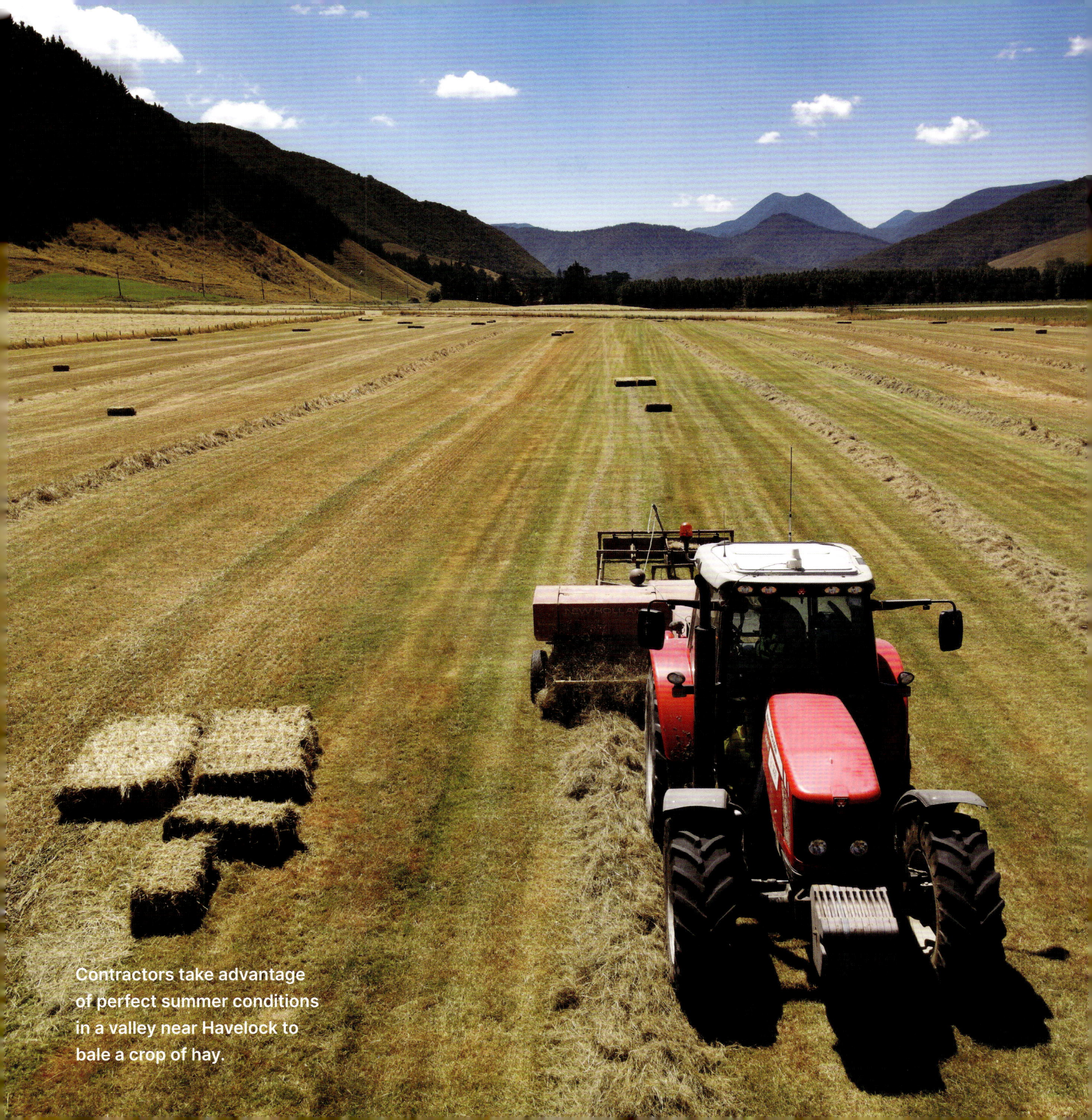

Contractors take advantage of perfect summer conditions in a valley near Havelock to bale a crop of hay.

# THE GOOD FARM

**Loren Gibbs and partner Michaela Good own The Good Farm in Welcome Bay, Tauranga, and run it on organic principles, selling the milk, veggies and eggs they produce to locals. Loren Gibbs explains:**

'My mum always said that food is medicine. So, if you are eating good food, you are getting good medicine.

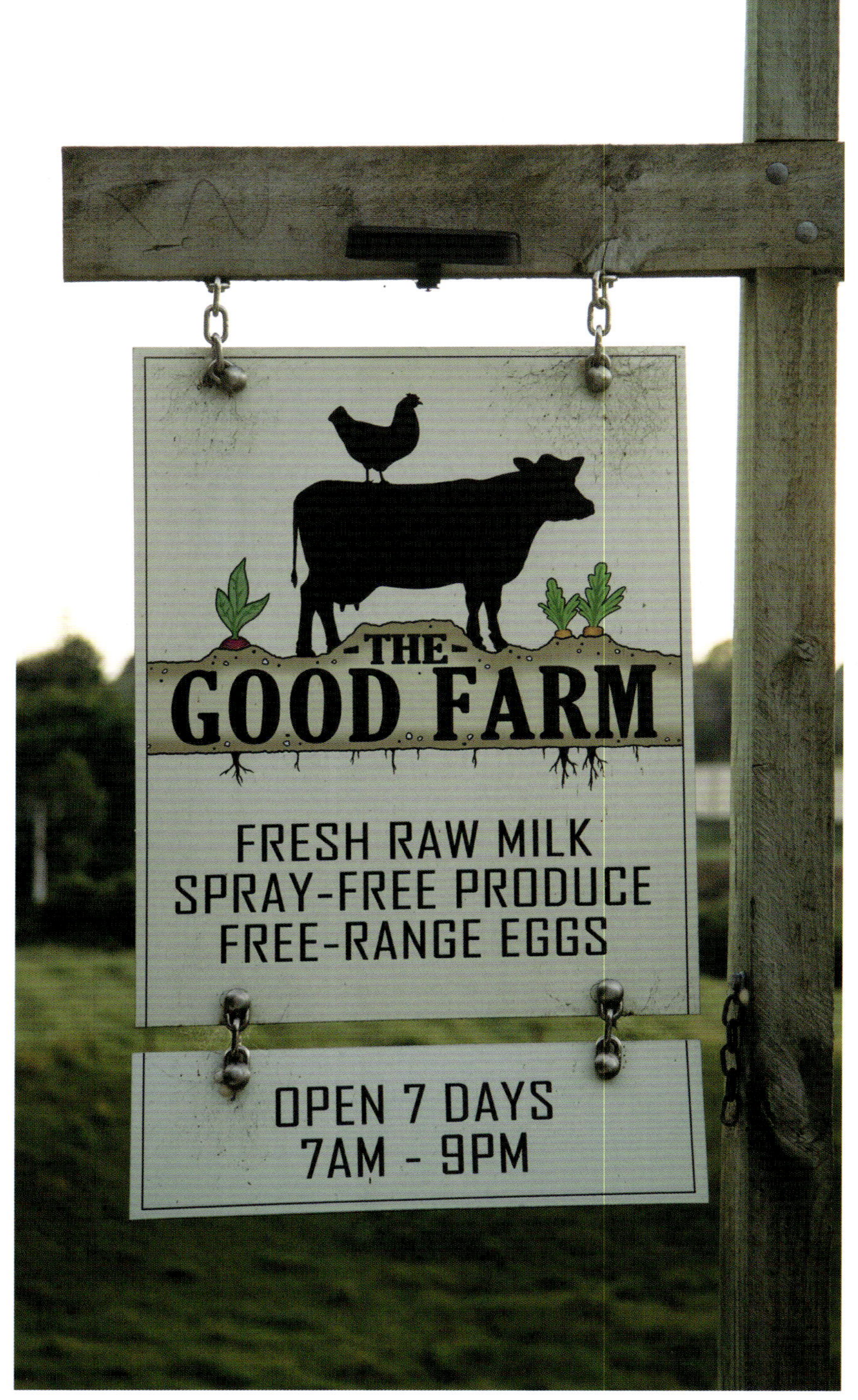

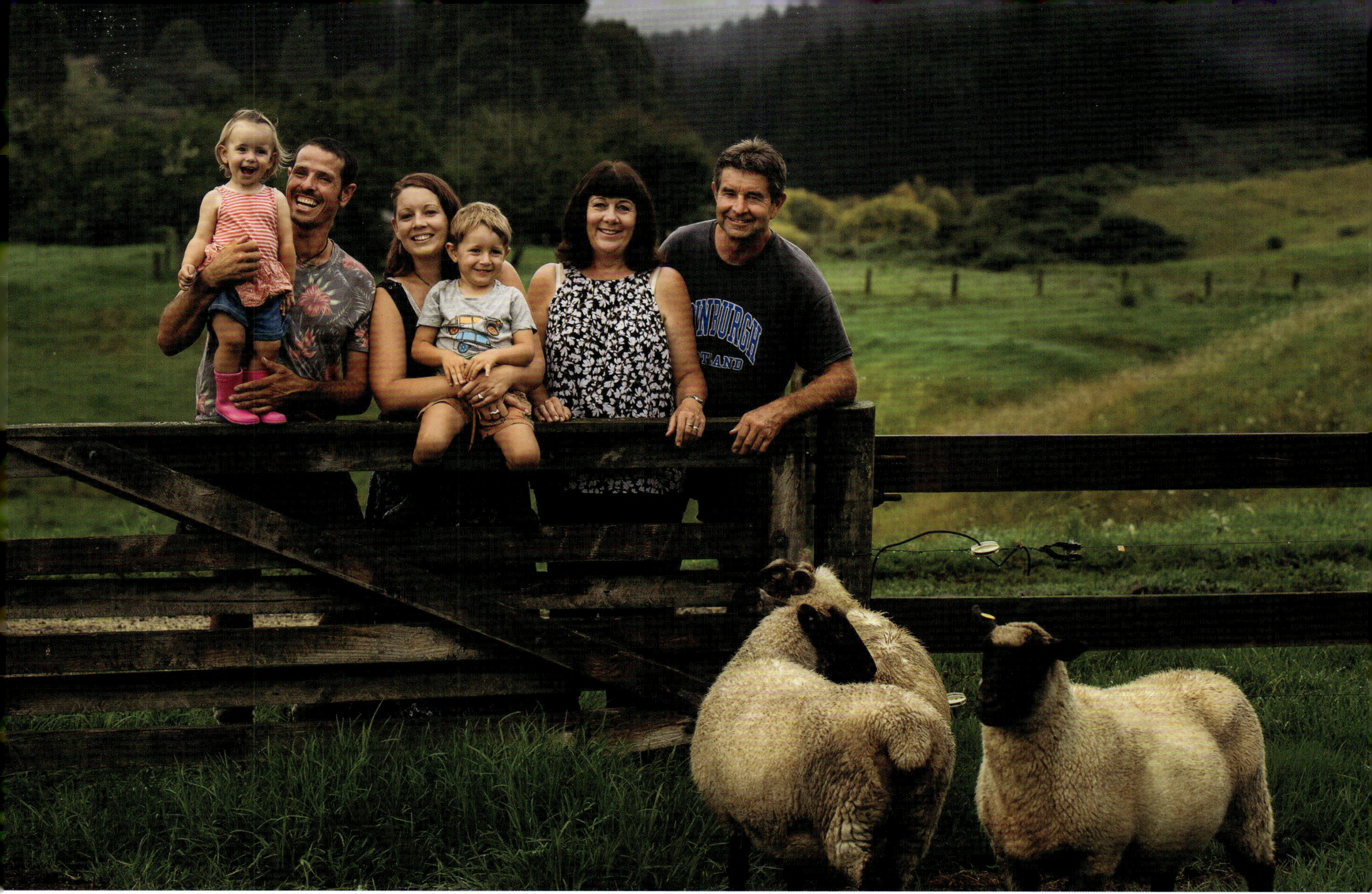

Loren Gibbs and Michaela Good holding their children, (left) Brianna Gibbs and Killian Gibbs. They are pictured with Michaela's parents Larisa and Daryl Anderson at The Good Farm in Welcome Bay, Bay of Plenty, home to the extended family.

'At The Good Farm, we are on 10 hectares, and we are running mainly a raw-milk dairy herd. We milk between 14 and 16 cows during the day. We are not certified organic, but we like to think that we work alongside the principles of organic agriculture and gardening. We are spray free on our pastures and our vegetable garden. We don't use synthetic fertilisers, any chemical pesticides or herbicides.

We have a farm shop and that's where we make most of our income. All the milk from our cows gets sold on the farm through a self-service dispenser. That's about 180 litres a day. All the produce from the veggie garden and our eggs get sold through the shop as well, on an honesty system that works well. We get hundreds of people through the shop every week and they come from all walks of life; they are not all a bunch of hippies. The only thing they have in common is that they all want fresh, raw milk and that they care about their food. That's the main thing.

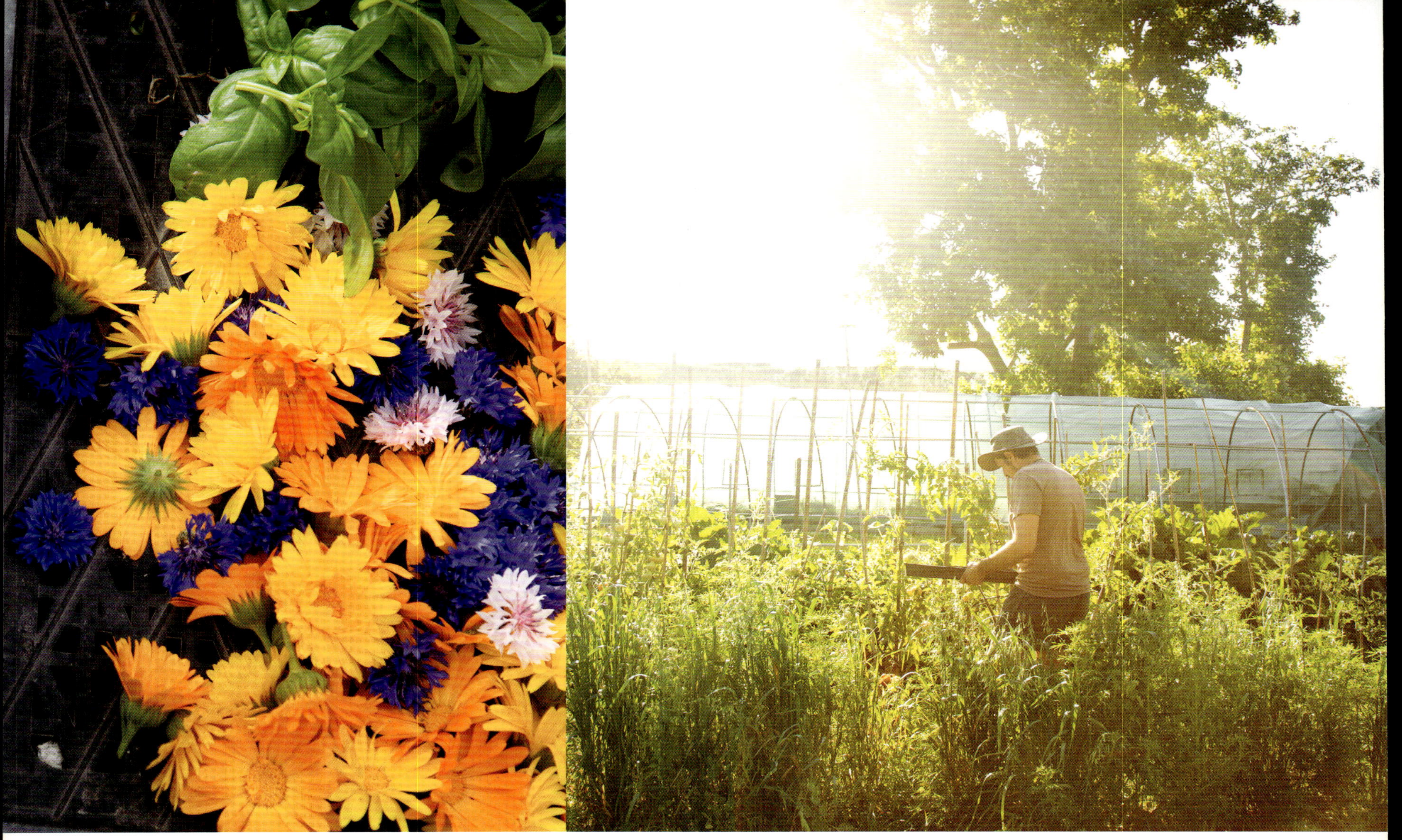

**A selection of vegetables, salad greens and edible flowers are picked and bagged for customers every couple of days during the peak of the growing season.**

'My wife and I returned from Australia and were looking for new careers. My wife's parents gave us this opportunity and we thought, "Why not!" I have always been interested in food, being a chef for 12 years. It was an opportunity to change lifestyles, change family life and still work within food. It also gives us an opportunity to know where our food comes from and how it's grown.

— Loren Gibbs

'We don't have a farming background. Loren had never milked a cow in his life, and we just had a few pots on the porch. It had never been in the plan. But maybe that's what makes it even better because we dived head first into it and love it.

We are into our third year here. People really love it. They love the raw milk and produce. I am very optimistic about the future, and we have lots of plans for the property. We have a love for this place.

— Michaela Good

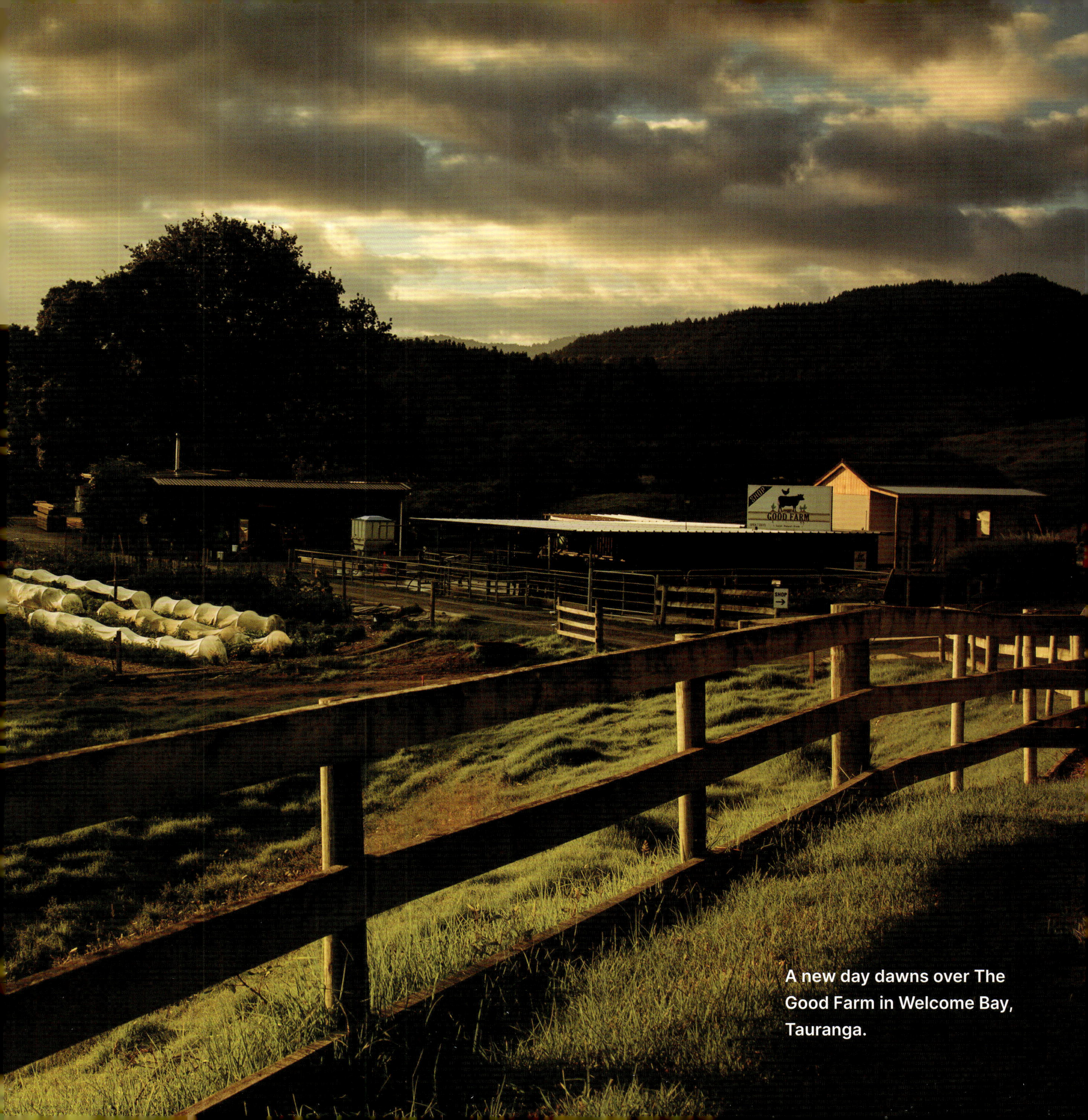


A new day dawns over The Good Farm in Welcome Bay, Tauranga.

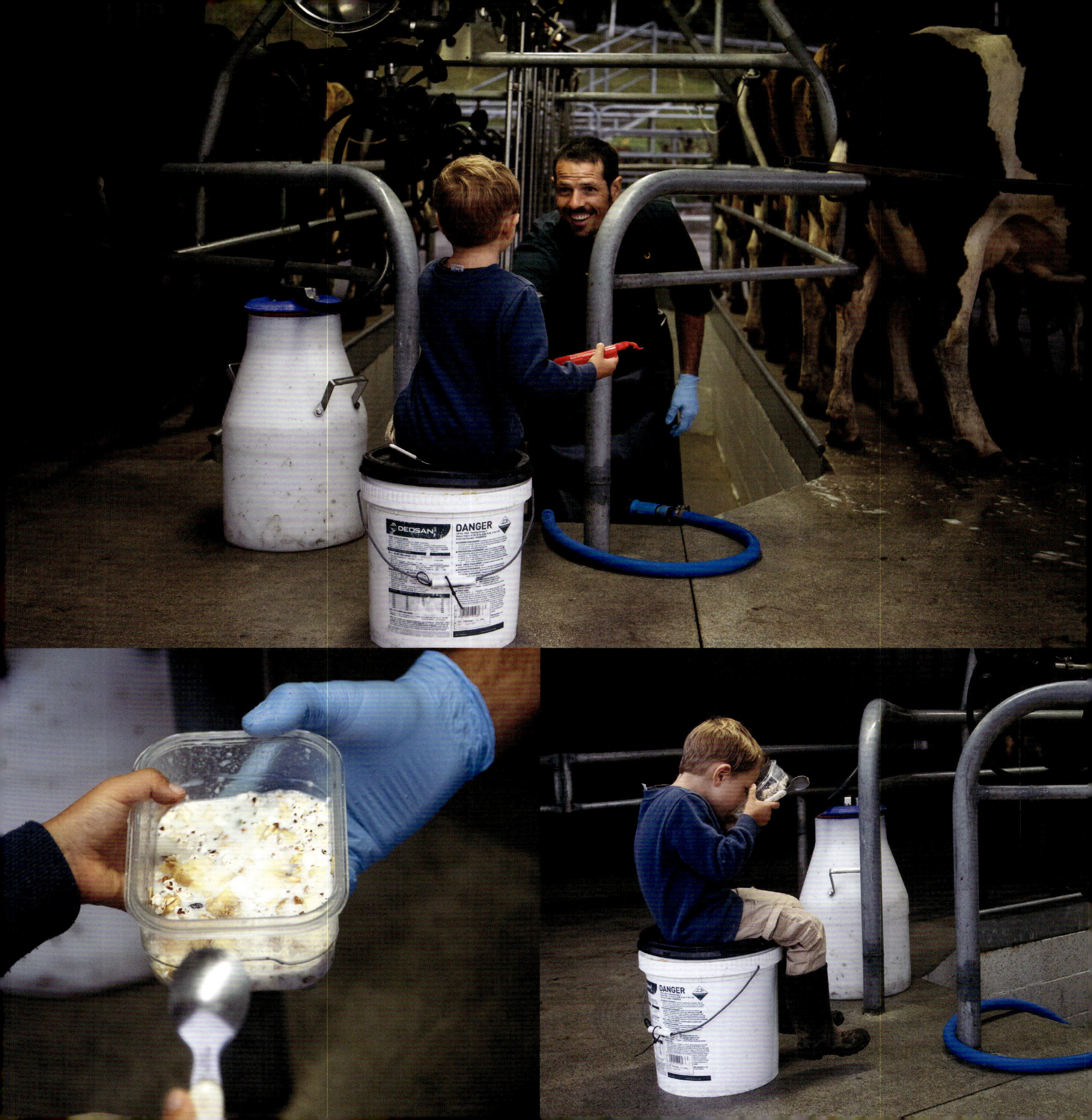
DEOSAN
DANGER
DANGER

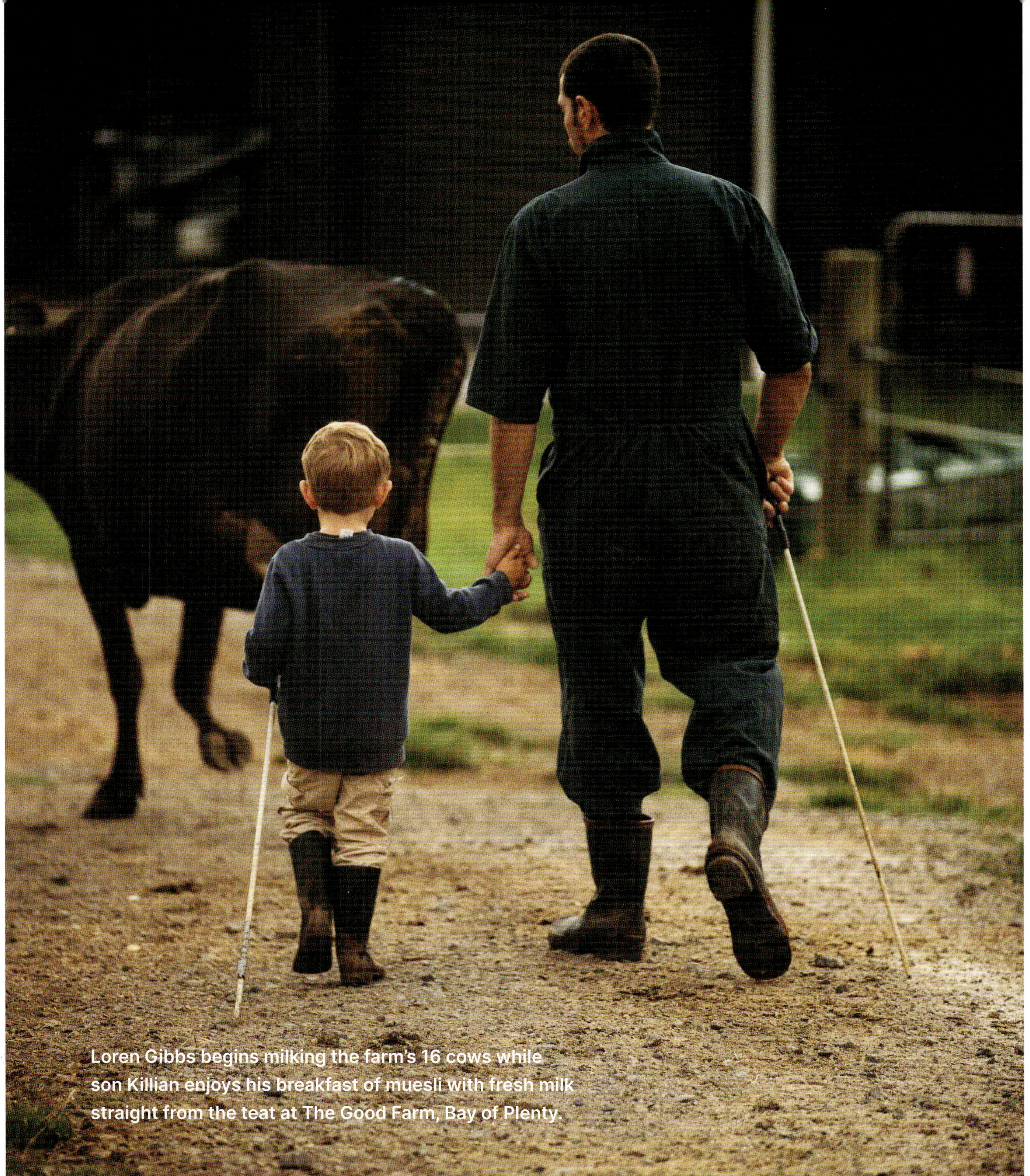

Loren Gibbs begins milking the farm's 16 cows while son Killian enjoys his breakfast of muesli with fresh milk straight from the teat at The Good Farm, Bay of Plenty.

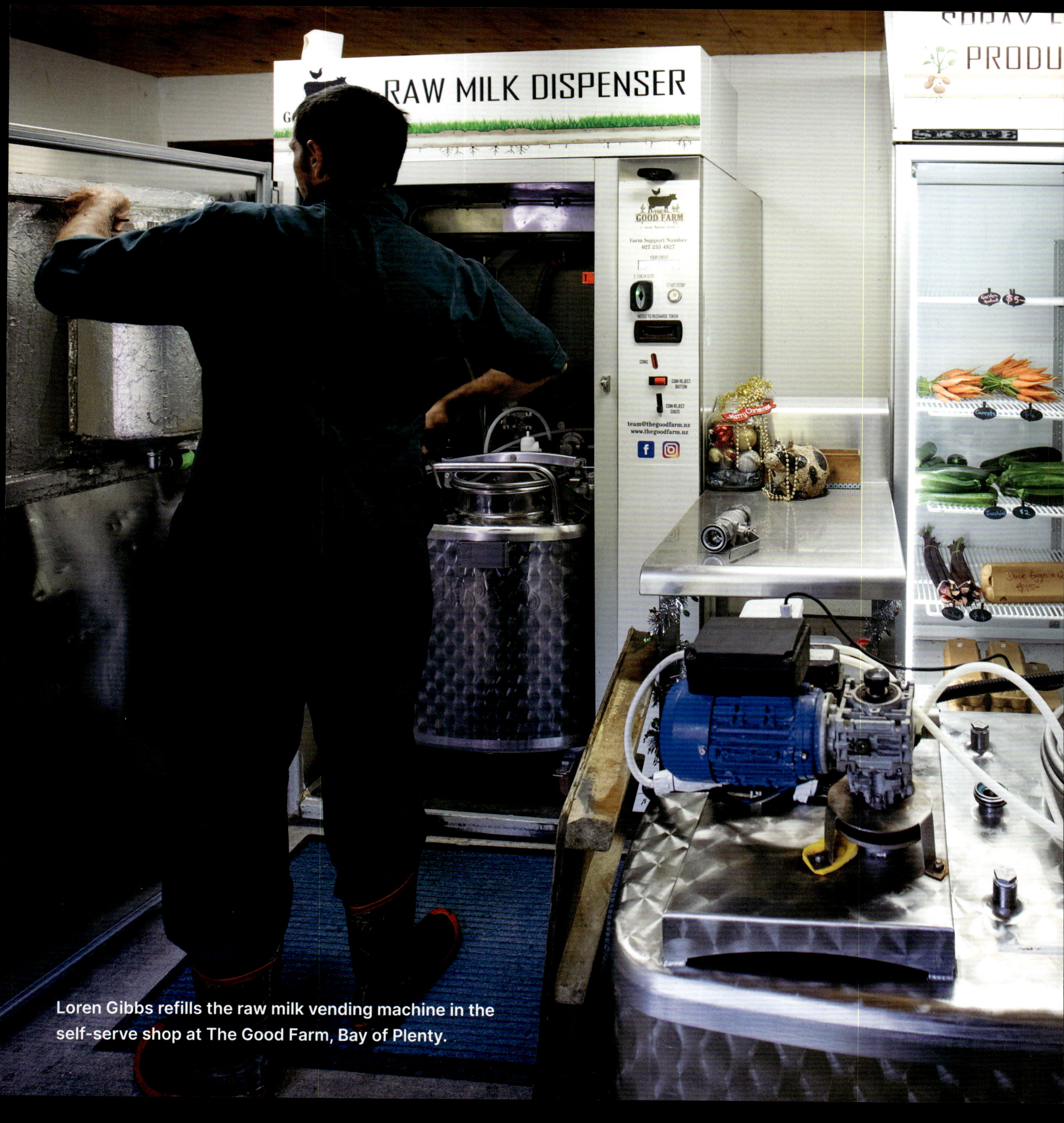


Loren Gibbs refills the raw milk vending machine in the self-serve shop at The Good Farm, Bay of Plenty.

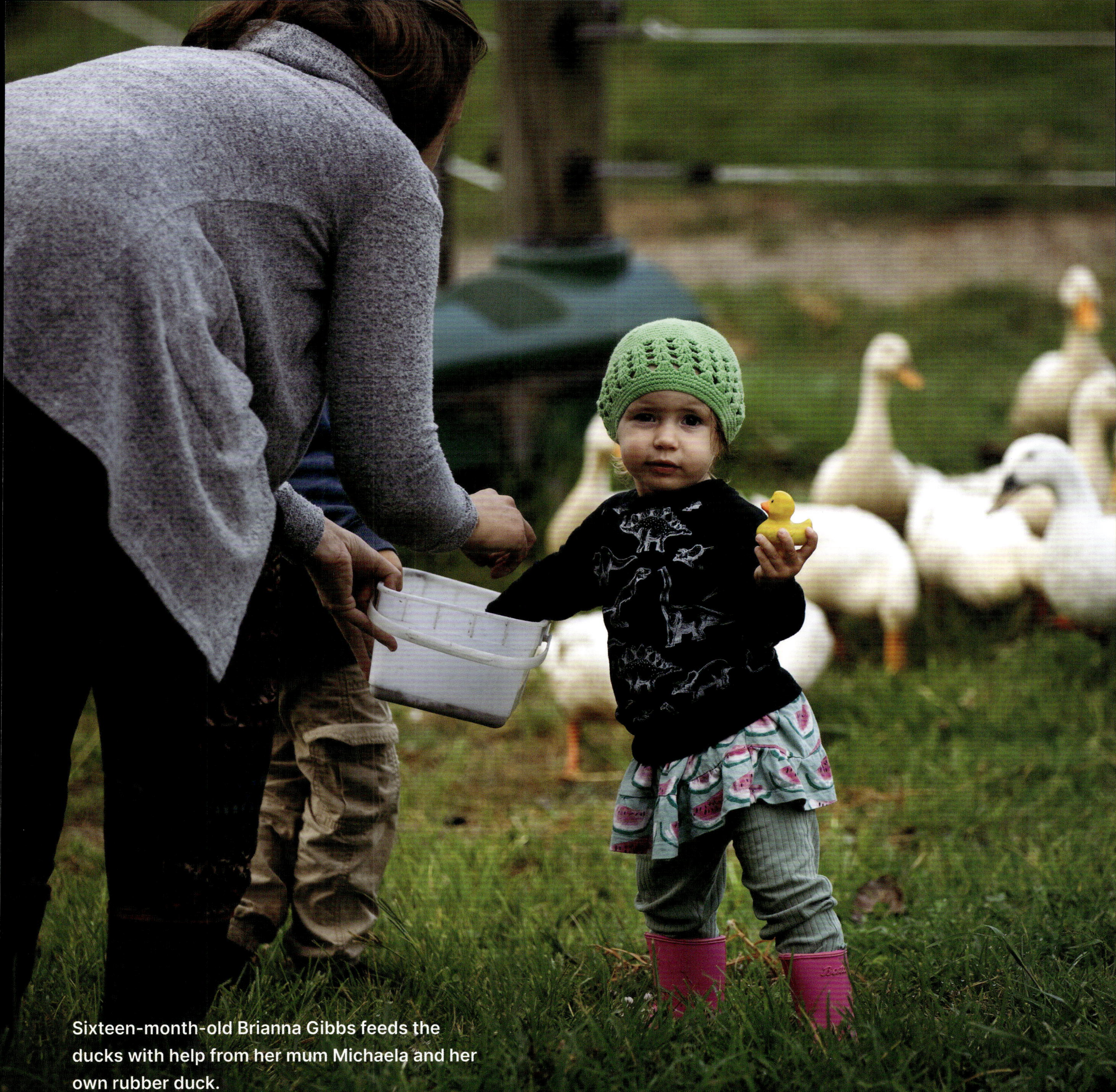

Sixteen-month-old Brianna Gibbs feeds the ducks with help from her mum Michaela and her own rubber duck.

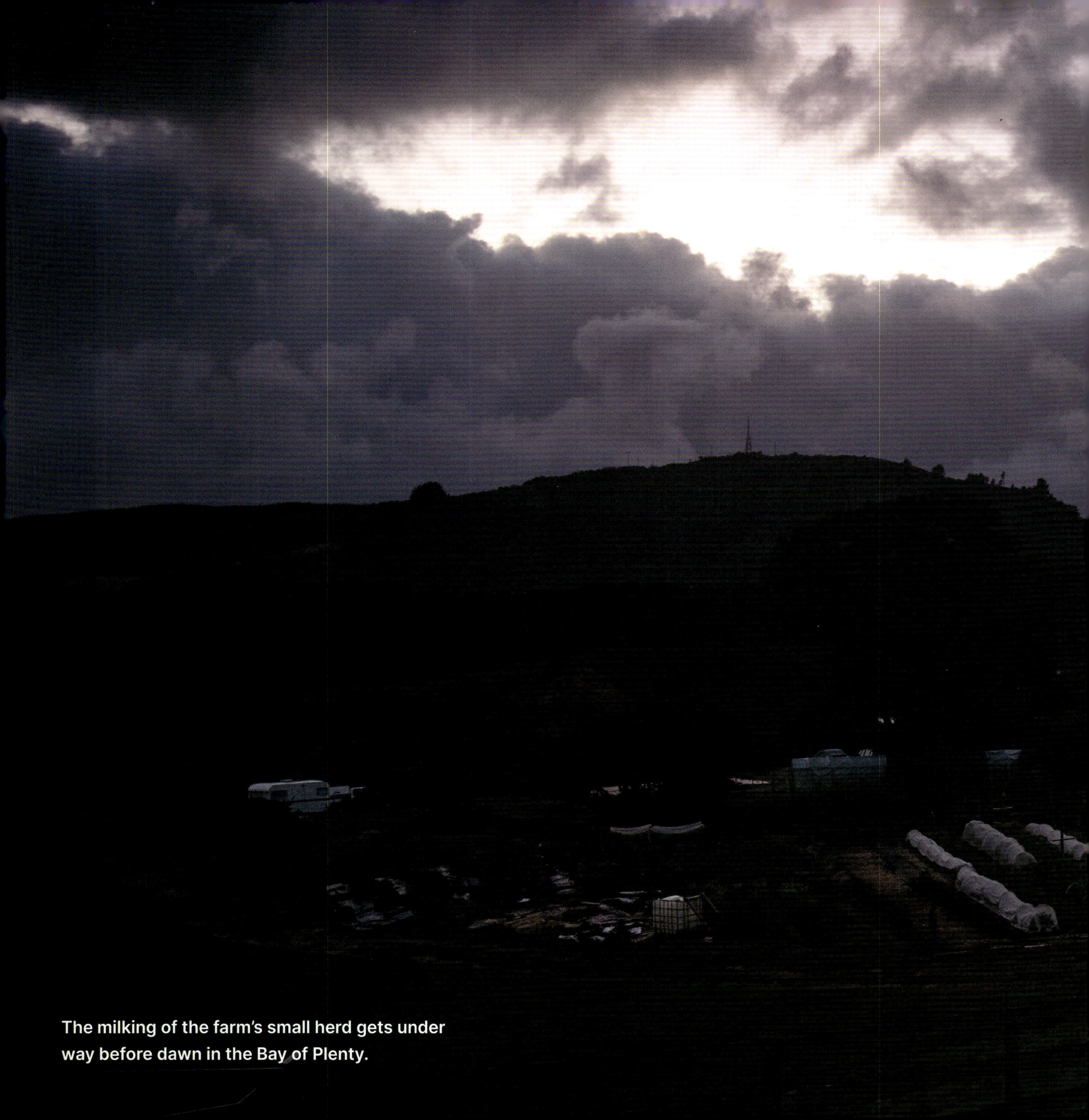

The milking of the farm's small herd gets under way before dawn in the Bay of Plenty.

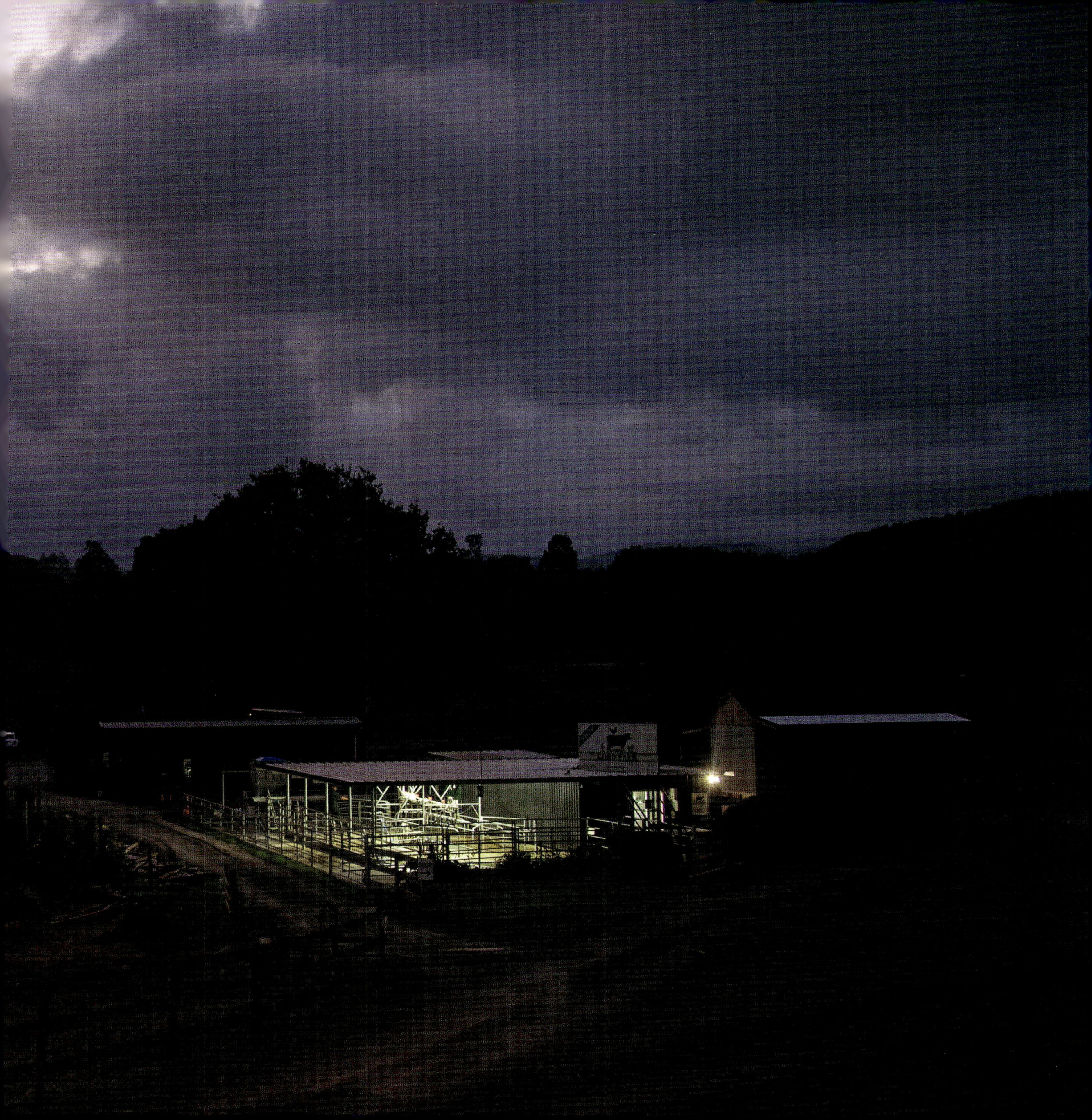

# SHEEP

The first sheep were introduced into New Zealand by Captain Cook in 1773. But they died shortly after being set ashore at Ship's Cove in Queen Charlotte Sound. The first five sheep arriving in 1814 were merinos from Australia. Other sheep were introduced by whalers and missionaries and by the 1840s major flocks were successfully established. By 1900 merinos remained in the high country but elsewhere had largely been replaced by cross-bred European breeds. The sheep population had reached around five million by this stage. 'More sheep than people' is still true today, although in 2020 numbers had declined to around 26 million from a peak of some 70 million in 1982. Falling prices for wool and meat, the break-up of larger farms and a major shift to dairying have all affected sheep production.

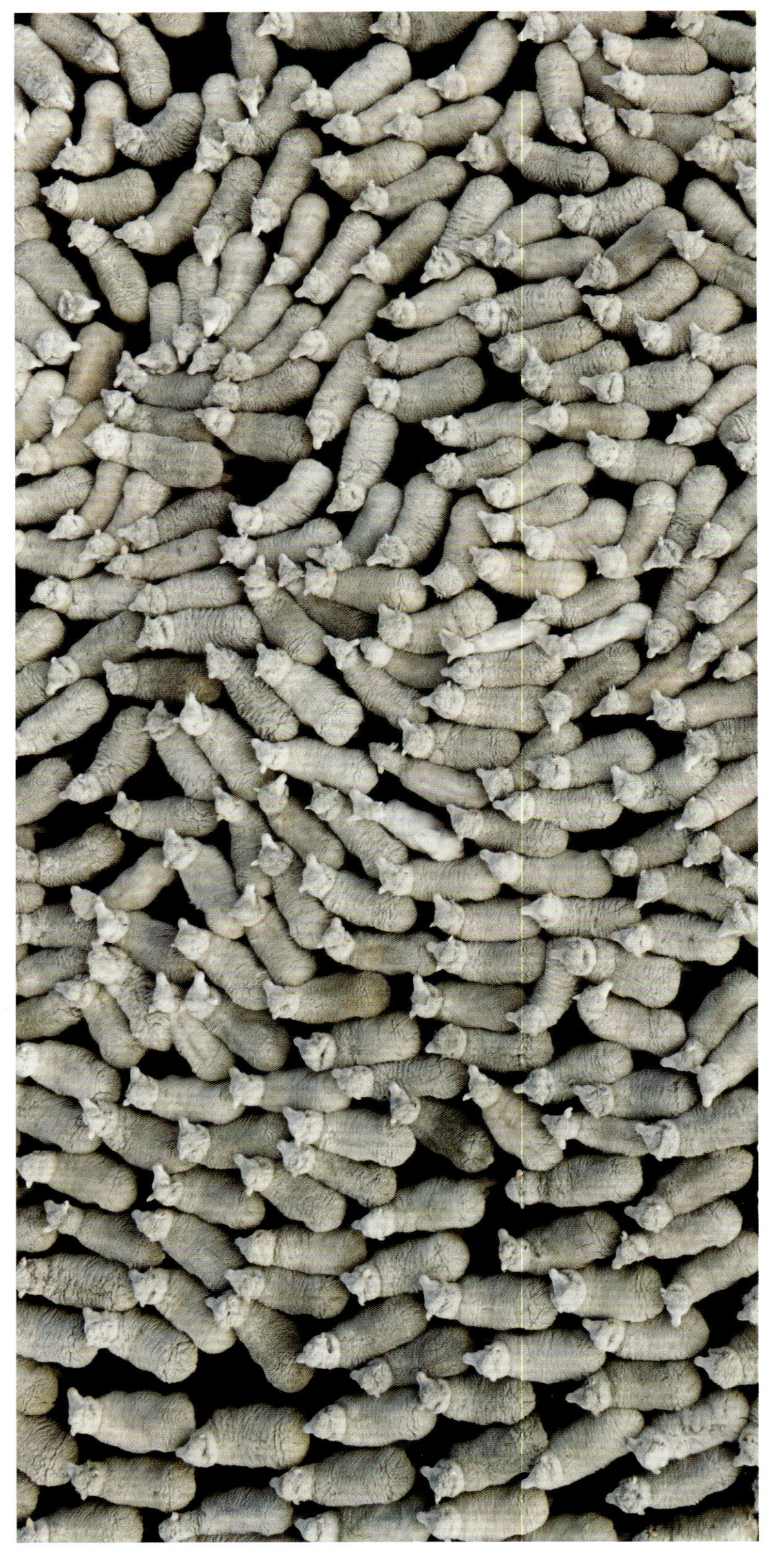

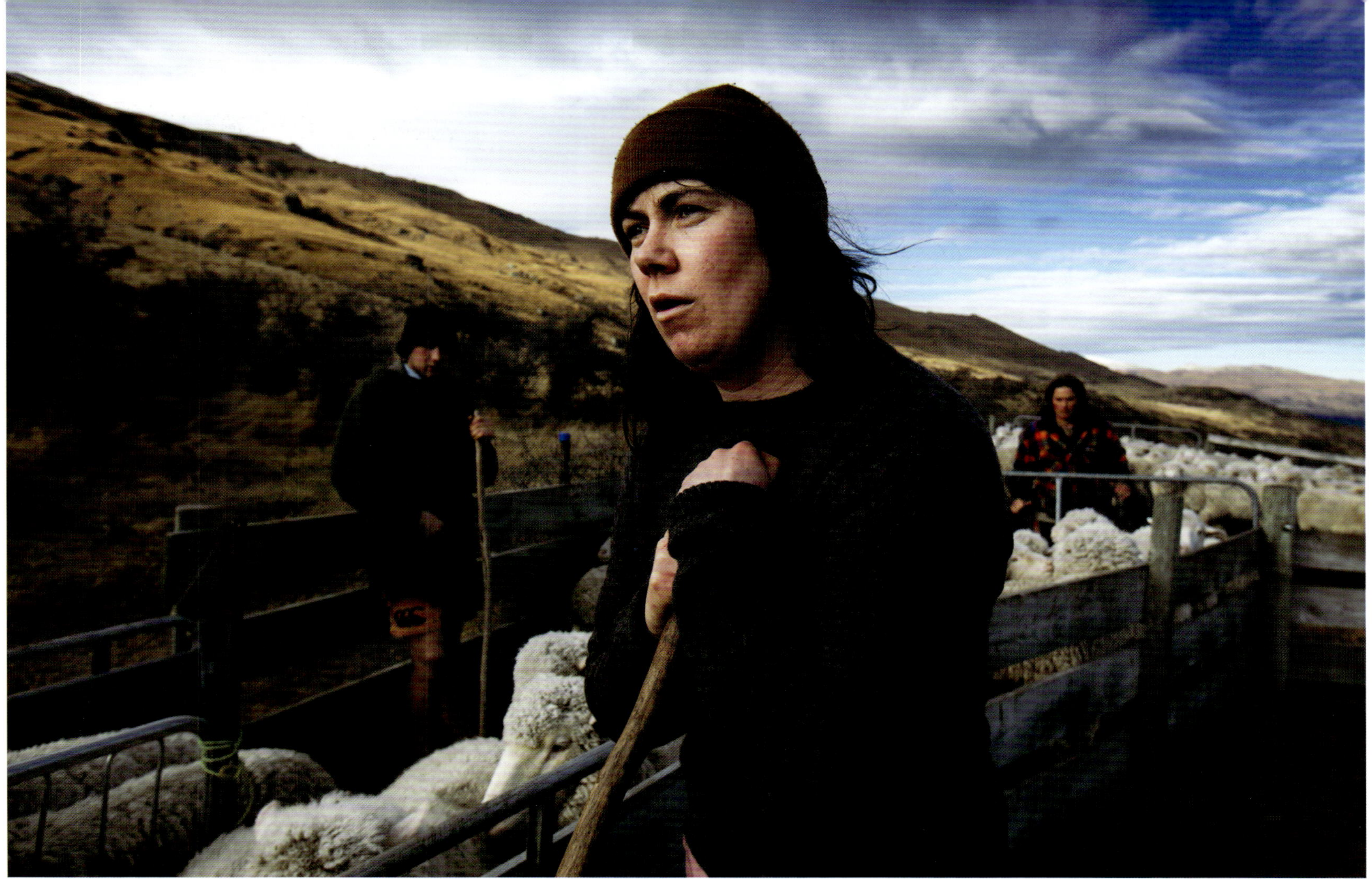

**The Scott family farm Loch Linnhe Station, near the southern end of Lake Wakatipu in Otago. Murray has been working here since 1977 and his wife Karen arrived in 1982.**

**Sophie Scott leans on her hill stick during a break in the work at the yards on Loch Linnhe Station, Otago.**

'We run 6000 ewes and 1500 hoggets, as well as rams and the usual killer mob. We have limited flat land so have all grass wintering with very little supplements such as hay being fed. That's a unique part about it.

The Queenstown International Airport is 25 minutes away, yet we feel like we are in the middle of nowhere. Our nearest neighbour is 10 kilometres away. — Murray Scott

'It has been such a privilege to live here and bring up the children here. I have loved every minute of it. Love the dogs, horses and the views. It's not an easy property to farm, but the lifestyle and property are pretty special. — Karen Scott

**Daughter Sophie returned to the farm several years ago and Karen and Murray have enjoyed watching her increasing contribution.**

'I have decided that farming will be my future. I am drawn to the landscape here and the way of life. It's a big station and it keeps me busy. I hope to take it over one day. — Sophie Scott

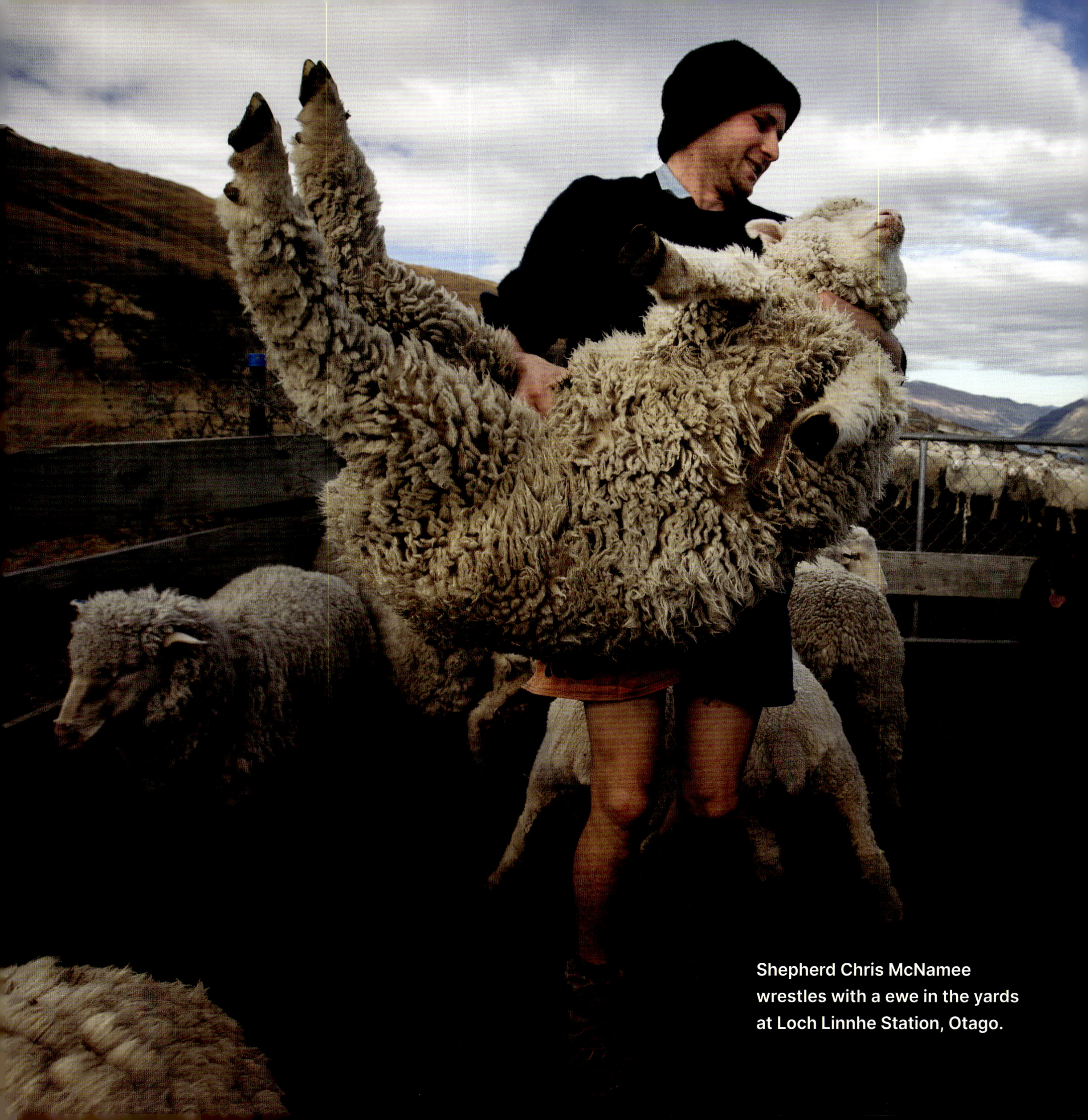

Shepherd Chris McNamee wrestles with a ewe in the yards at Loch Linnhe Station, Otago.

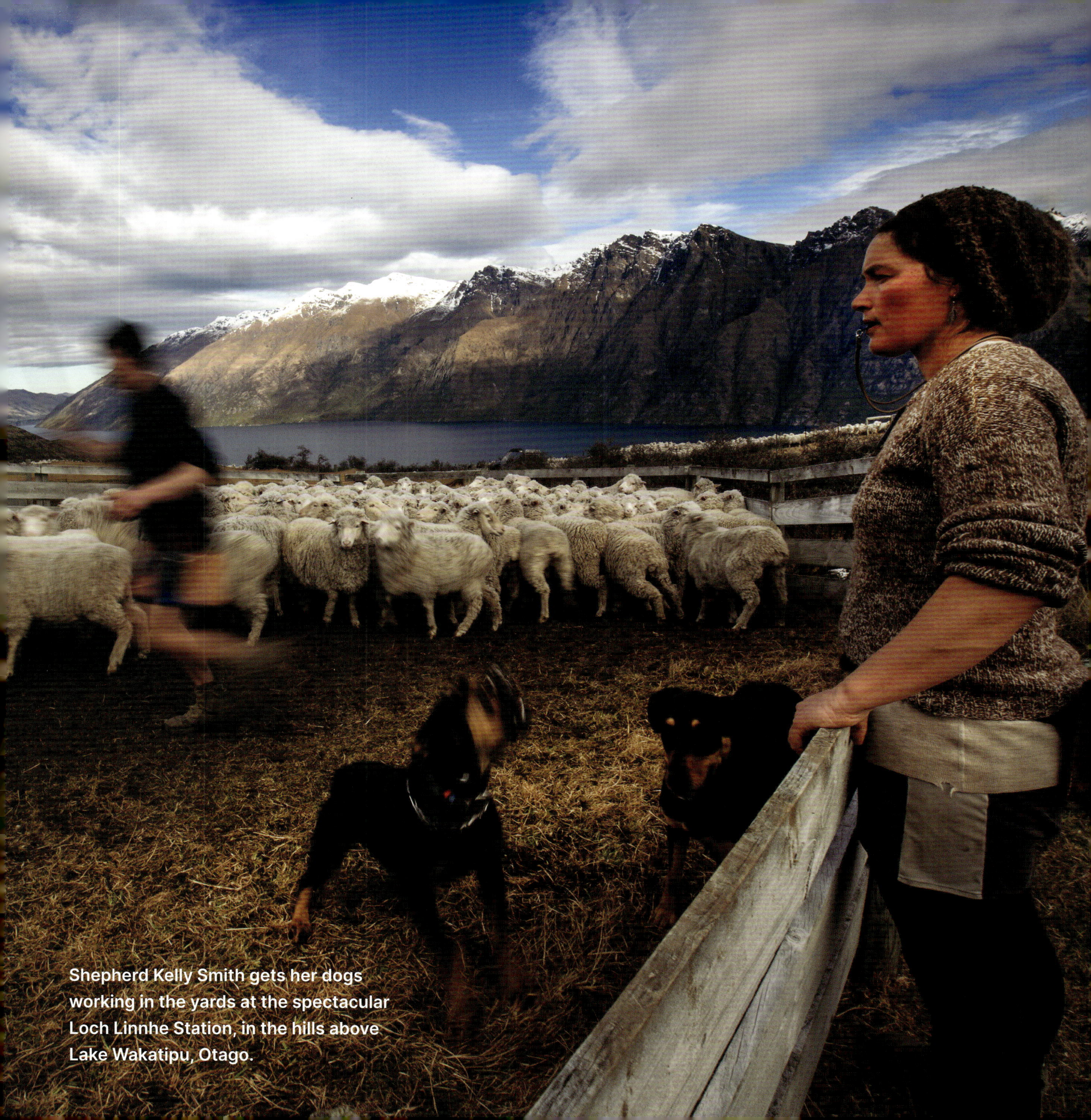

Shepherd Kelly Smith gets her dogs working in the yards at the spectacular Loch Linnhe Station, in the hills above Lake Wakatipu, Otago.

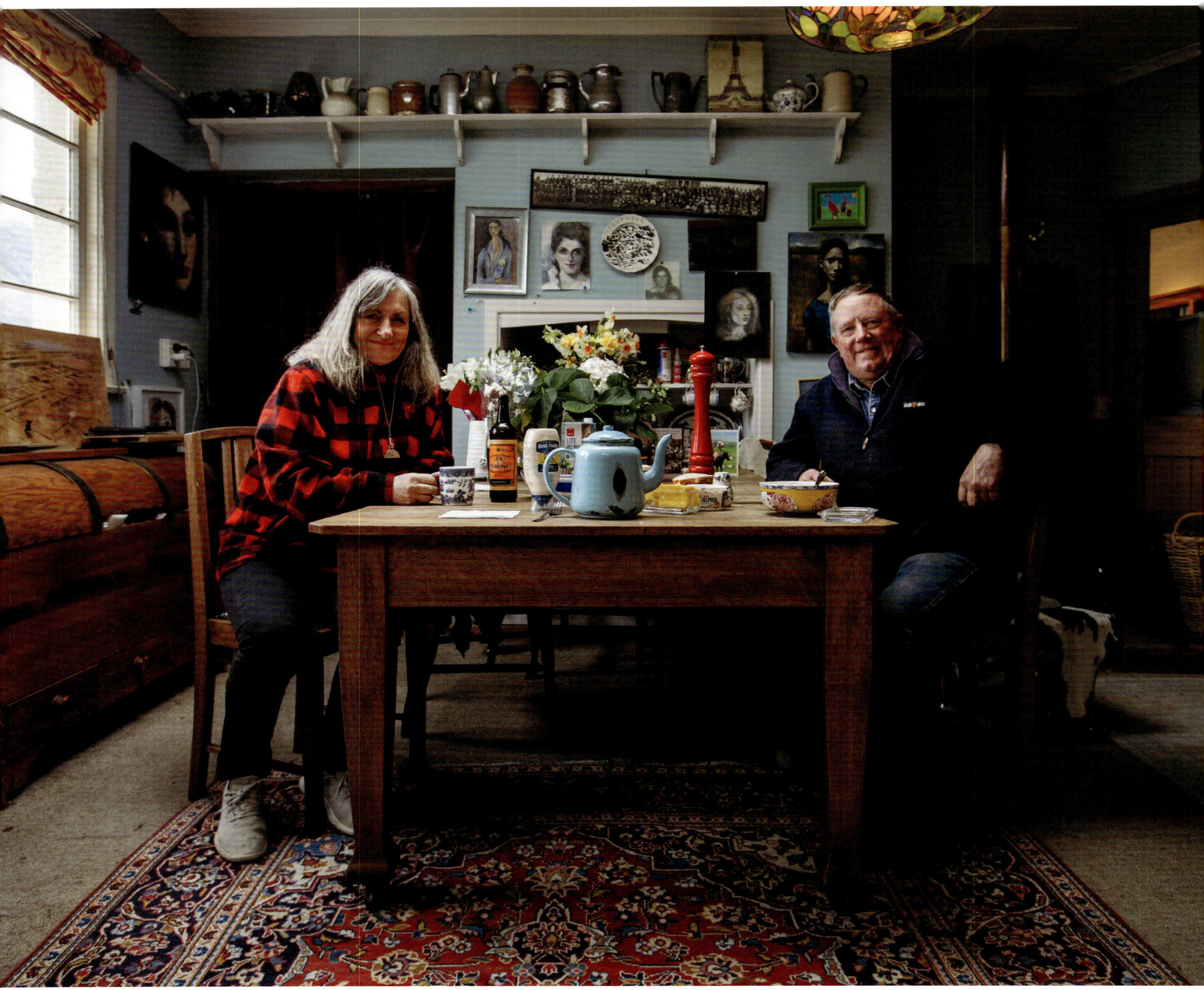

Karen and Murray Scott in the station homestead.

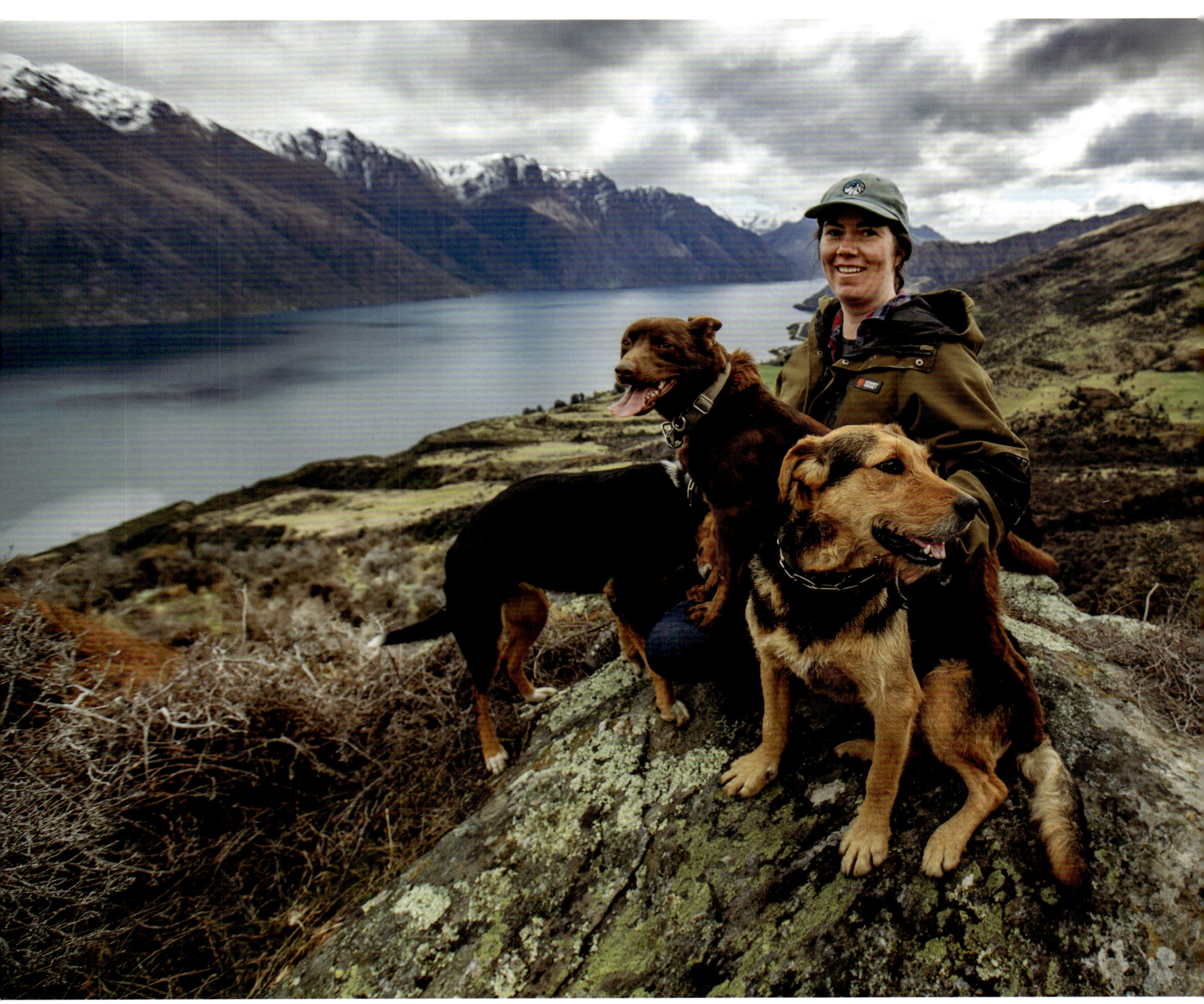

Sophie Scott with her dogs on her family's Loch Linnhe Station.

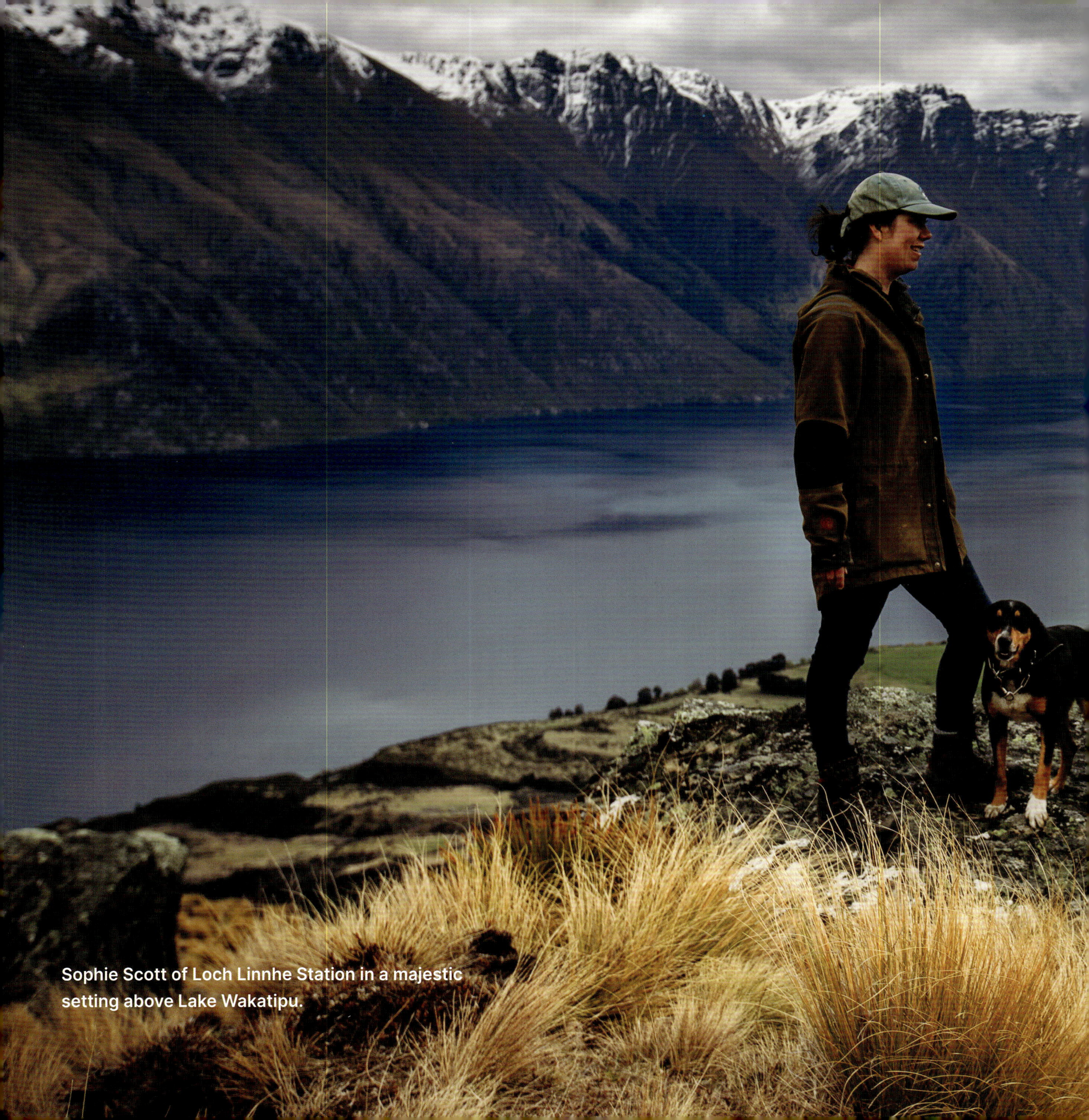

Sophie Scott of Loch Linnhe Station in a majestic setting above Lake Wakatipu.

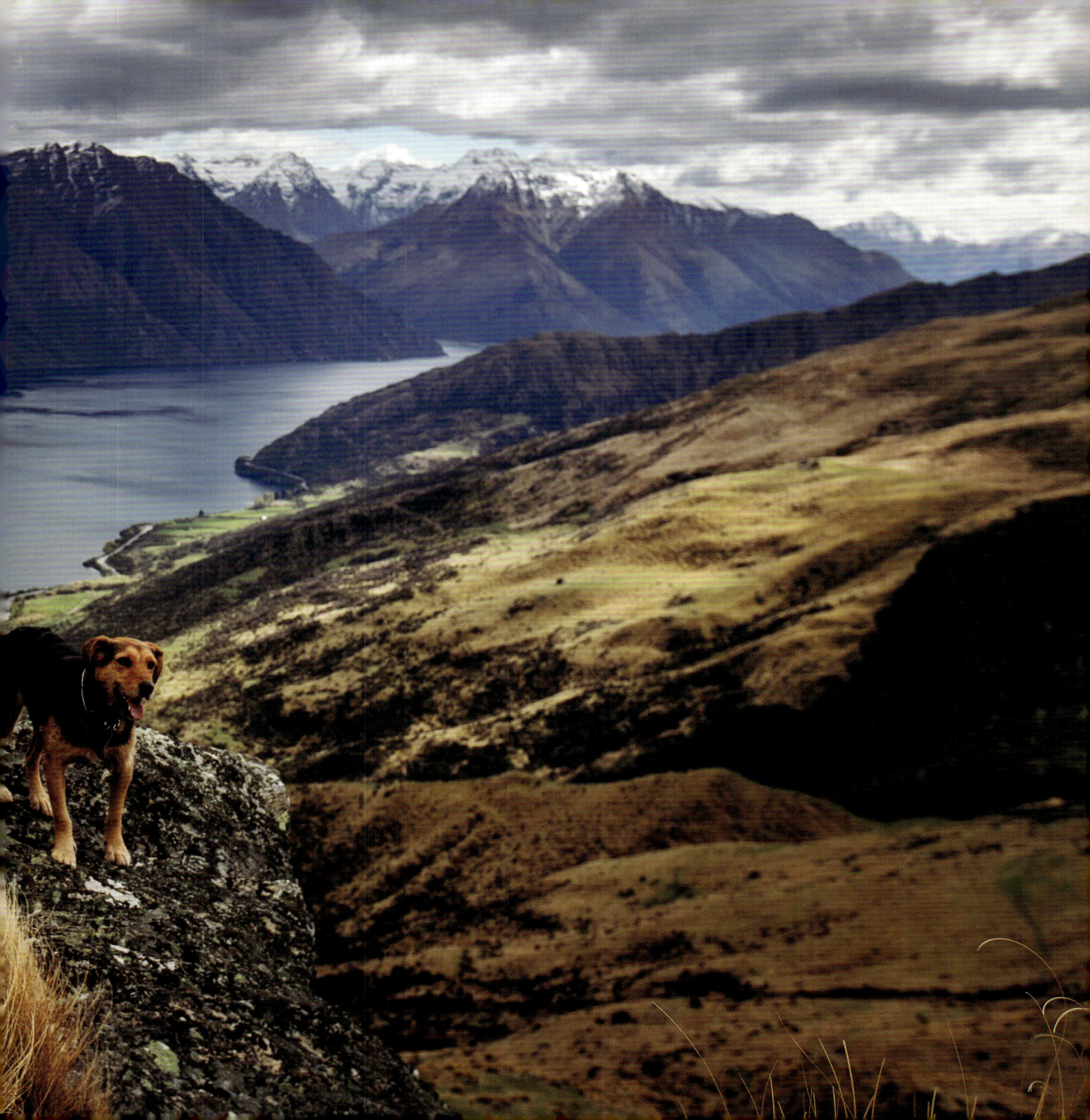

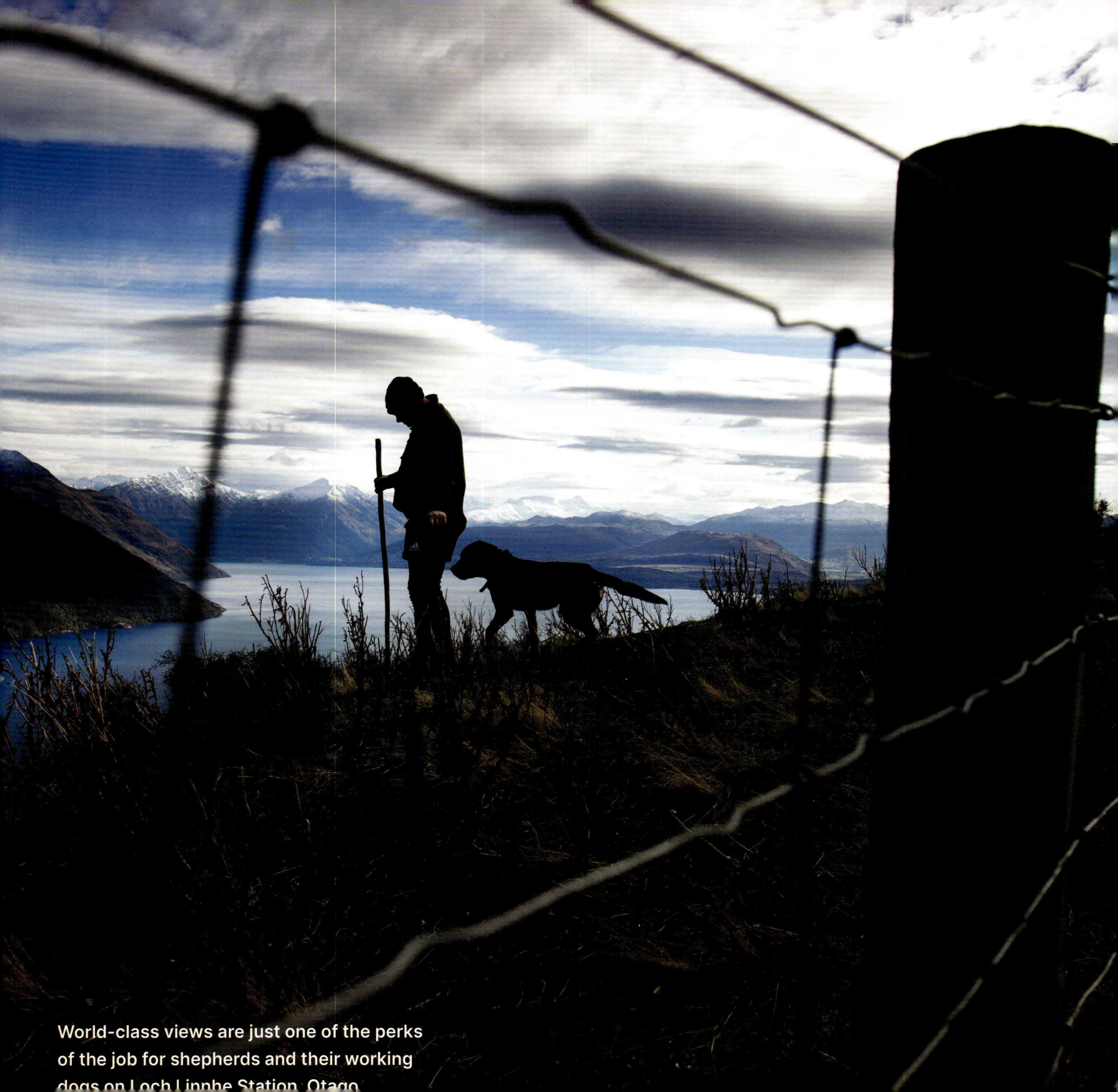

World-class views are just one of the perks of the job for shepherds and their working dogs on Loch Linnhe Station, Otago.

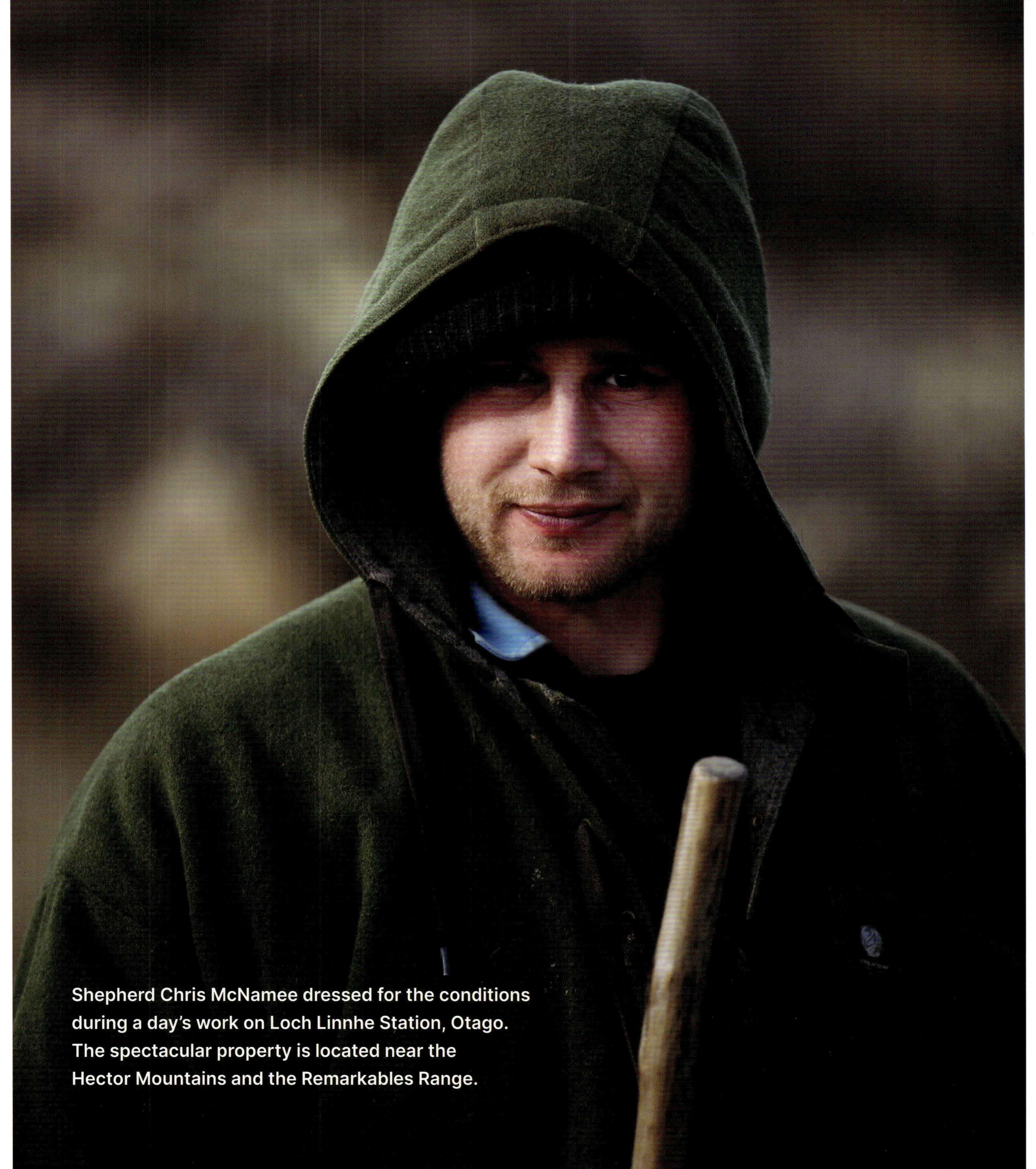

Shepherd Chris McNamee dressed for the conditions during a day's work on Loch Linnhe Station, Otago. The spectacular property is located near the Hector Mountains and the Remarkables Range.

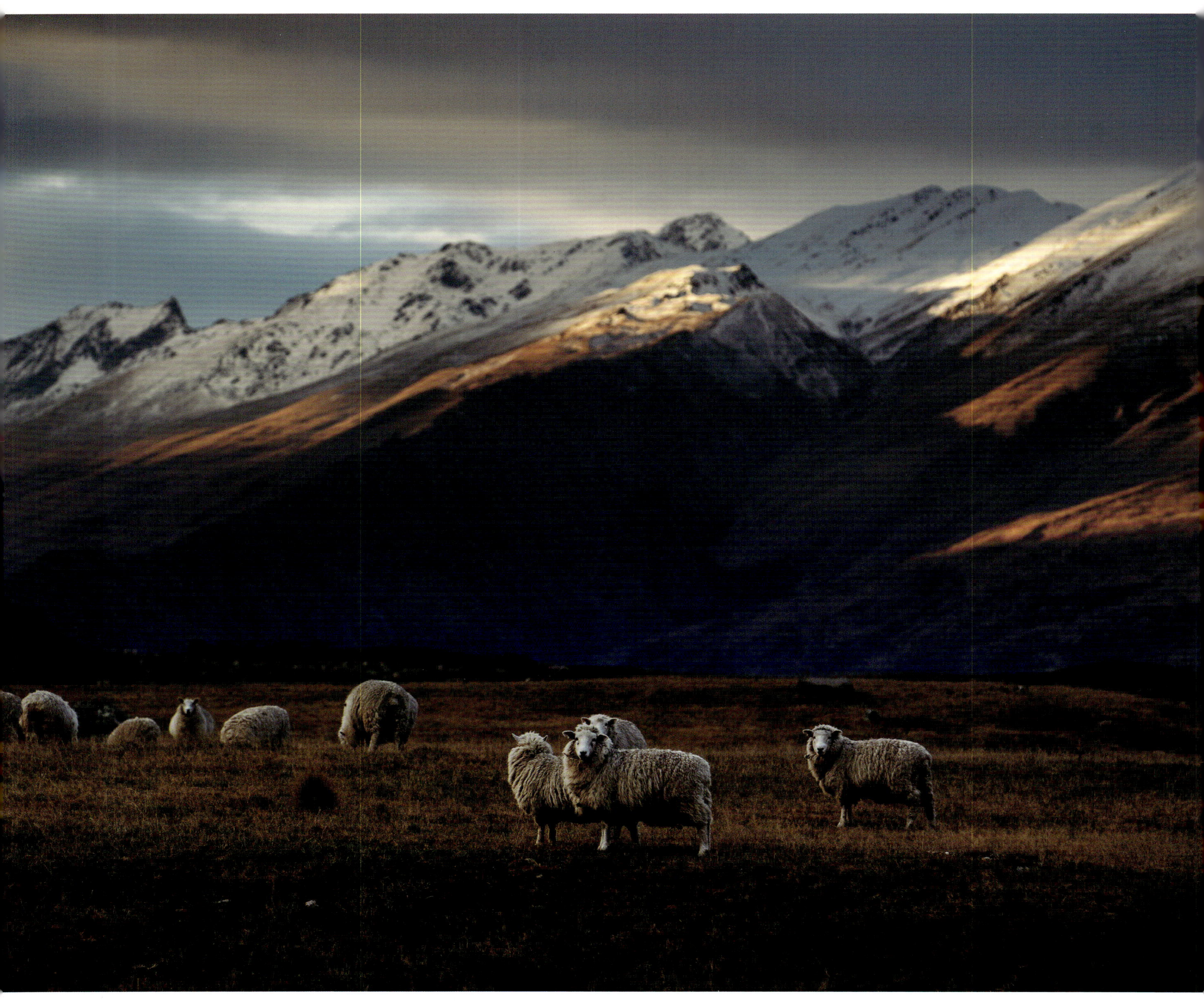

Sheep grow a thick fleece of wool to survive in the shadow of the Hector Mountains on a property at Kingston, Otago.

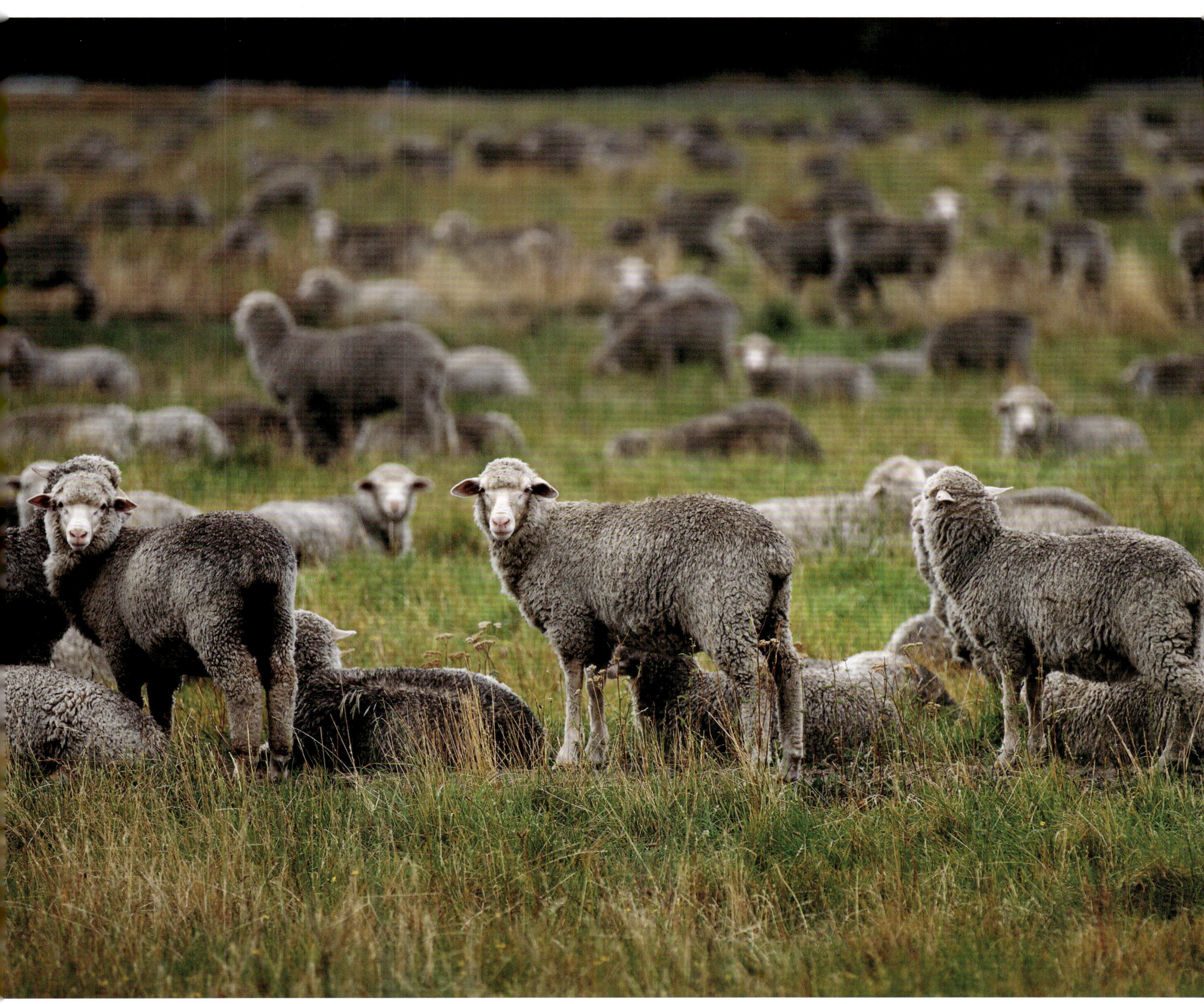

Merinos enjoy some time on the flats near Alexandra, Otago.

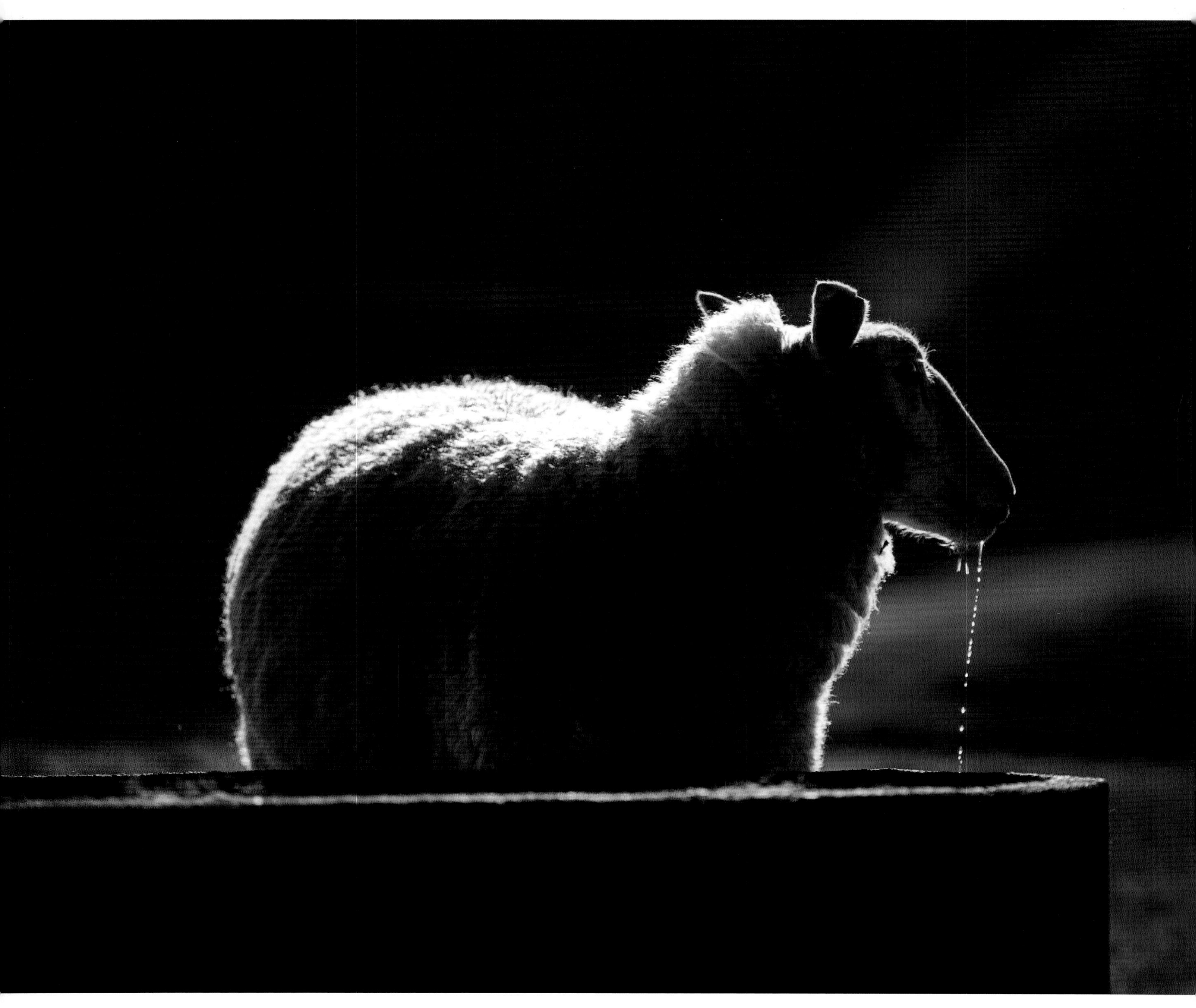

A thirsty ewe drinks from a trough on a property at Matatā, Bay of Plenty.

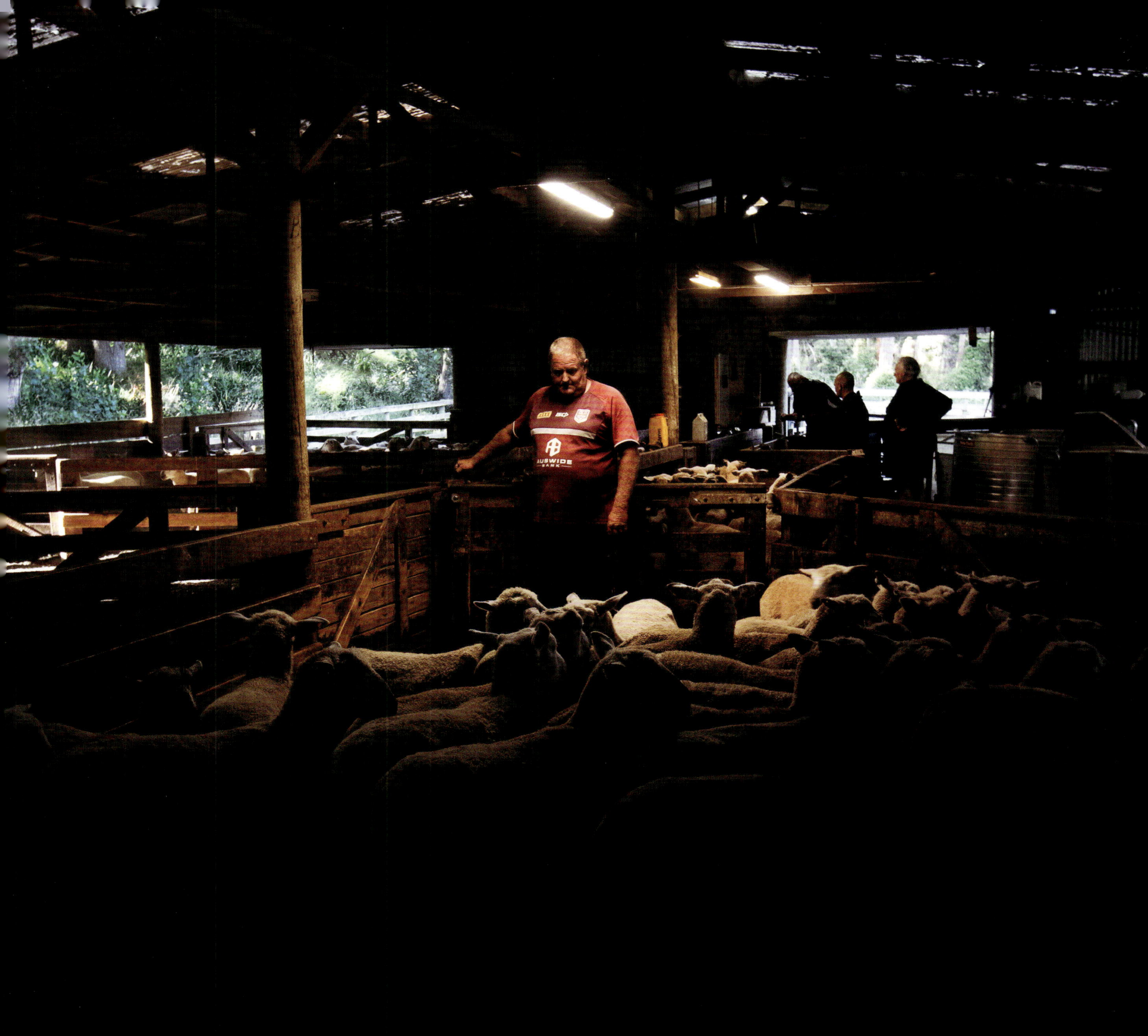


Sheep are drafted under the covered yards at Ranworth Farm in Te Ākau, Waikato.

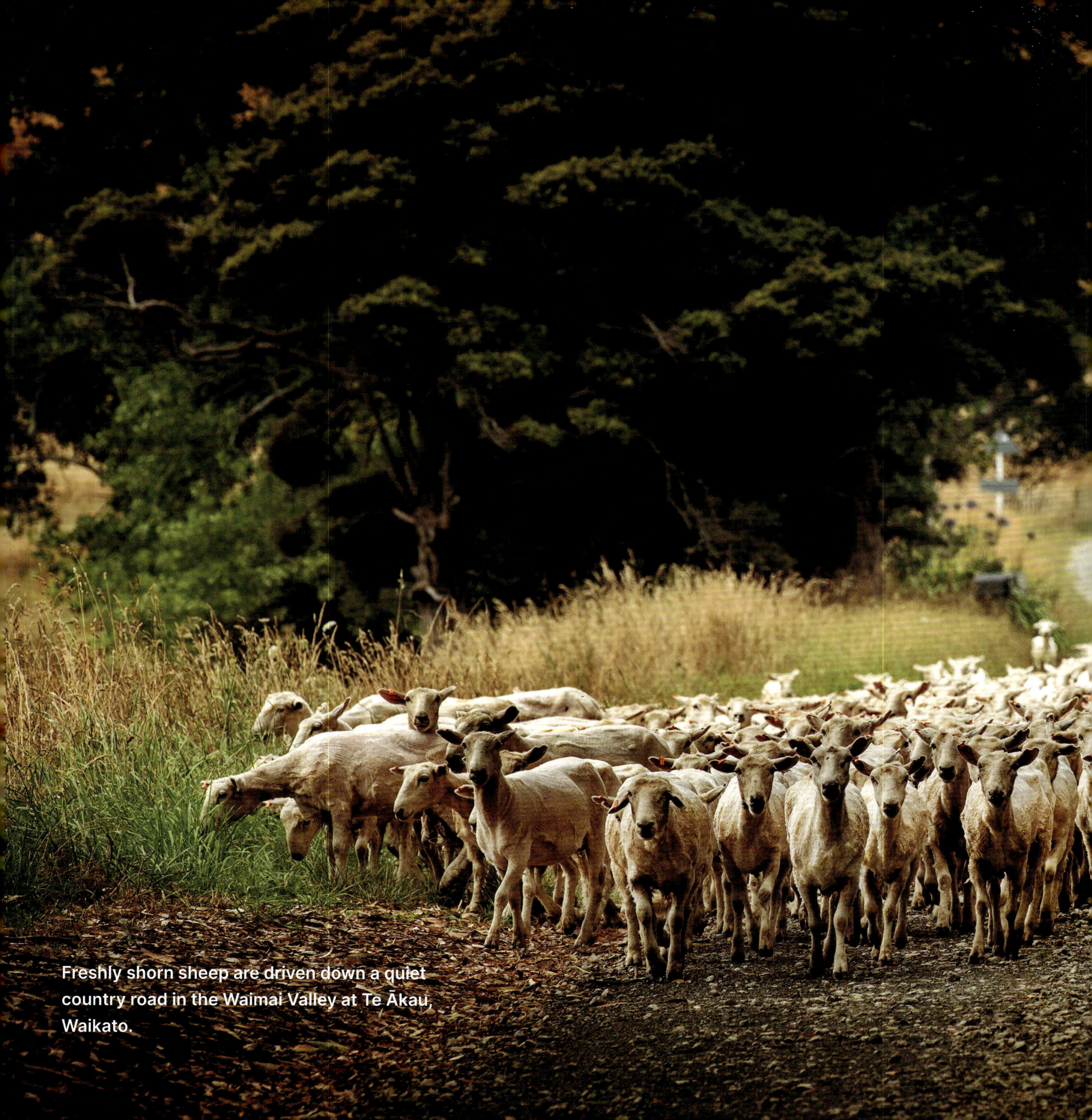

Freshly shorn sheep are driven down a quiet country road in the Waimai Valley at Te Ākau, Waikato.

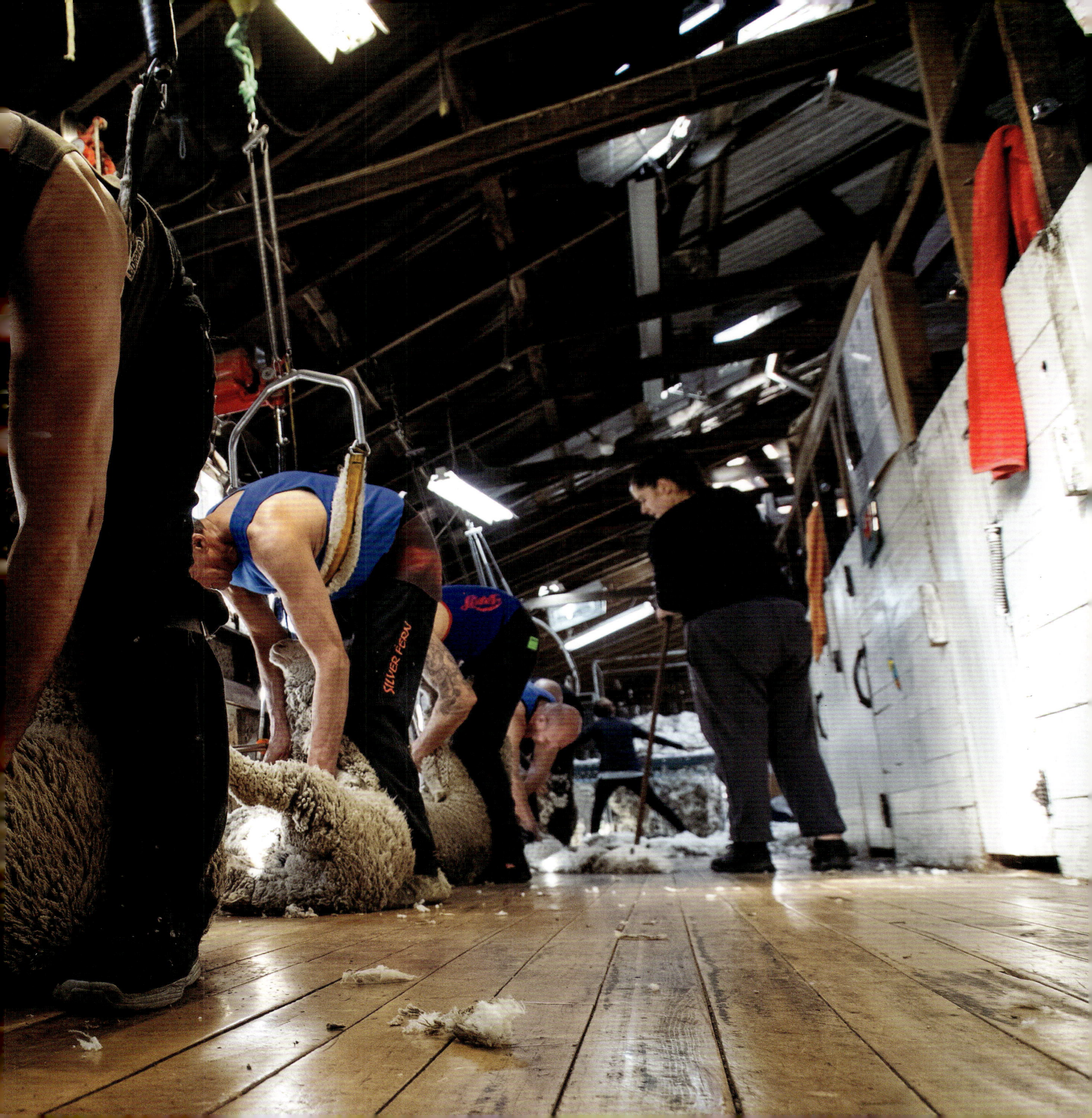
SILVER FERN

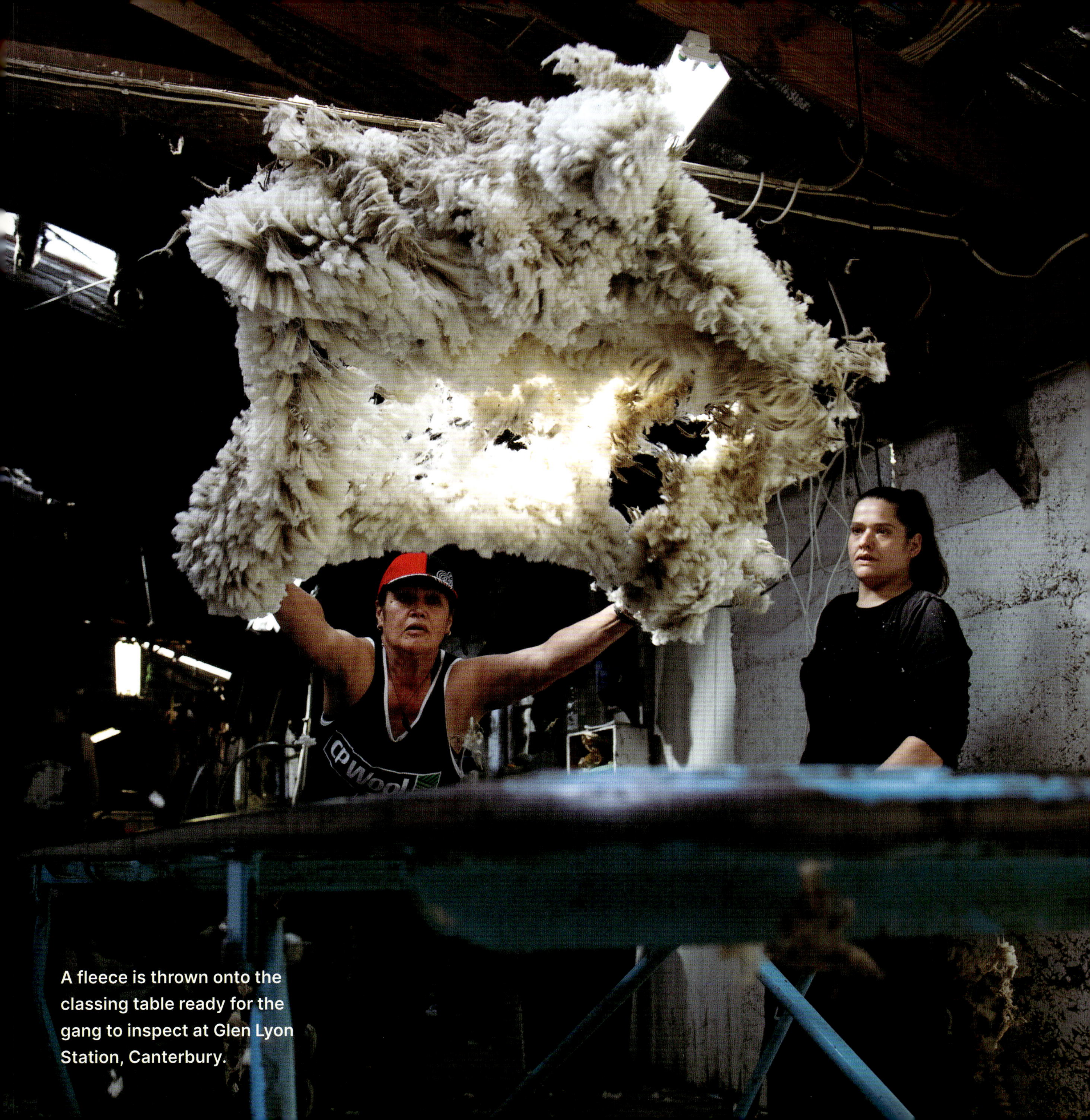

A fleece is thrown onto the classing table ready for the gang to inspect at Glen Lyon Station, Canterbury.

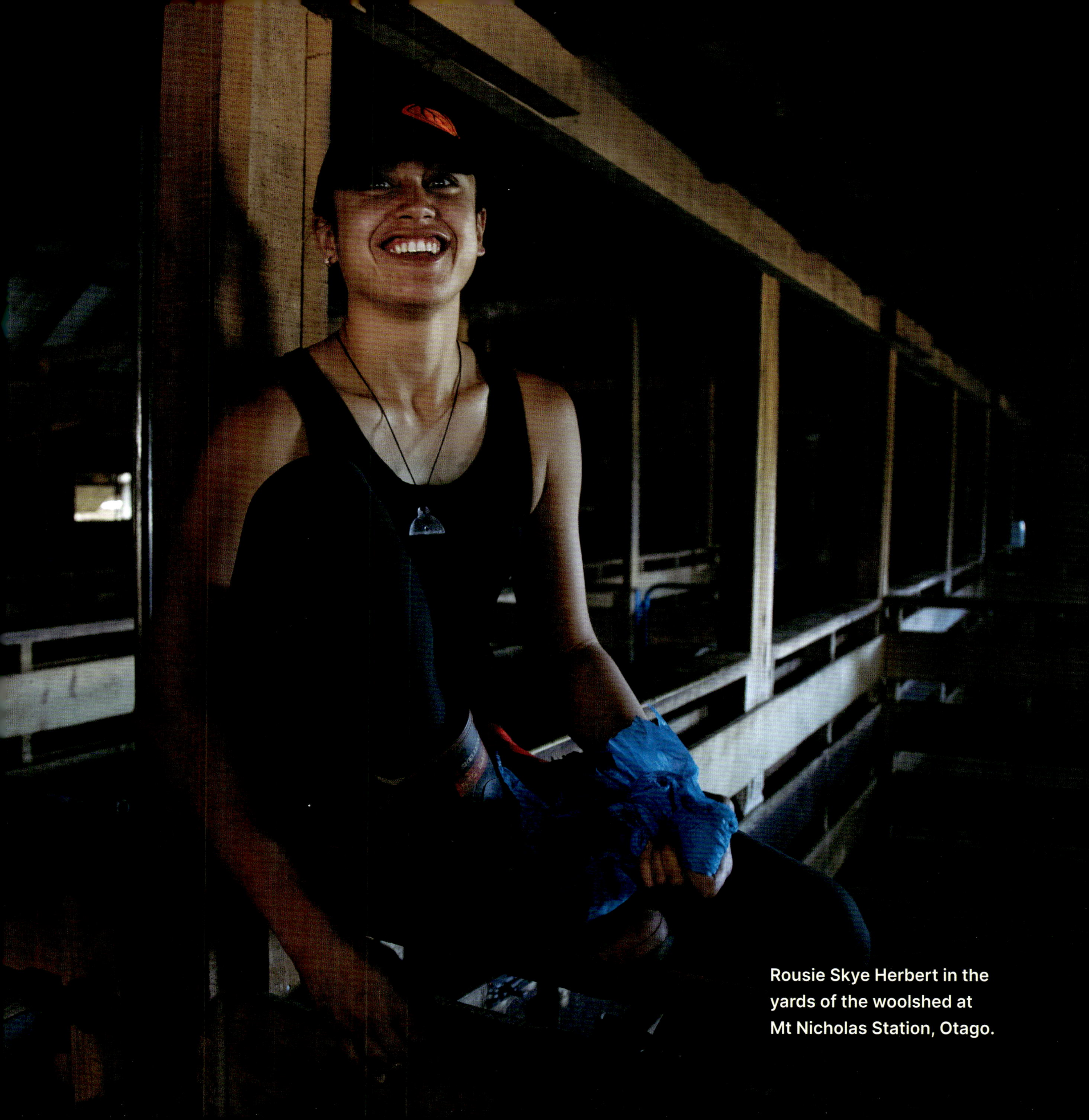

Rousie Skye Herbert in the yards of the woolshed at Mt Nicholas Station, Otago.

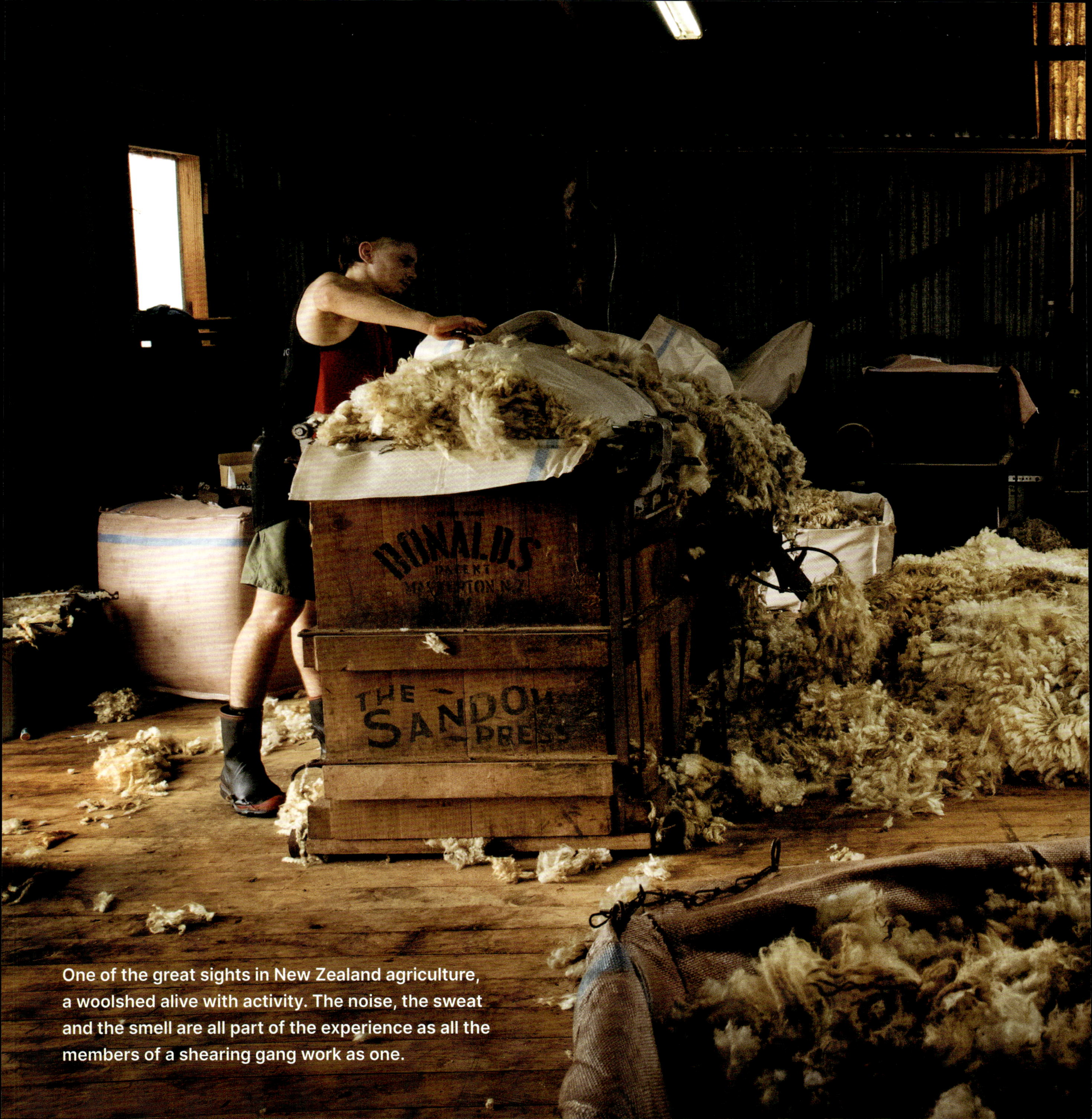


One of the great sights in New Zealand agriculture, a woolshed alive with activity. The noise, the sweat and the smell are all part of the experience as all the members of a shearing gang work as one.

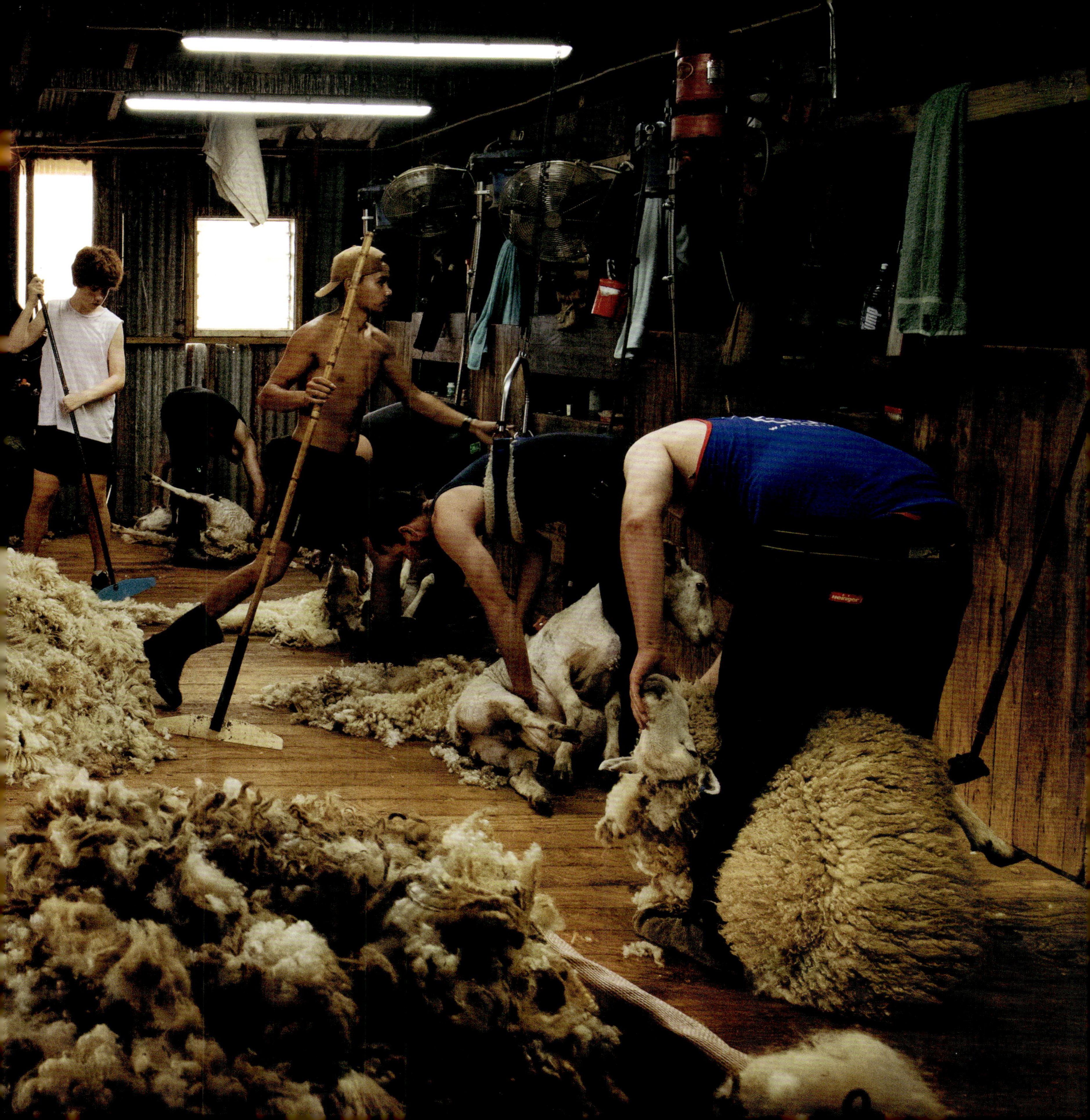

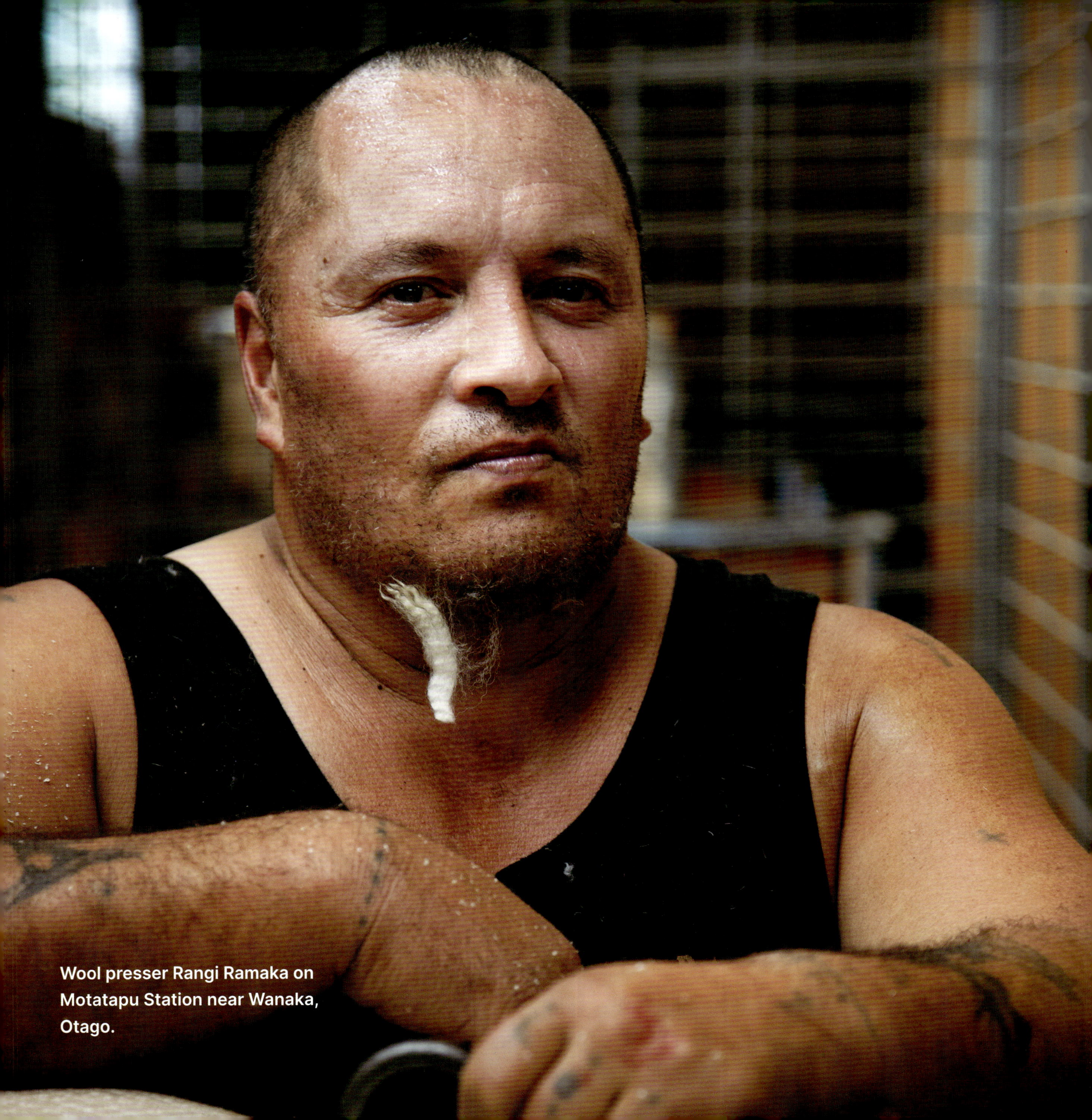

Wool presser Rangi Ramaka on Motatapu Station near Wanaka, Otago.

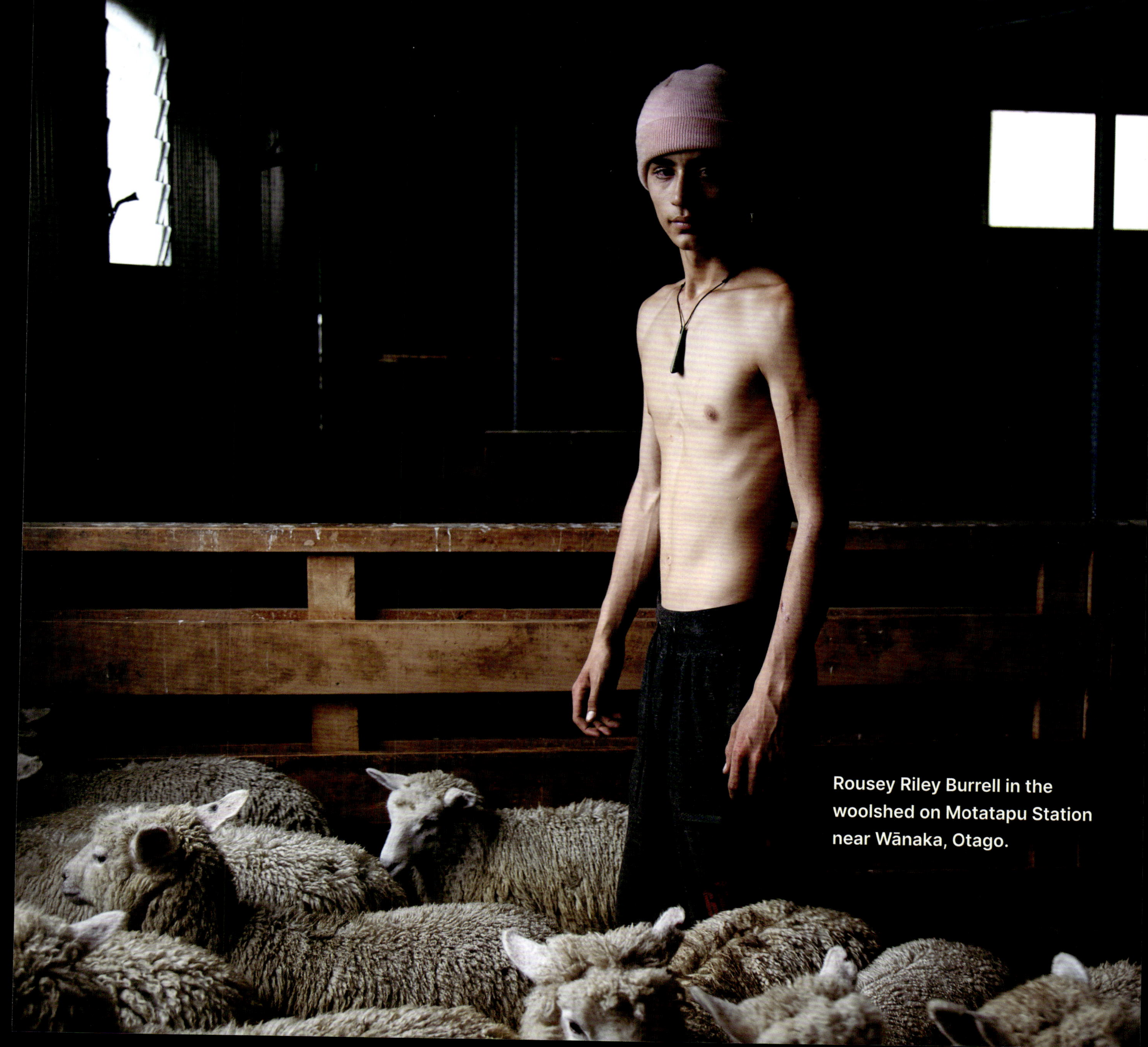

Rousey Riley Burrell in the woolshed on Motatapu Station near Wānaka, Otago.

# LOGAN WILLIAMS

**LOGAN WILLIAMS (Ngāi Tahu) is an internationally acclaimed entrepreneur and inventor, who operates between San Francisco and Christchurch. He undertook a project for New Zealand Merino Company, with government support, to tackle the issue of declining income from strong (or coarse) wool. New Zealand has been a leading exporter of this wool to textile manufacturers. However, while fine wool prices have risen considerably in the past 20 years, strong wool has been a different story, with it costing more to shear a sheep than the wool returns.**

**Logan's response was, within just four months, to invent a product called Keravos, made with strong wool and polylactic acid (PLA) from corn starch to produce wool pellets. PLA is widely used around the world as a plastic substitute.**

**Using injection moulding, the Keravos pellets can be turned into numerous products such as pontoons, kayaks and cooler bins, to name just a few.**

'We have a simple company where we take any kind of wool — dags, bellies, sides, pieces —and we combine them with polymers to make pellets. The pellets are the building blocks for everything we make. We have made everything from knives with Victory, Dynex cladding and we have just made the world's first woollen catamaran, which is pretty cool. Our goal is to dominate the strong wool industry with hundreds of consumer products and displace plastic as much as possible. It should transform the industry.

I think in New Zealand the agriculture sector offers the most opportunity commercially. We have all of these farmers producing bulk commercial services at the lowest possible price all around the world. We should be taking those low-value commodities and elevating them to high-performance consumer products.

— Logan Williams

**Logan Williams holding his invention, Keravos pellets, made from strong wool and acid derived from corn starch.**

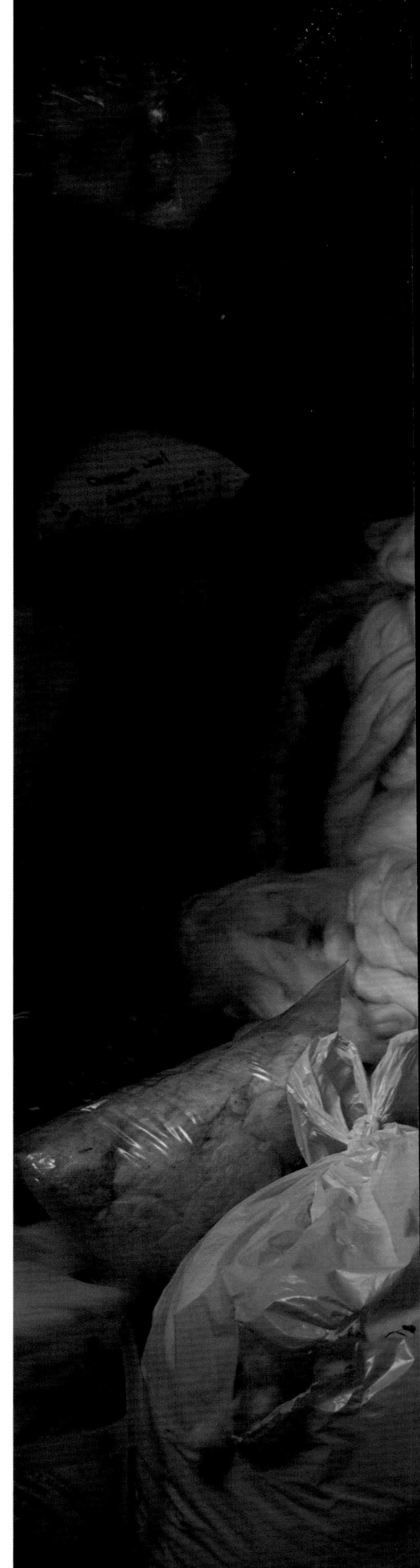

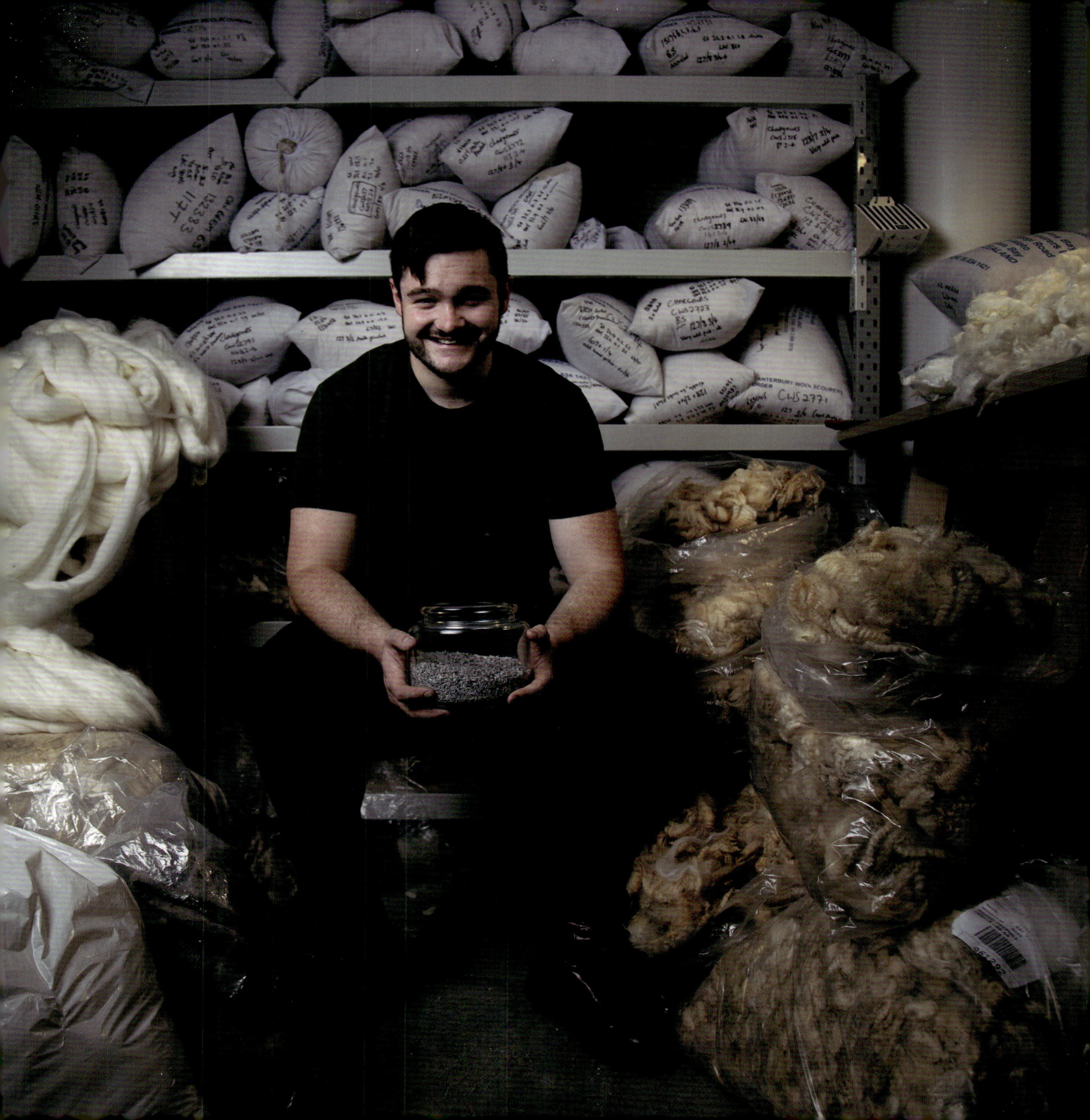

# WINE

Winemaking and viticulture were established early in New Zealand, with British Resident James Busby producing wine on his land near Waitangi in Northland for locally stationed British soldiers in 1836. In Hawke's Bay in 1851, French Marist missionaries established a vineyard for making communion wine. It is now part of the Mission Estate Winery, the oldest commercial vineyard in New Zealand. Immigrants arriving in New Zealand from the Dalmatian coast of Croatia in the late nineteenth and early twentieth centuries brought with them a love of wine and viticultural knowledge and planted vineyards in West and North Auckland, producing mostly table wine and fortified wine. New Zealand has experimented with various wine varieties, with 'vine-pulls' of unsuccessful varieties occurring along the way. Today Marlborough sauvignon blanc dominates, along with dense, concentrated pinot noir from Marlborough, Martinborough and Central Otago. In 2020, New Zealand produced 329 million litres from 39,935 hectares of vineyard area, of which about two-thirds is dedicated to sauvignon blanc. Nearly 90 per cent of total production is exported, mainly to the United States, Britain and Australia, reaching a record NZ$1.92 billion in export revenue in 2020.

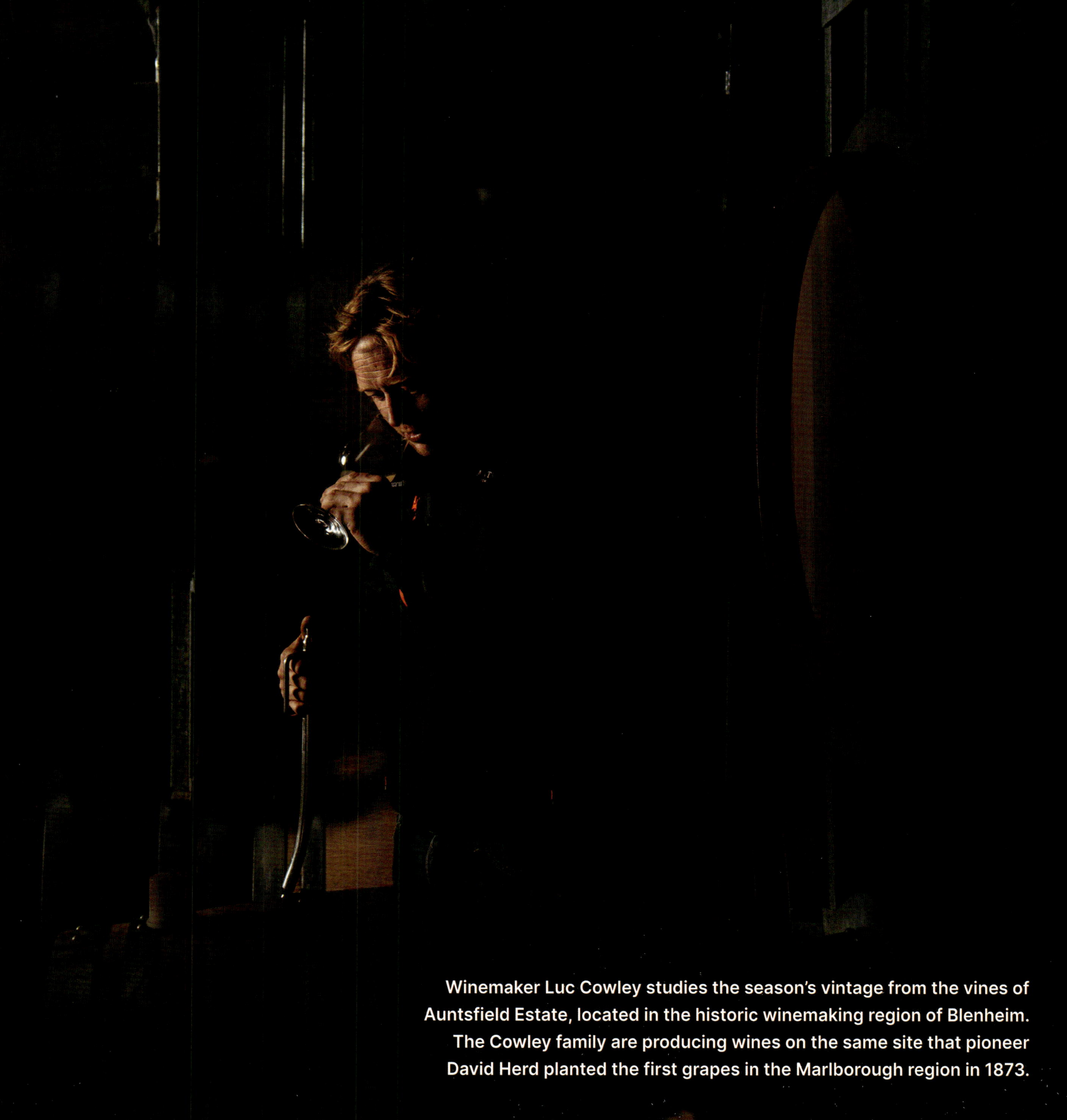

Winemaker Luc Cowley studies the season's vintage from the vines of Auntsfield Estate, located in the historic winemaking region of Blenheim. The Cowley family are producing wines on the same site that pioneer David Herd planted the first grapes in the Marlborough region in 1873.

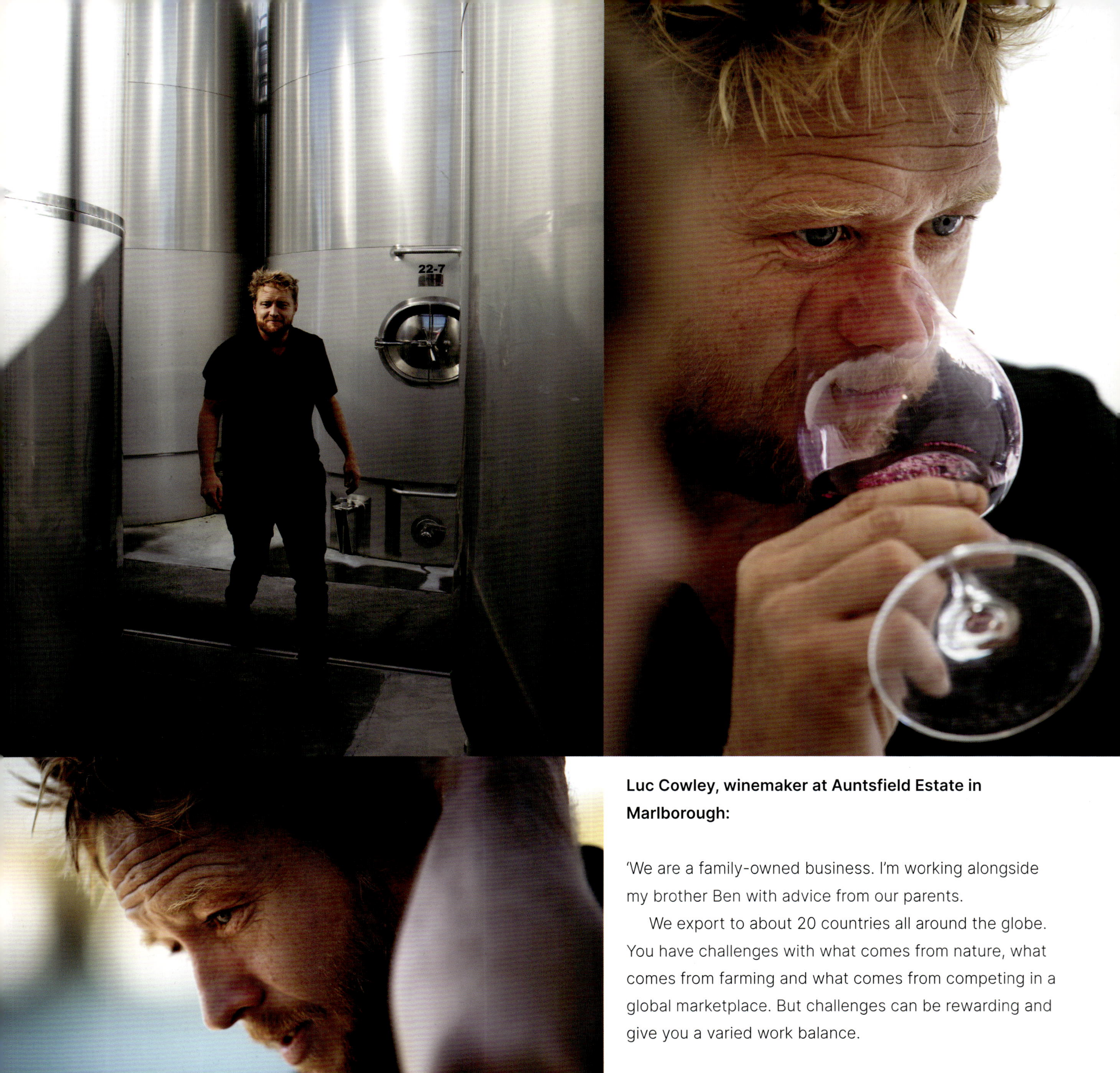


**Luc Cowley, winemaker at Auntsfield Estate in Marlborough:**

'We are a family-owned business. I'm working alongside my brother Ben with advice from our parents.

We export to about 20 countries all around the globe. You have challenges with what comes from nature, what comes from farming and what comes from competing in a global marketplace. But challenges can be rewarding and give you a varied work balance.

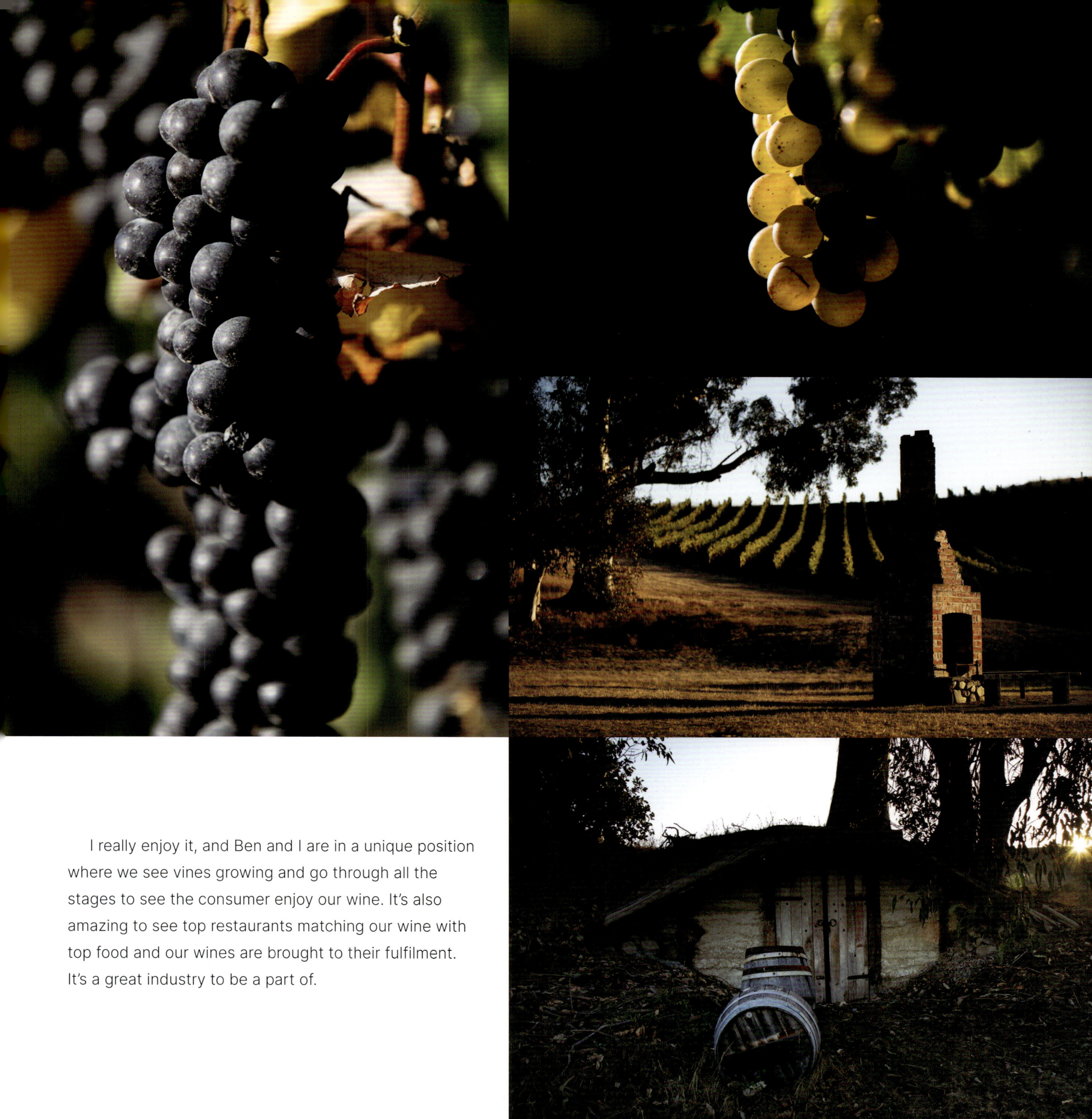

I really enjoy it, and Ben and I are in a unique position where we see vines growing and go through all the stages to see the consumer enjoy our wine. It's also amazing to see top restaurants matching our wine with top food and our wines are brought to their fulfilment. It's a great industry to be a part of.

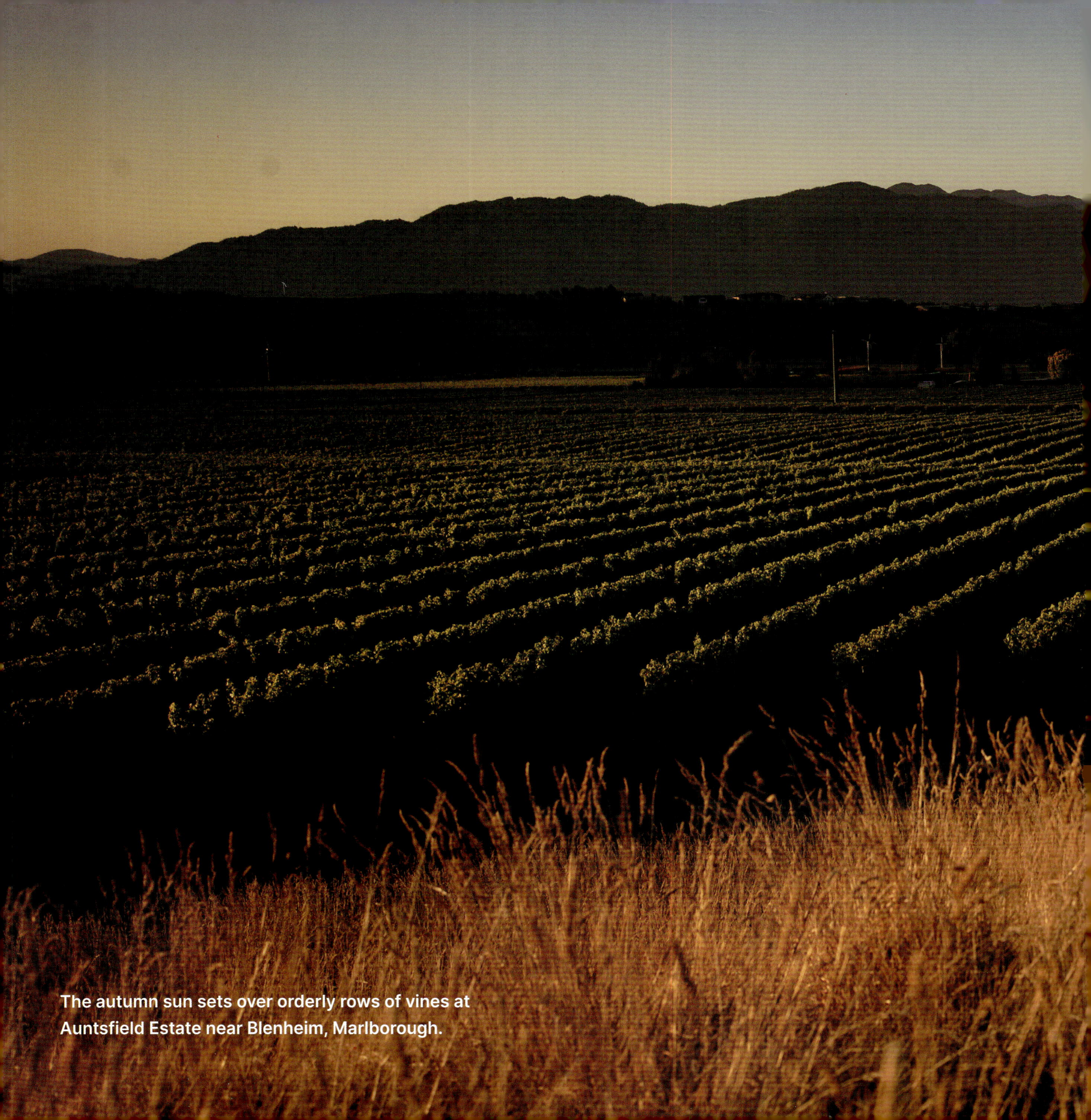

The autumn sun sets over orderly rows of vines at Auntsfield Estate near Blenheim, Marlborough.

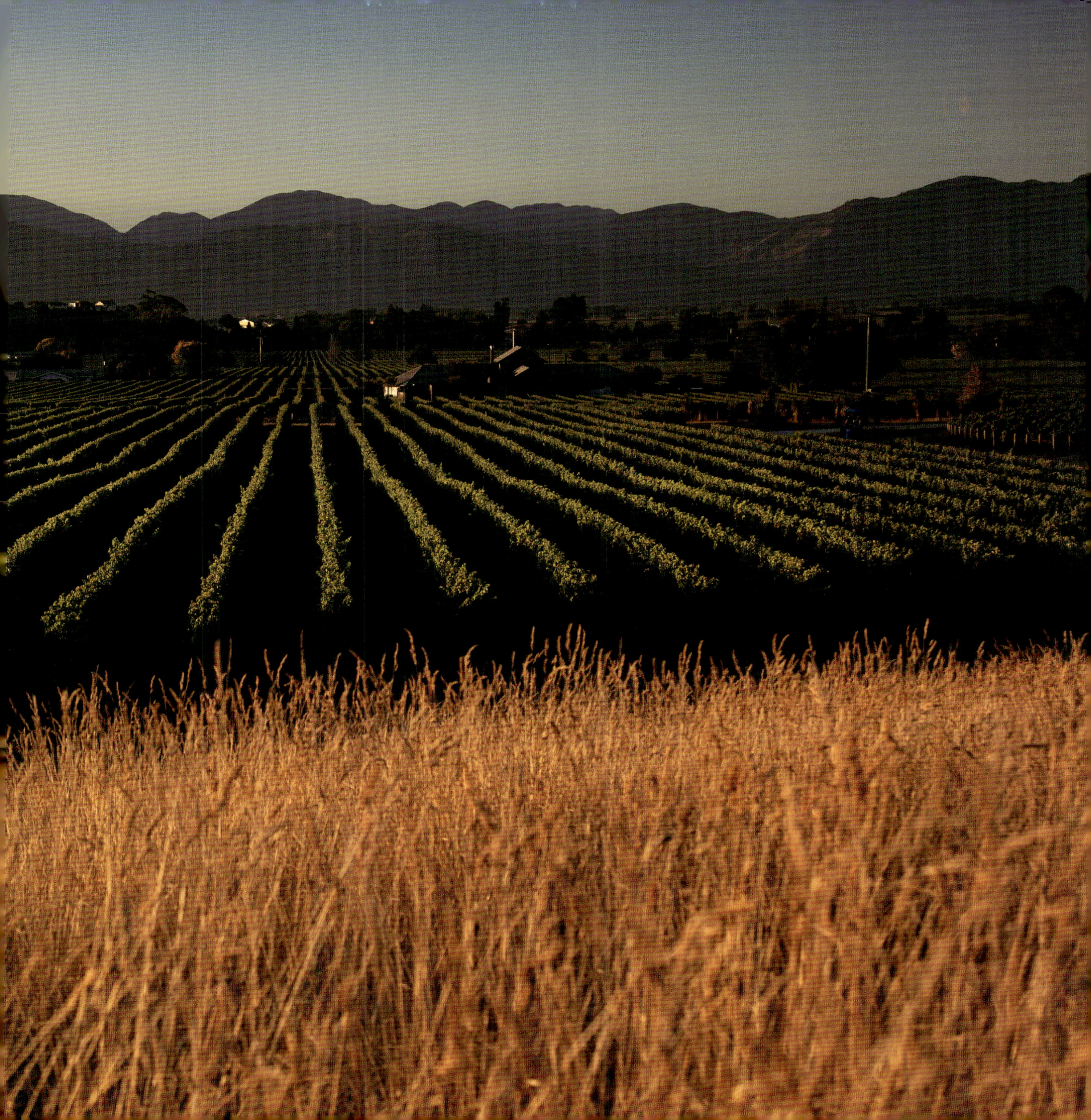

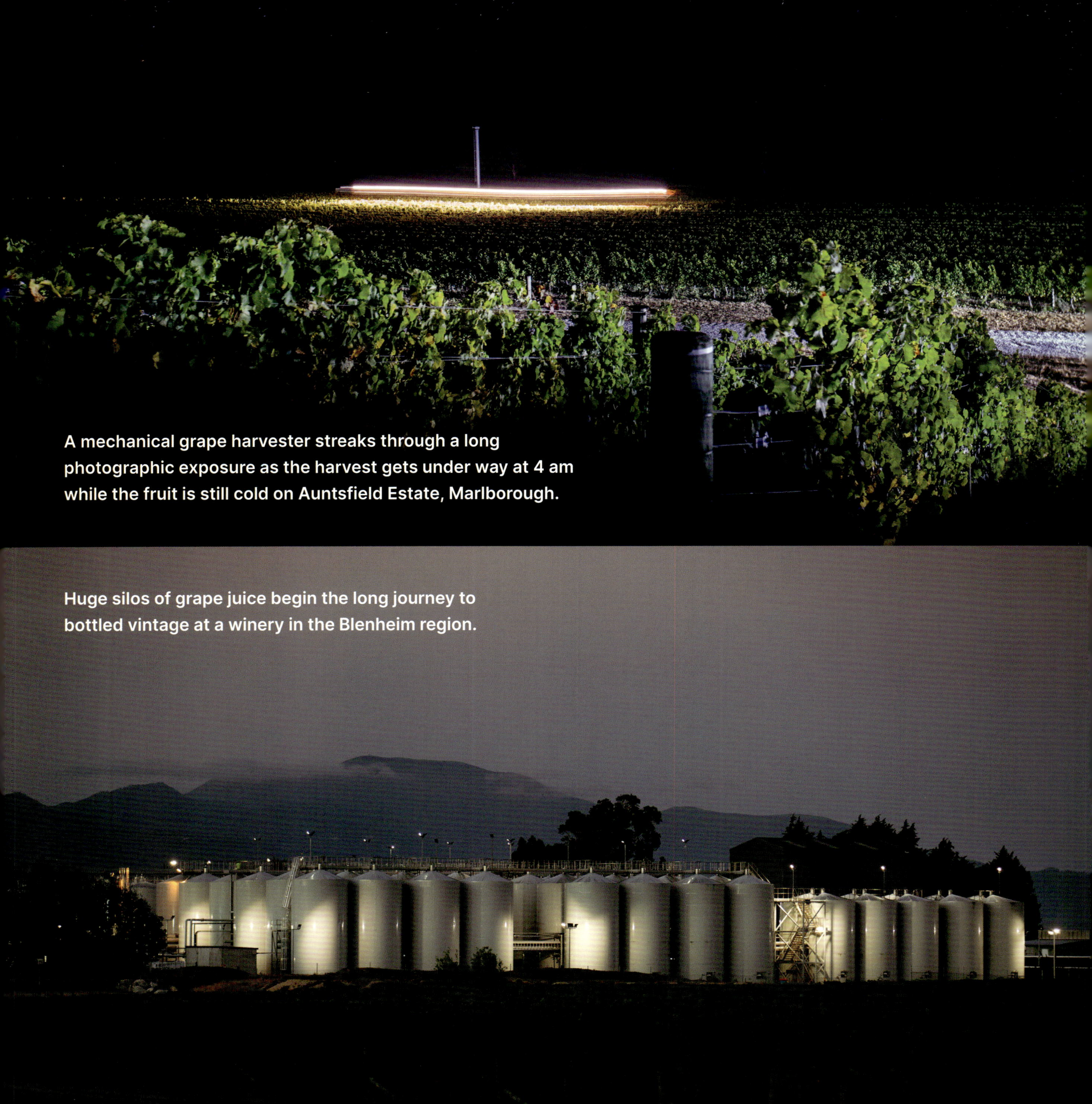

A mechanical grape harvester streaks through a long photographic exposure as the harvest gets under way at 4 am while the fruit is still cold on Auntsfield Estate, Marlborough.

Huge silos of grape juice begin the long journey to bottled vintage at a winery in the Blenheim region.

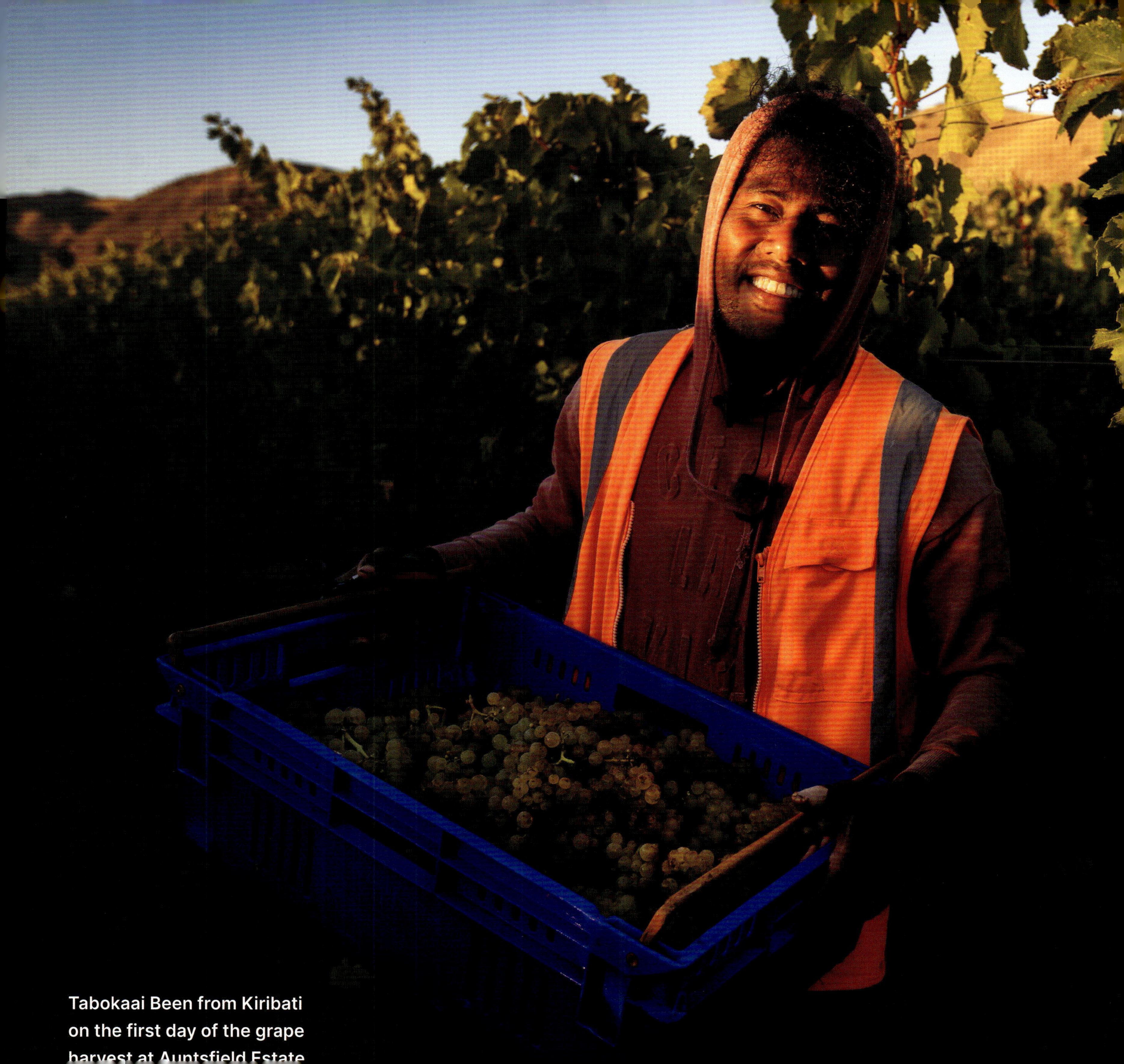

Tabokaai Been from Kiribati on the first day of the grape harvest at Auntsfield Estate

# DAIRYING

**Dairy communities are an integral part of rural life. New Zealand's abundant pastures have meant that in 30 years to 2020, dairy exports have grown from just over NZ$2 billion per year to almost $20 billion, and dairy is the country's largest export goods sector. All that is produced by some six million dairy cows, with the greatest concentration in the Waikato and other parts of western and northern North Island, along with the West Coast and Southland in the South Island.**

**New Zealand contributes around 3 per cent of the world's milk output. Local dairy companies produce a wide range of dairy products, from milk and milk powders, butter and cheese, to infant formula, specialty creams, and specialist nutritional products. In recent years, China, Australia, USA, Japan and Malaysia have been key markets.**

**Ruby White, 13 years old, from Te Aroha, Waikato, on what she loves about dairy farming:**

'It's just the cows and you are always out and about. The cows are real precious and very special to me. As long as the animals are happy then I am happy. I like going on my nana and grandad's farm and I like working there too. They have taught me a lot. From when I was a baby I used to come on the farm with my mum in the backpack and I have just loved it ever since.

I rear the calves over calving. My job is to make sure that they are all healthy and all happy. That they are all fed properly. That's all I care about. I come over most mornings and I am here every night. There are a lot to feed. I love it. It is hard to say goodbye when they go to grazing. I want to keep doing this and carry on the family business. I would like to have my own farm.

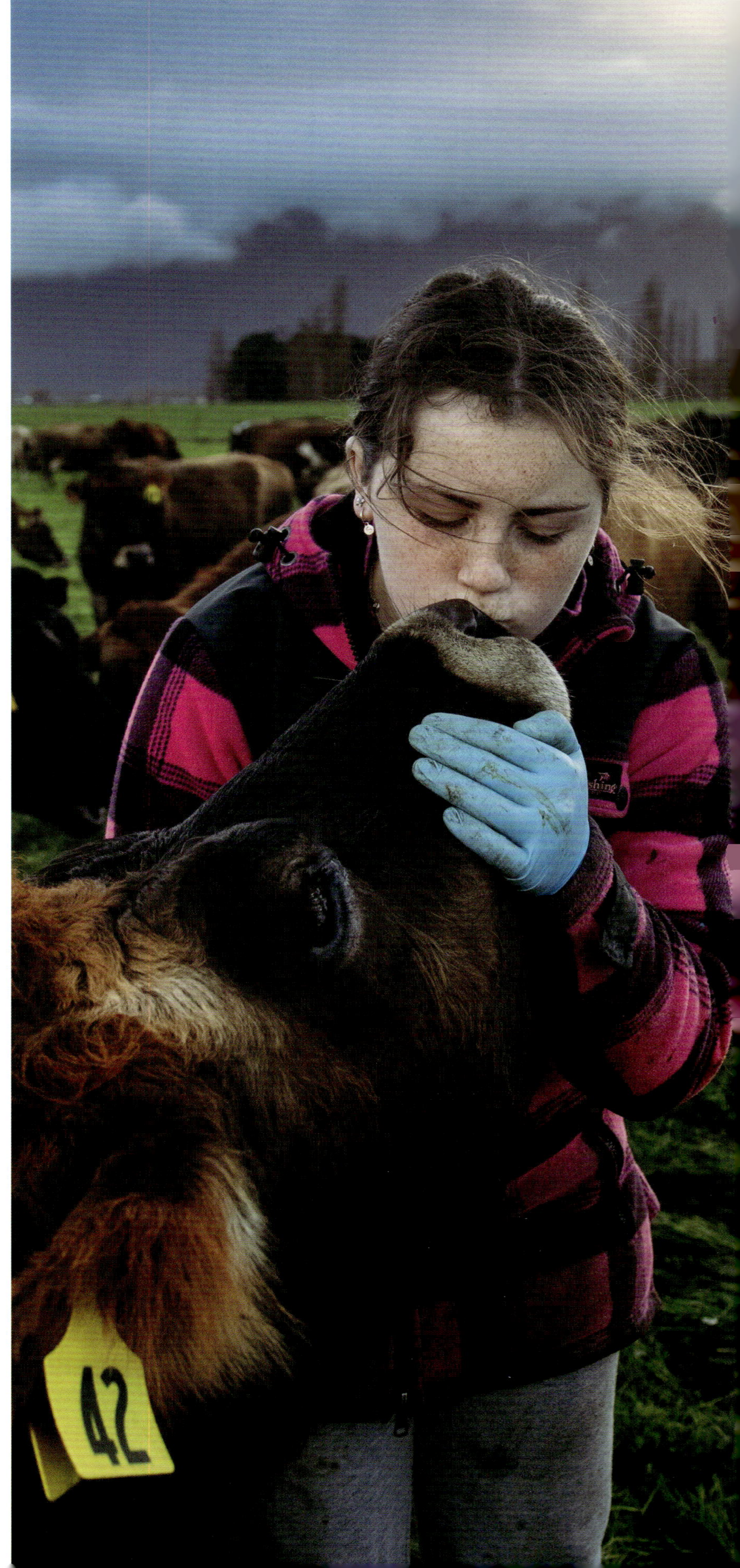


**Ruby White shares a moment with Pippy, a special cow in the herd that she and her mother Tania White milk at Te Aroha, Waikato.**

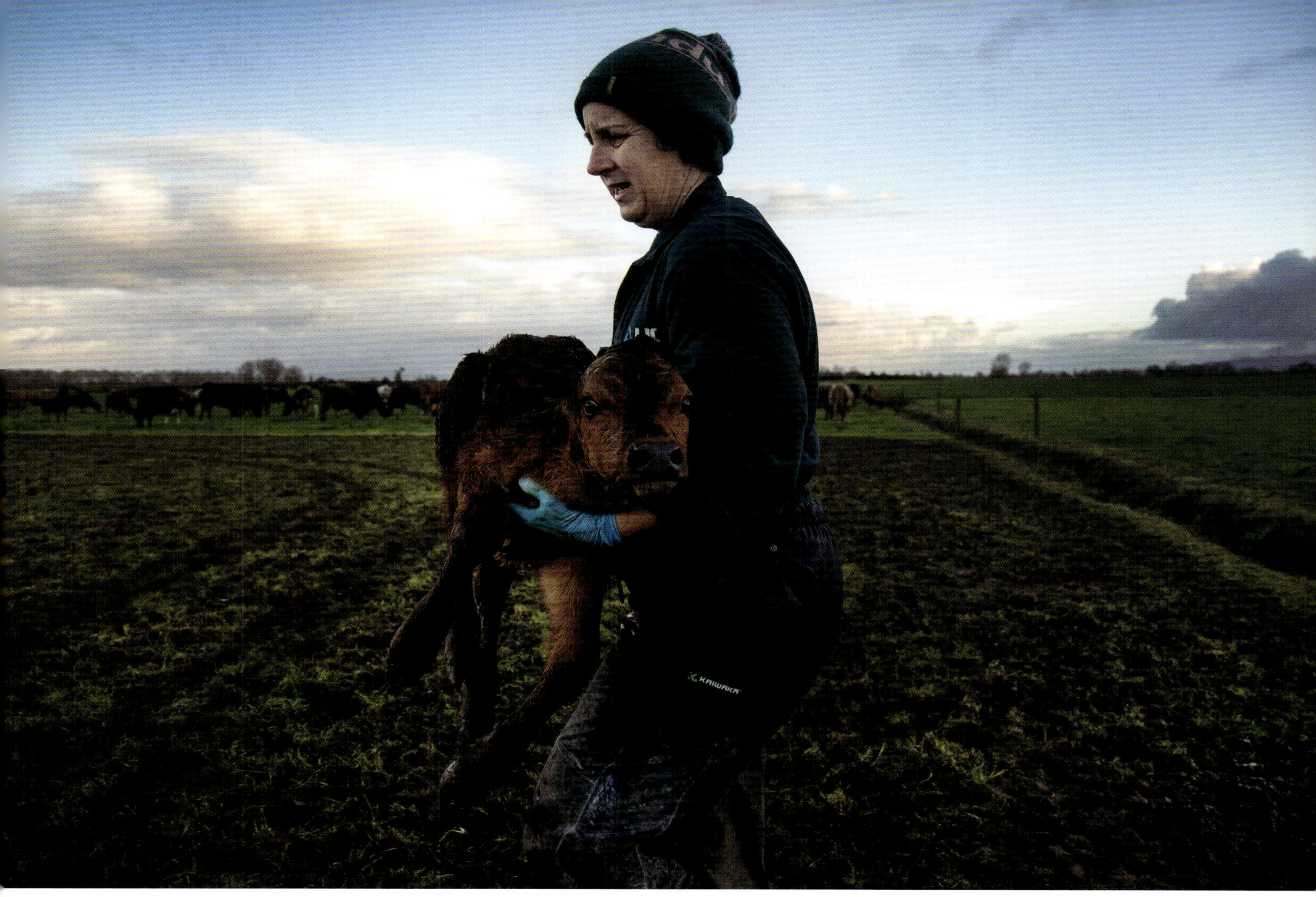


## *This is my life. I can't imagine doing anything else.*

**Tania White, dairy farmer, Te Aroha:**

'I have been in dairy farming my whole life. I remember as a child coming home from school and if Mum and Dad were in town, I would race inside, grab a drink and then bring in the cows and start milking. I was about 10 at the time. We just loved it. We loved the life. I wake up Ruby in the night during calving and she helps me with milking and spraying etc. It makes me happy that she wants to do this in the future. It's a good safe life.

I work seven days a week and I don't normally have time off during the year. I might try to take the kids off for a couple of days over Christmas. But apart from that I generally don't.

I am an artificial breeding technician and so I get to visit a lot of farms. This is my life. I can't imagine doing anything else.

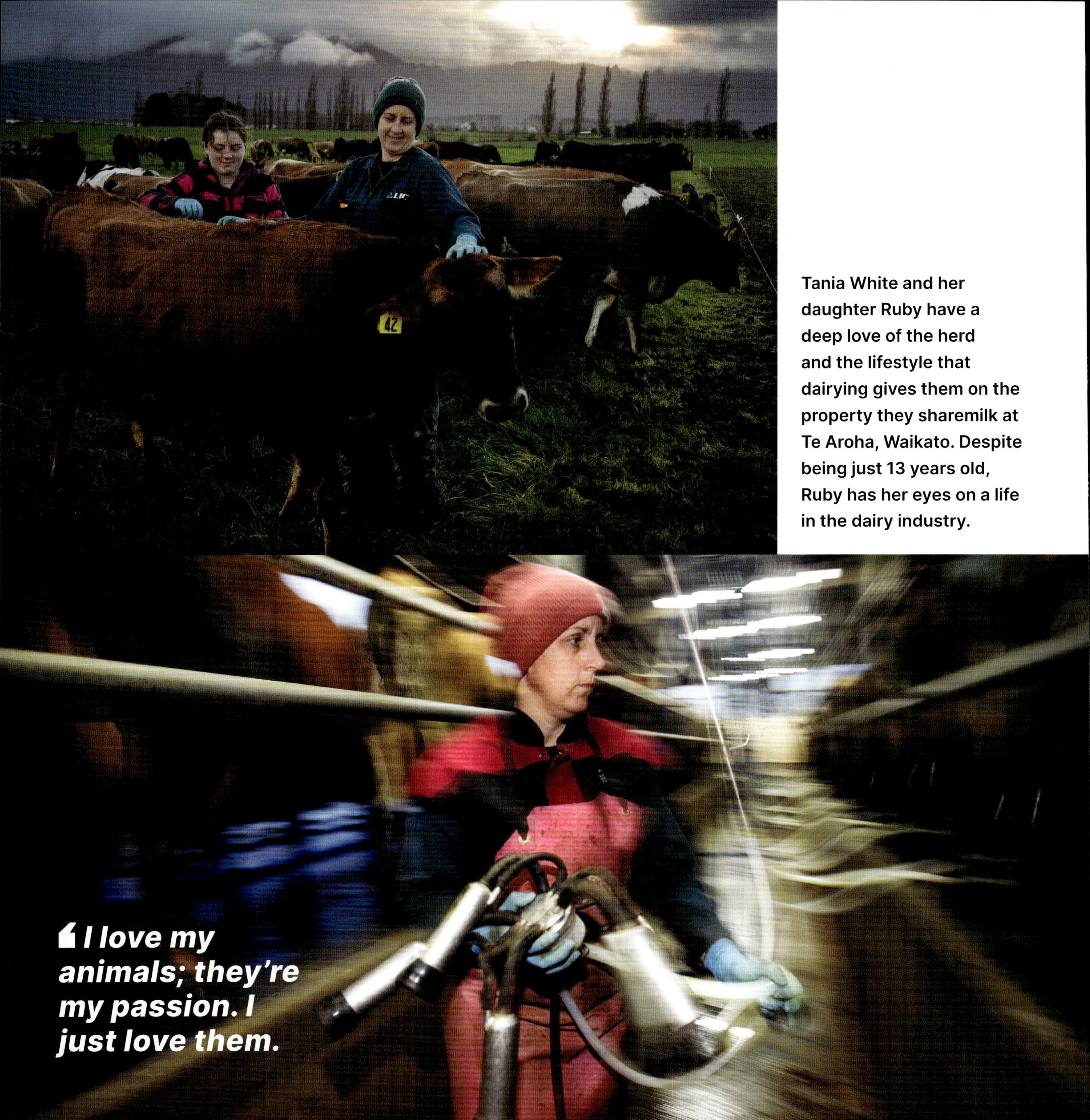


Tania White and her daughter Ruby have a deep love of the herd and the lifestyle that dairying gives them on the property they sharemilk at Te Aroha, Waikato. Despite being just 13 years old, Ruby has her eyes on a life in the dairy industry.

***'I love my animals; they're my passion. I just love them.***

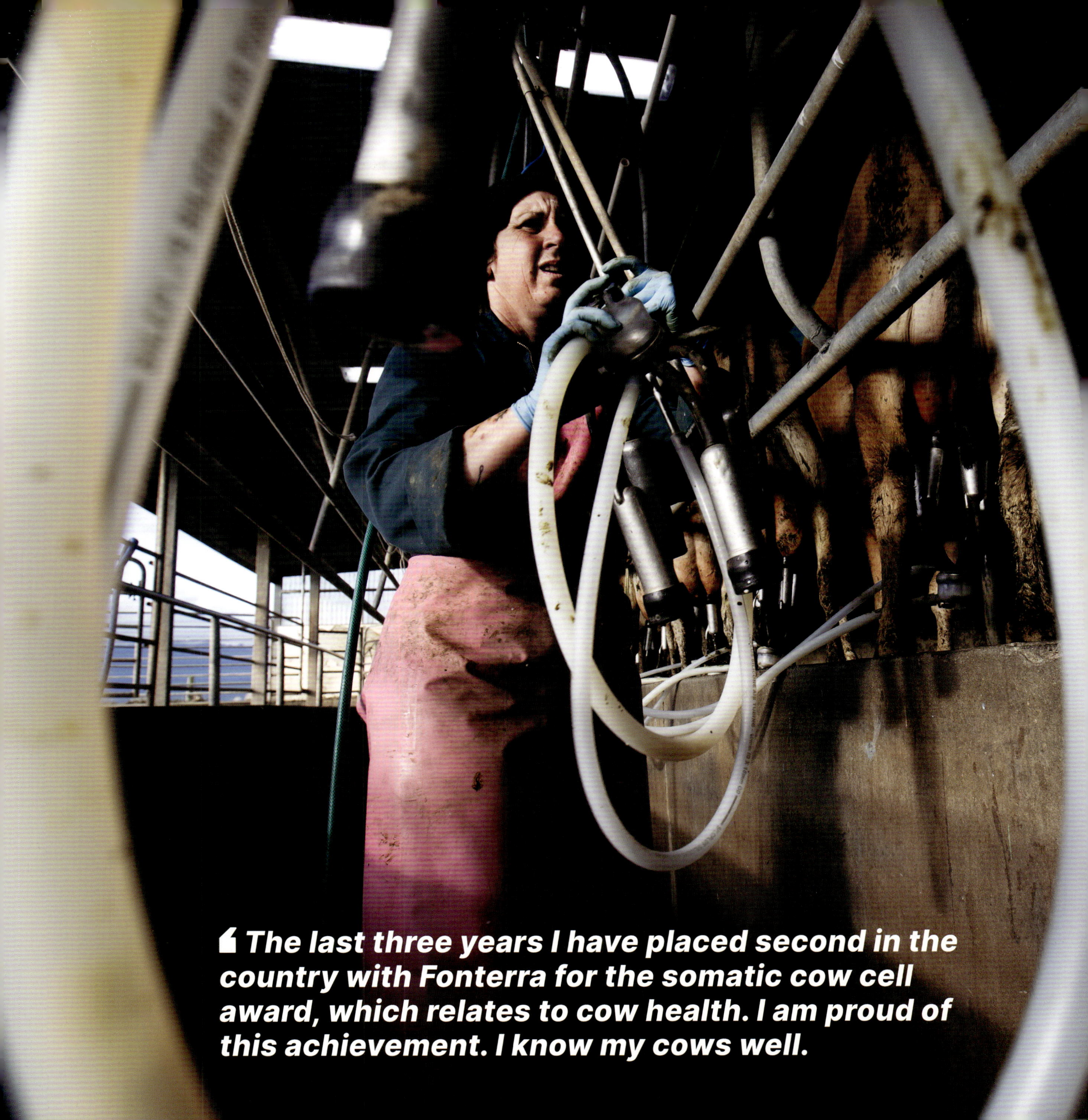

***The last three years I have placed second in the country with Fonterra for the somatic cow cell award, which relates to cow health. I am proud of this achievement. I know my cows well.***

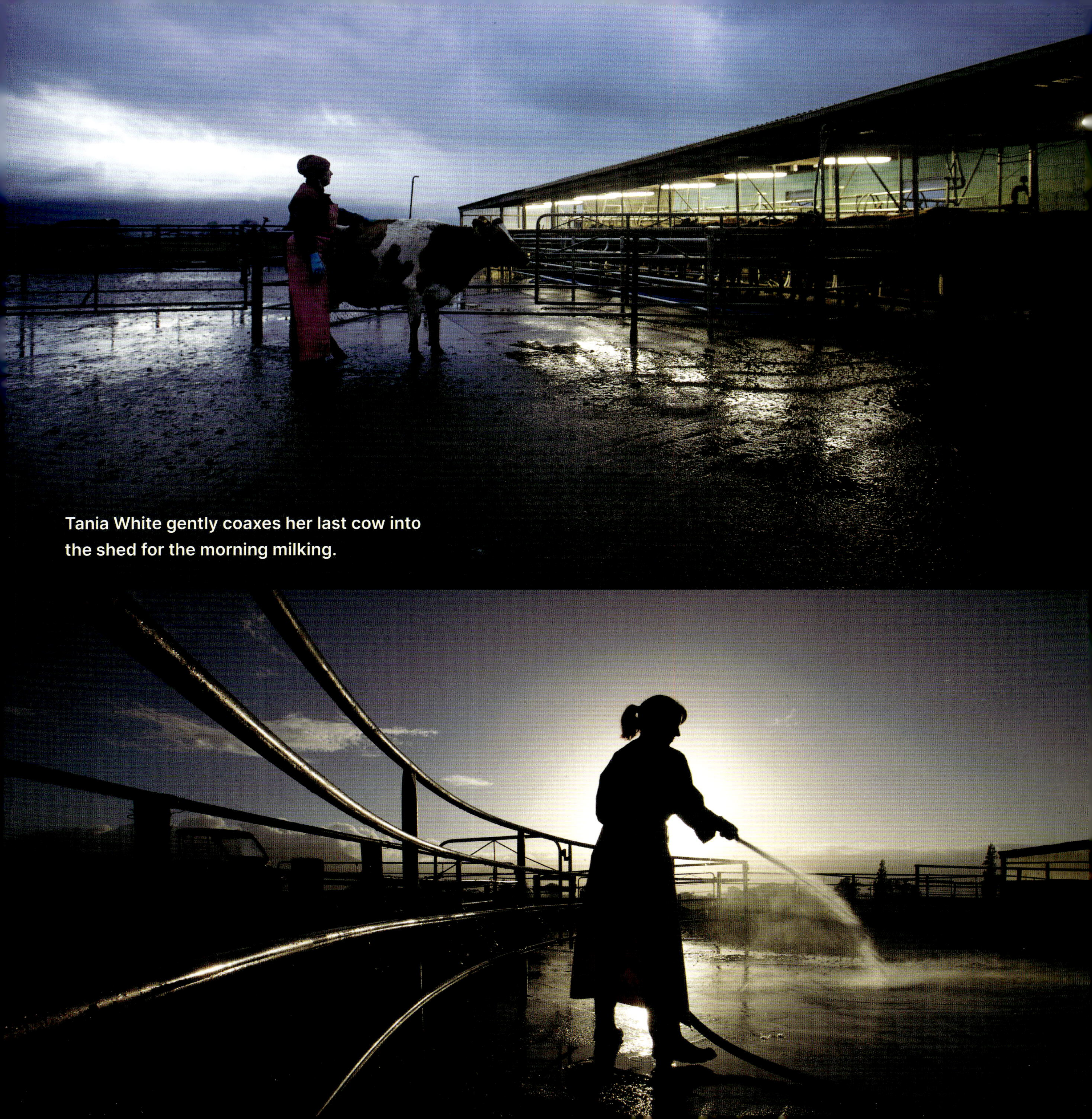

Tania White gently coaxes her last cow into the shed for the morning milking.

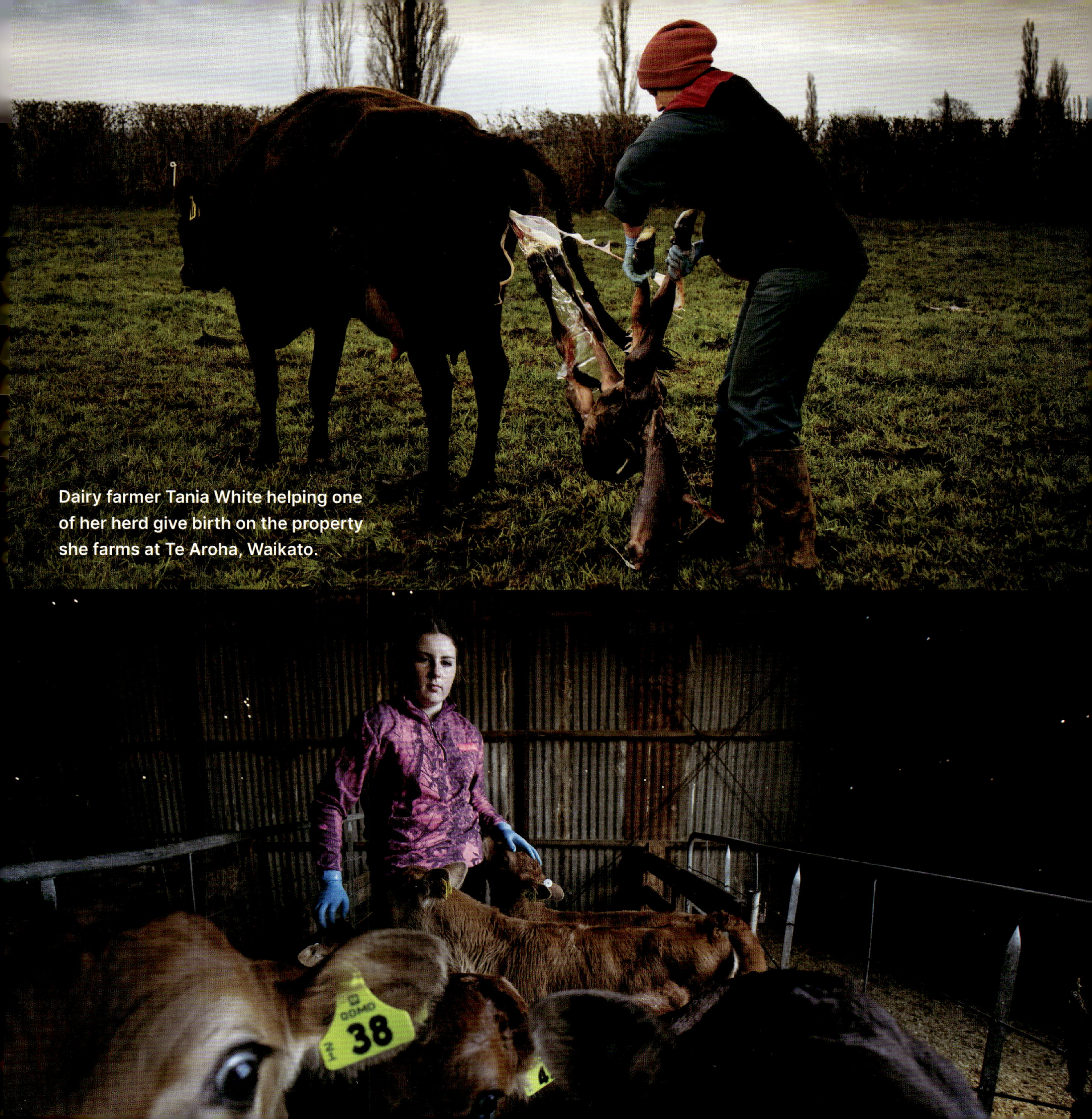


Dairy farmer Tania White helping one of her herd give birth on the property she farms at Te Aroha, Waikato.

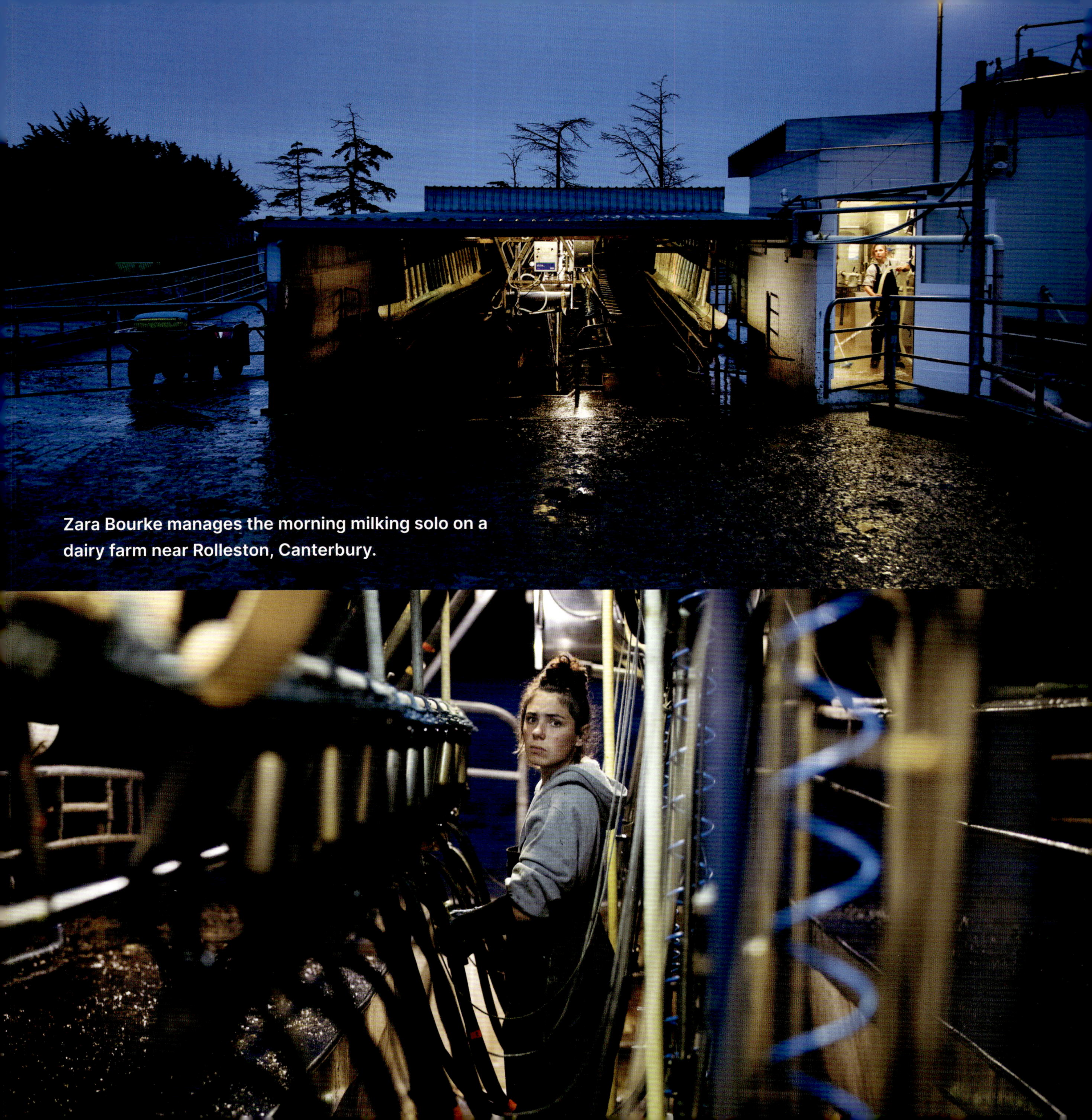

Zara Bourke manages the morning milking solo on a dairy farm near Rolleston, Canterbury.

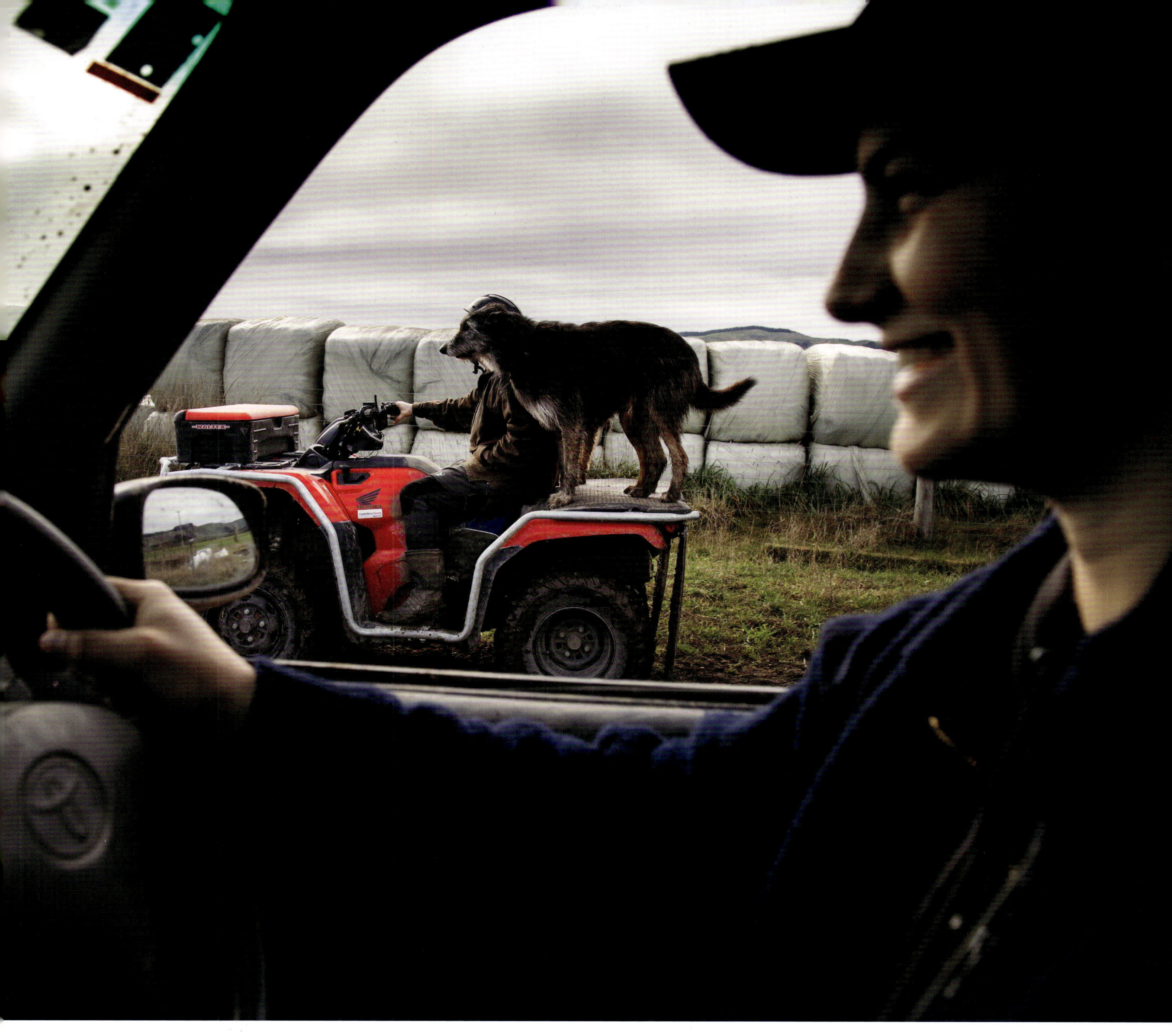

Jessie Vaughan pilots the ute while farm manager Anna Fitzgerald and her sidekick head out on the quadbike to feed cows on a dairy farm near Gore Bay, Canterbury.

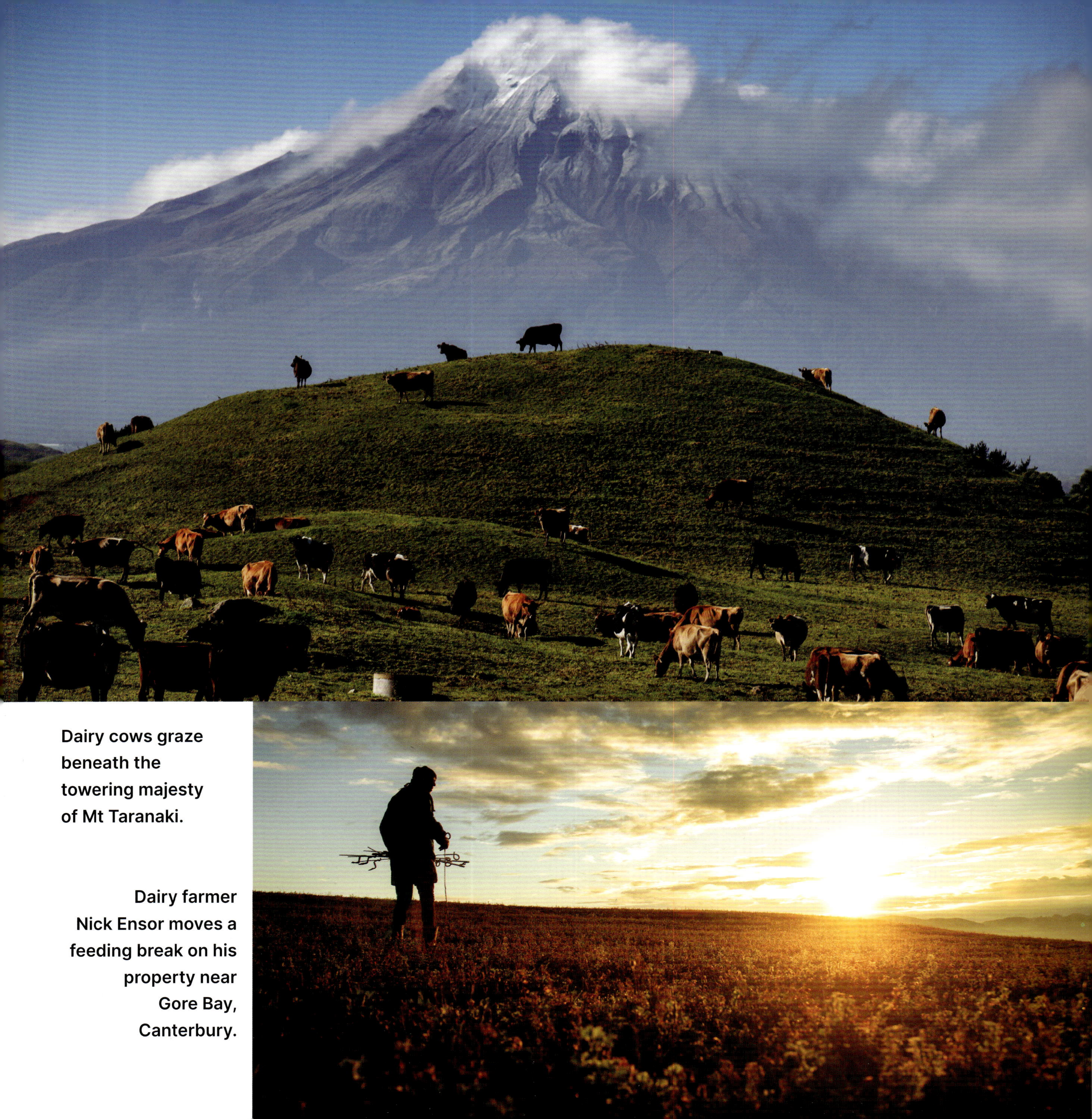

Dairy cows graze beneath the towering majesty of Mt Taranaki.

Dairy farmer Nick Ensor moves a feeding break on his property near Gore Bay, Canterbury.

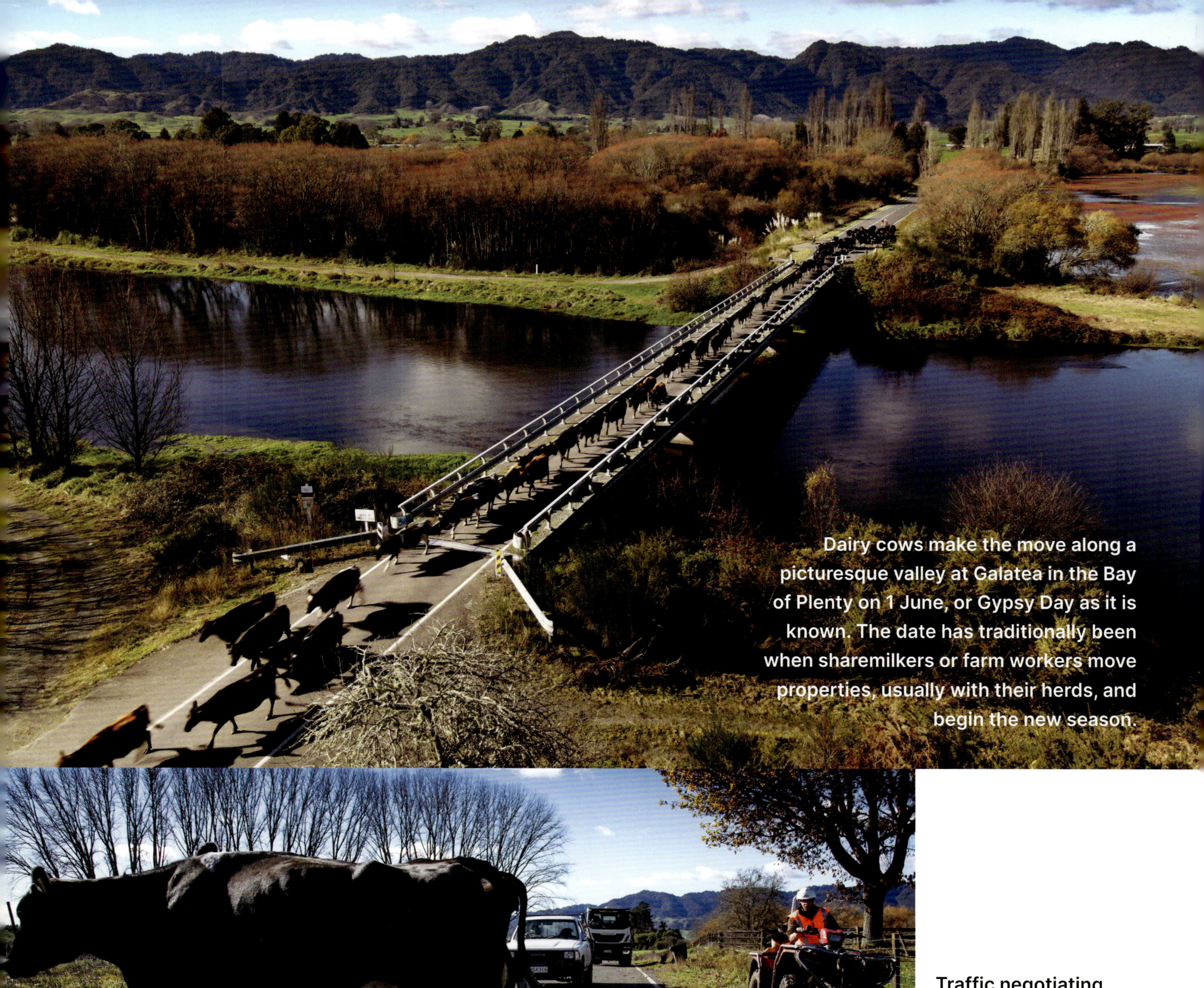

Dairy cows make the move along a picturesque valley at Galatea in the Bay of Plenty on 1 June, or Gypsy Day as it is known. The date has traditionally been when sharemilkers or farm workers move properties, usually with their herds, and begin the new season.

Traffic negotiating cows as farmers and their herds move on Gypsy Day.

# FARM DOGS

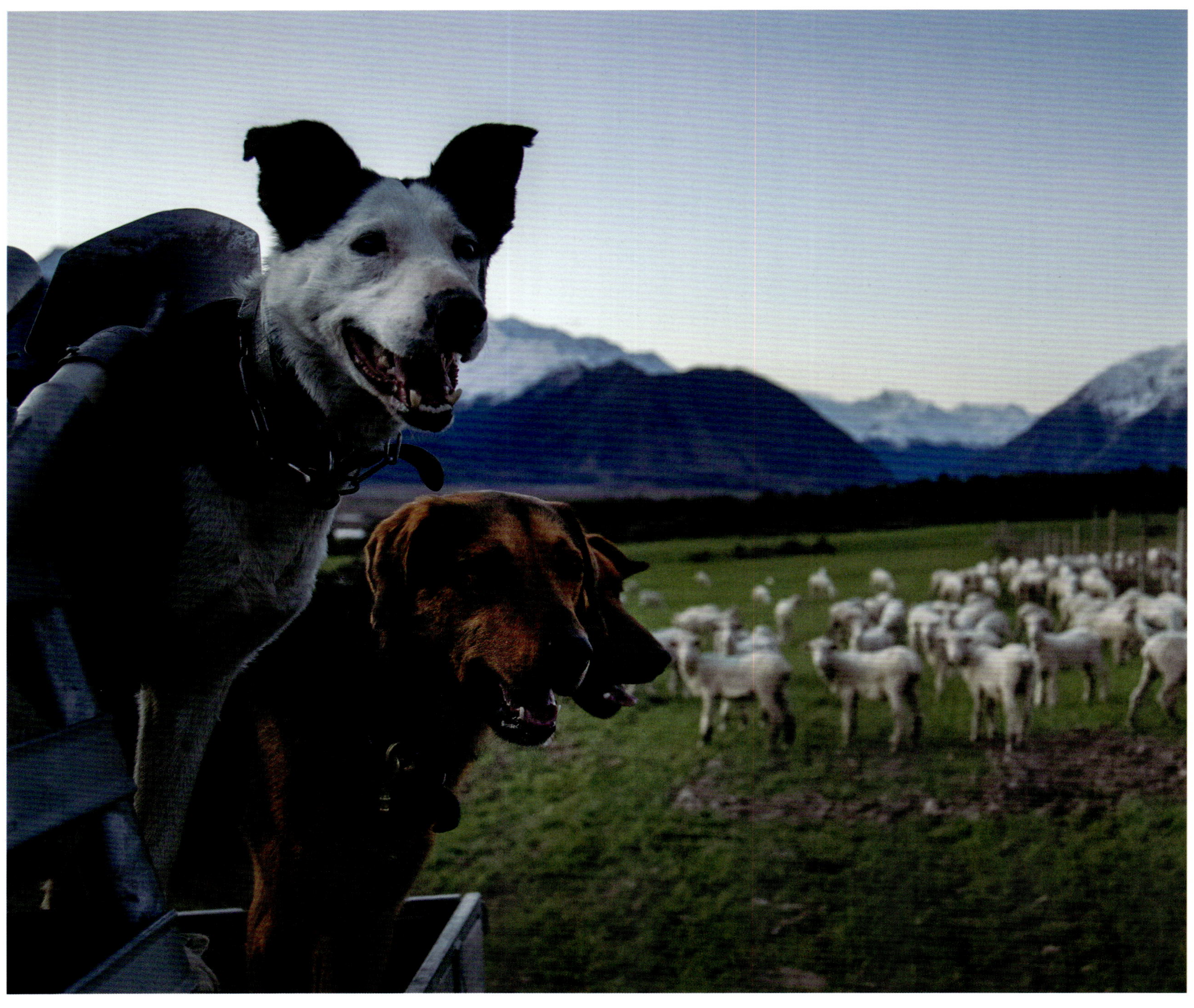

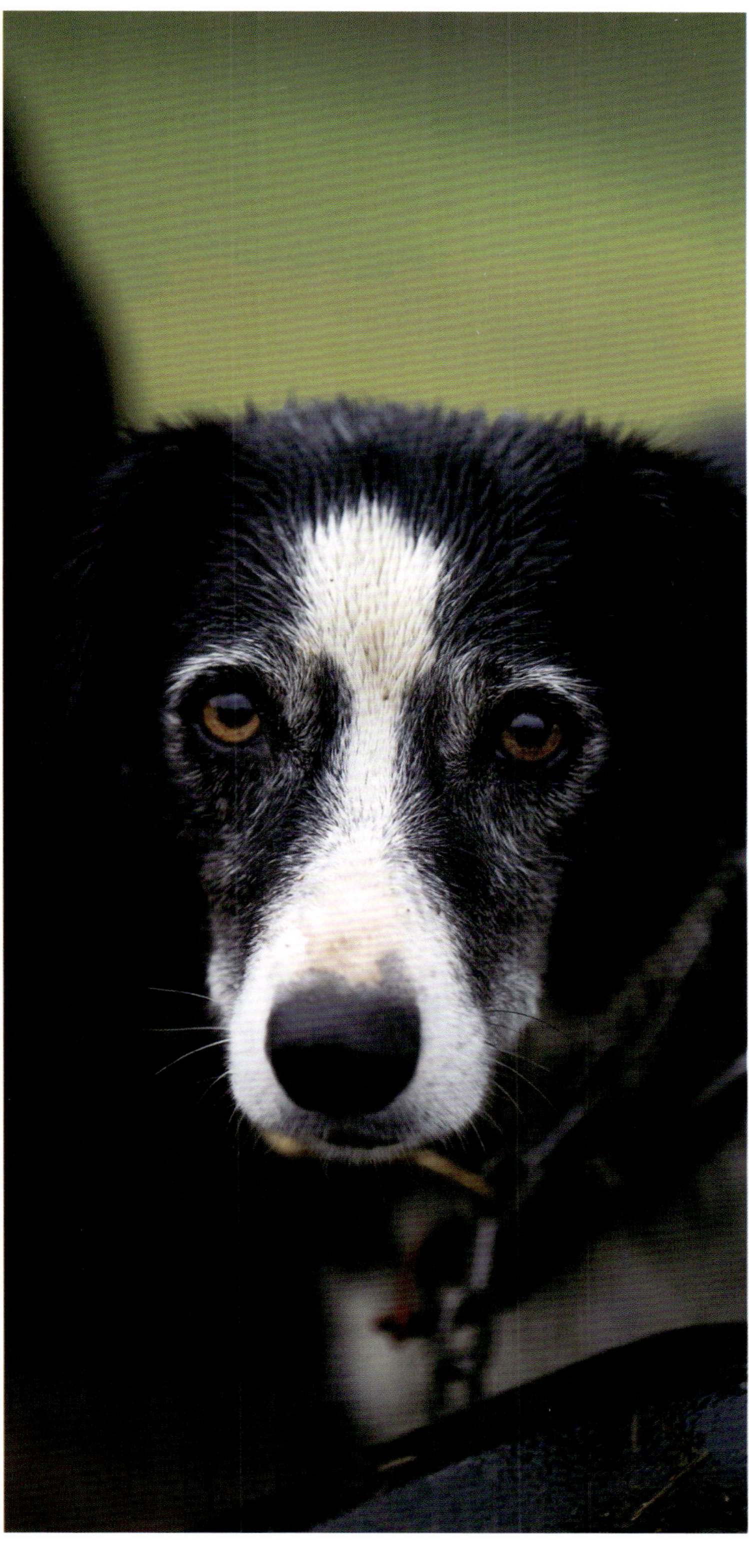

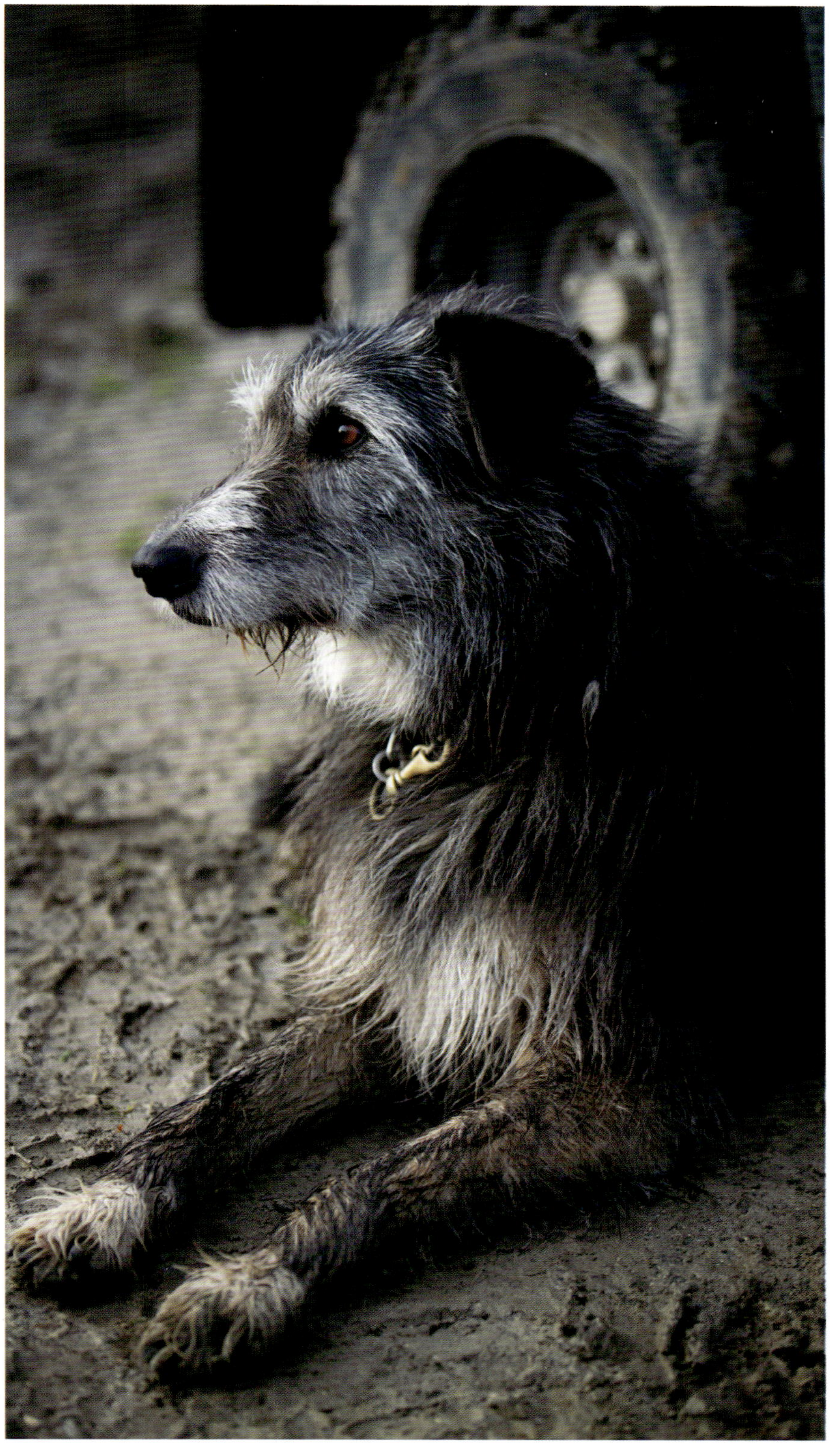

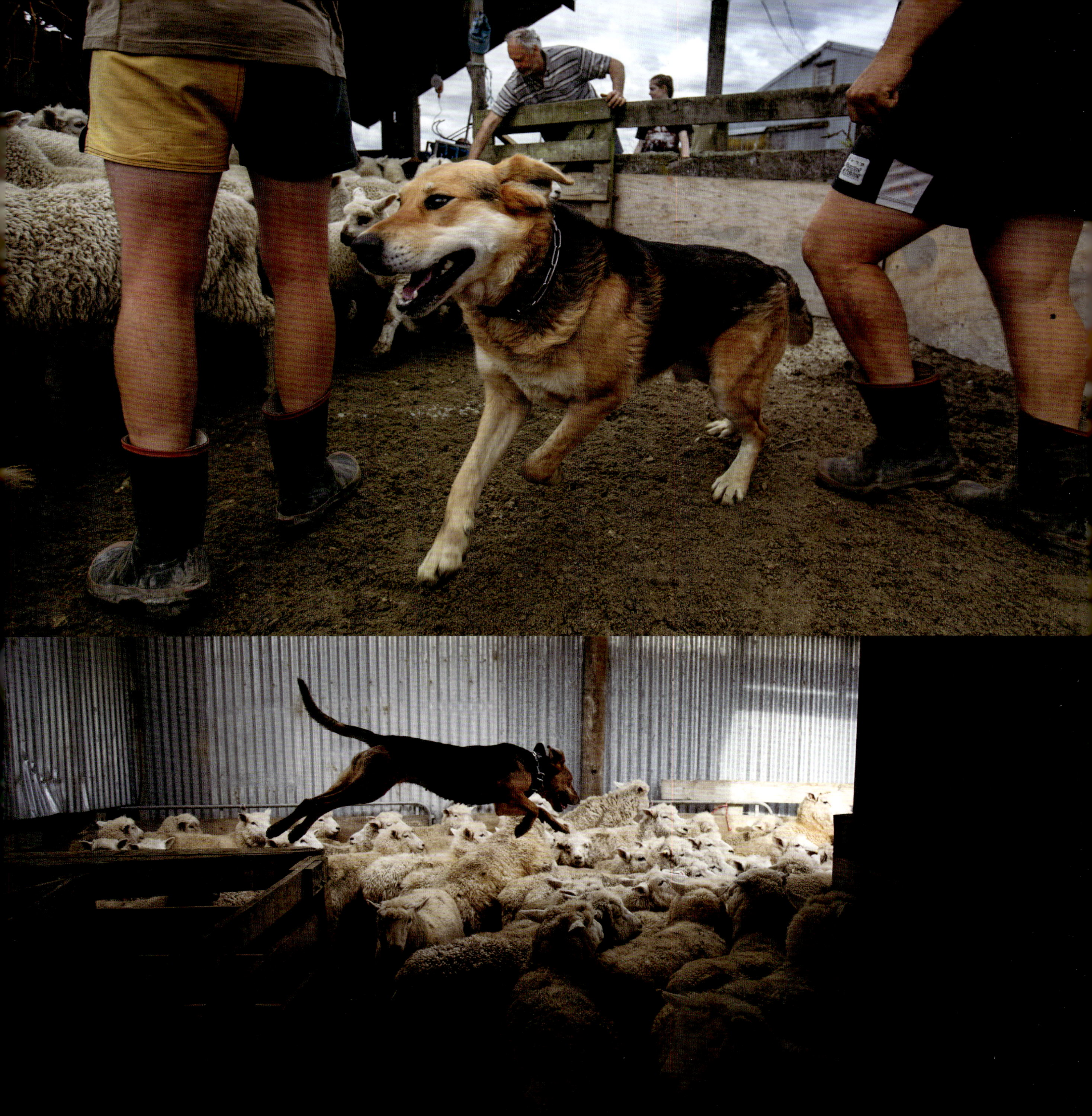

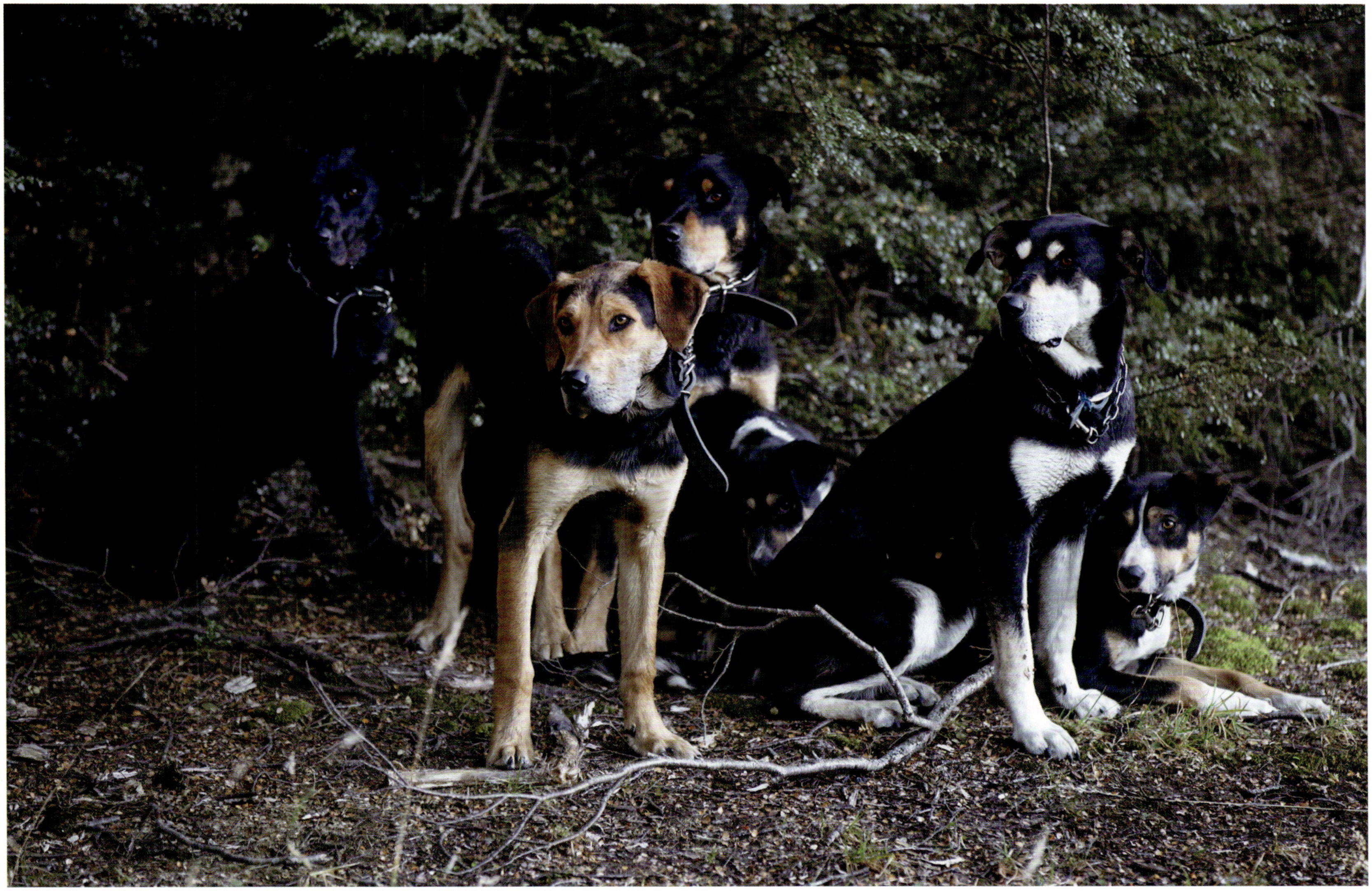

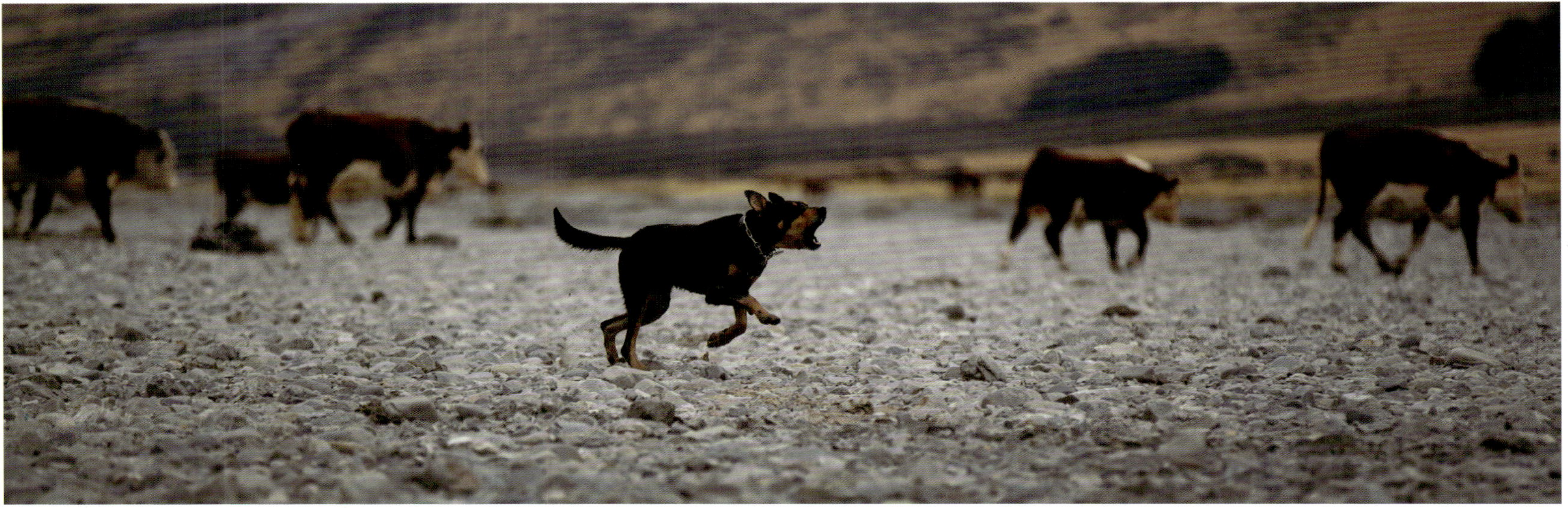

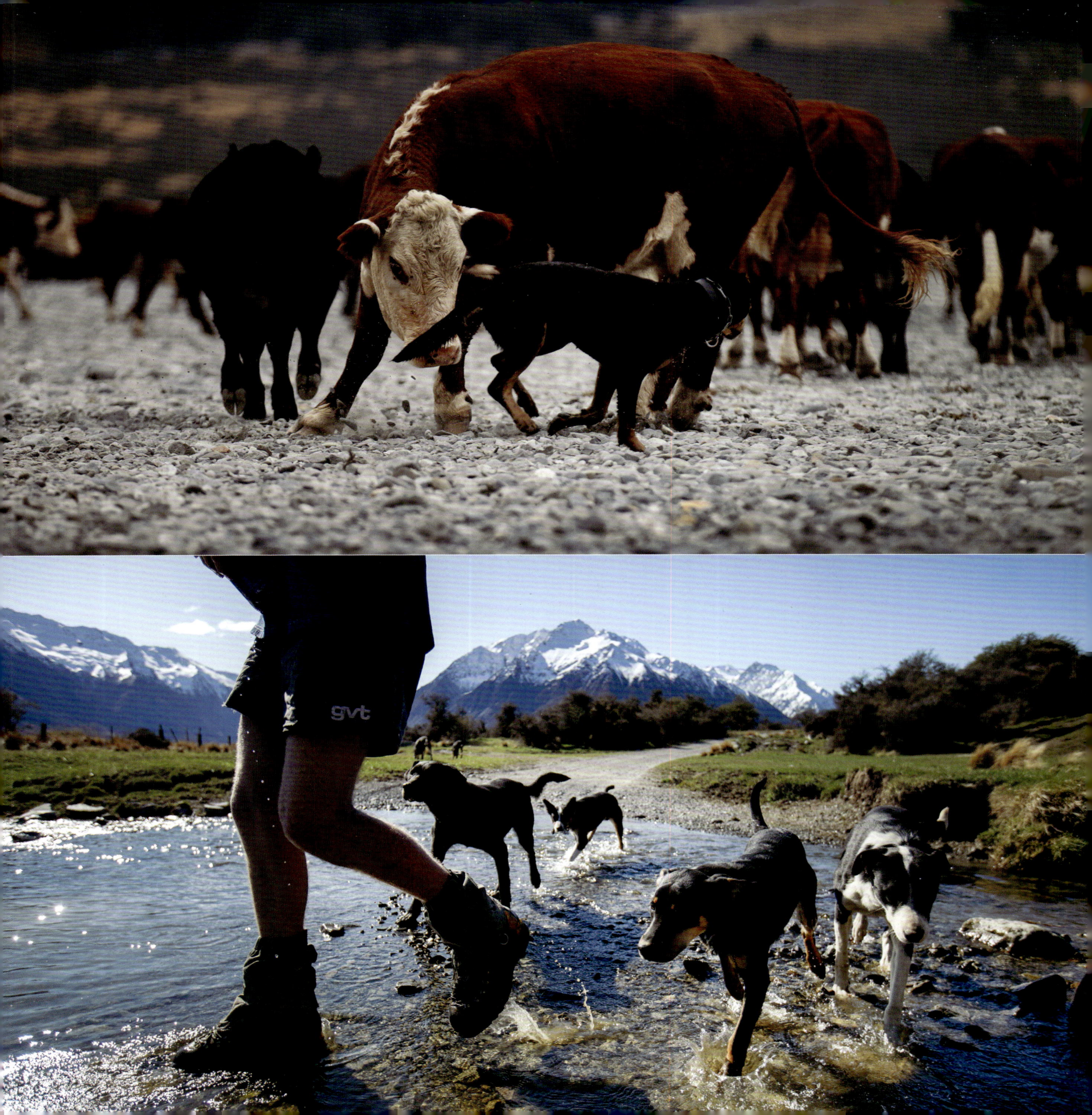
gvt

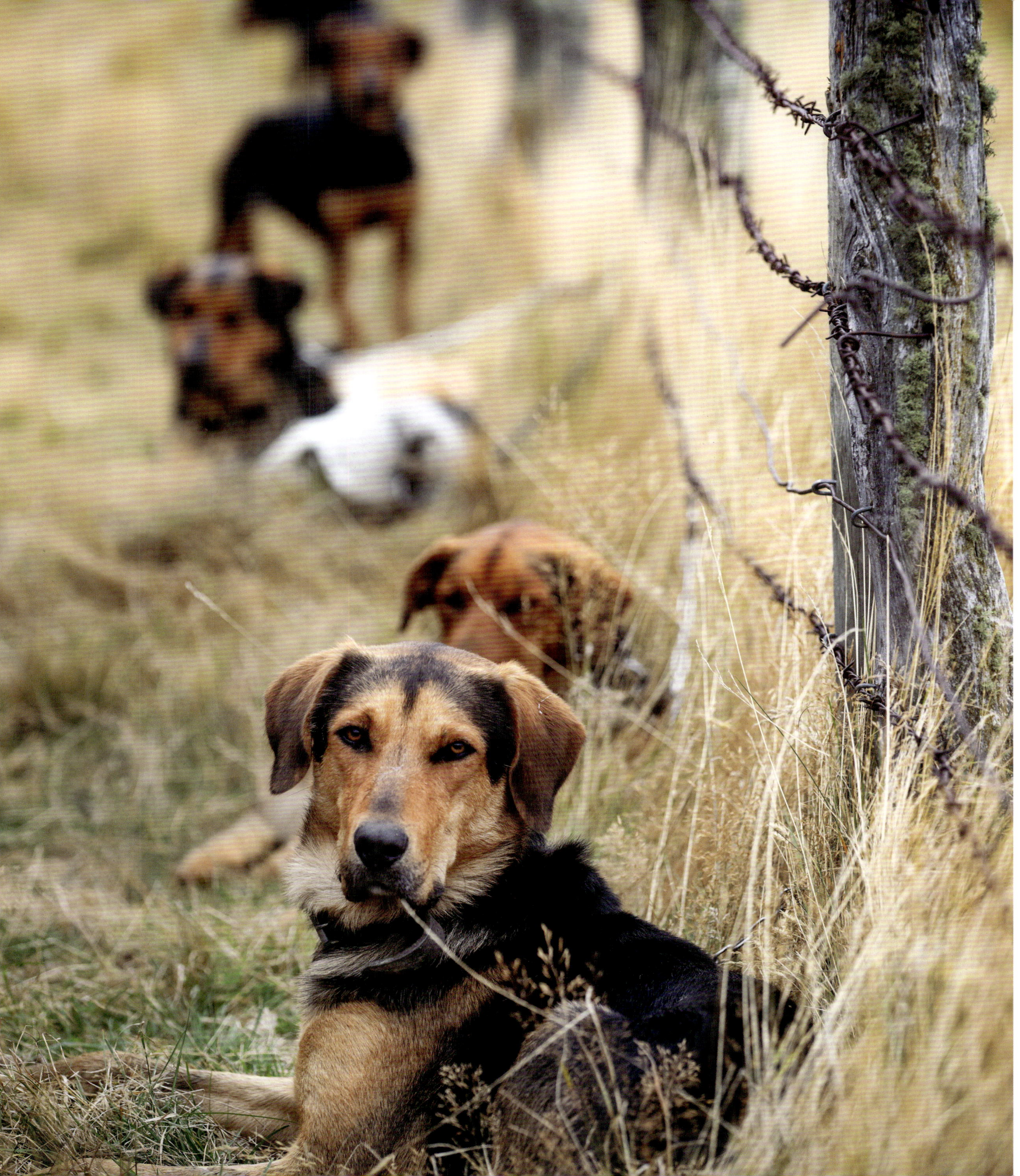

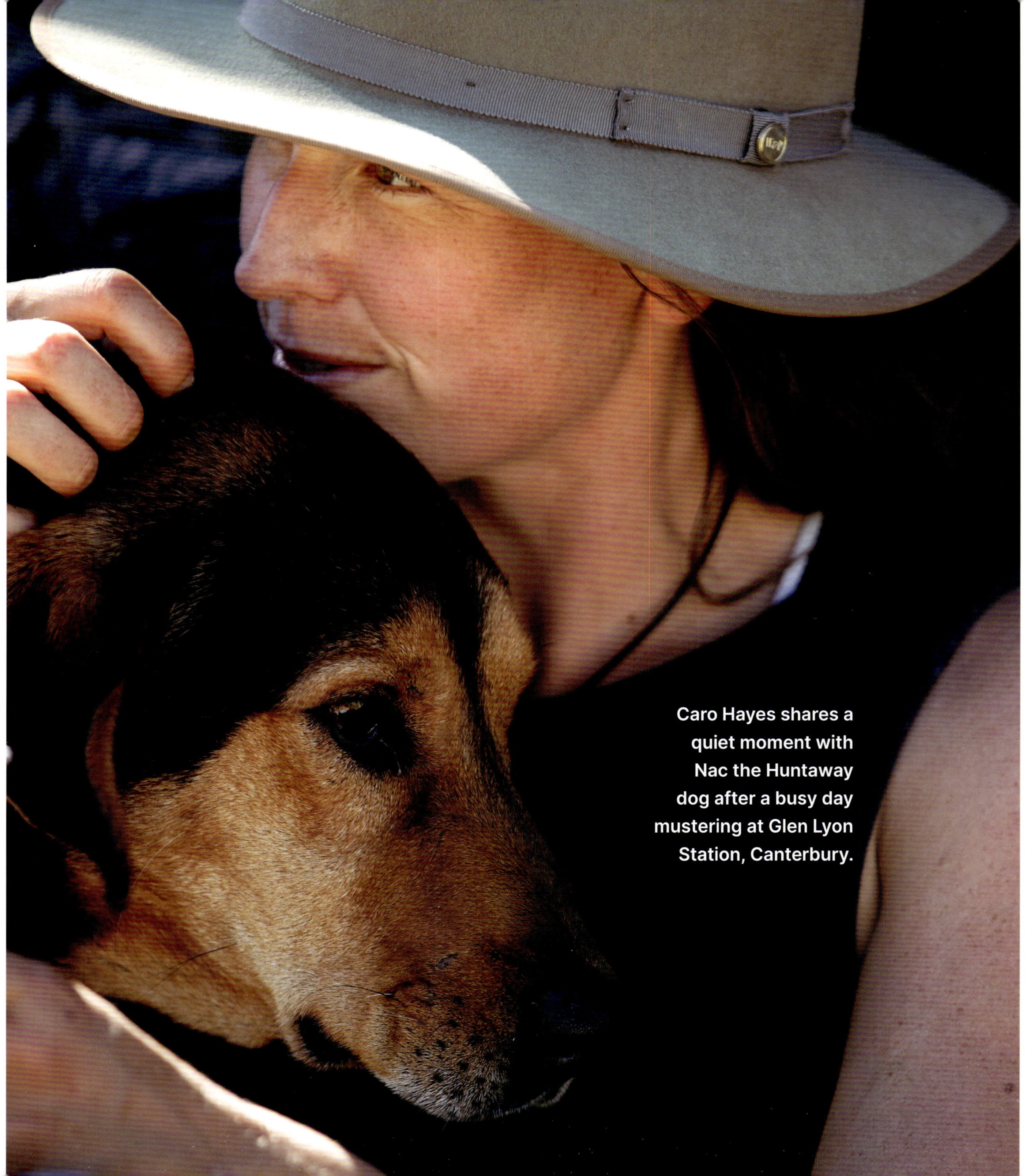

Caro Hayes shares a quiet moment with Nac the Huntaway dog after a busy day mustering at Glen Lyon Station, Canterbury.

# DEER FARMING

Aristocrats in nineteenth-century Europe hunted deer for sport, so New Zealand settlers followed suit and introduced deer for hunting purposes, mostly on public land. Eleven species were imported from Europe, America and Asia, most between 1860 and 1920. By the early decades of the twentieth century, deer had spread throughout the forests. Herds of wild deer wreaked havoc in native forest, on pastures as well as affecting young exotic trees in plantation forests. Government 'cullers' were employed to reduce numbers. In the late 1960s, however, commercial sales of venison kicked off a local deer-meat industry, first by shooting wild stocks and then through deer farming for venison and antler products. In 2020 there were about two million deer on New Zealand farms.

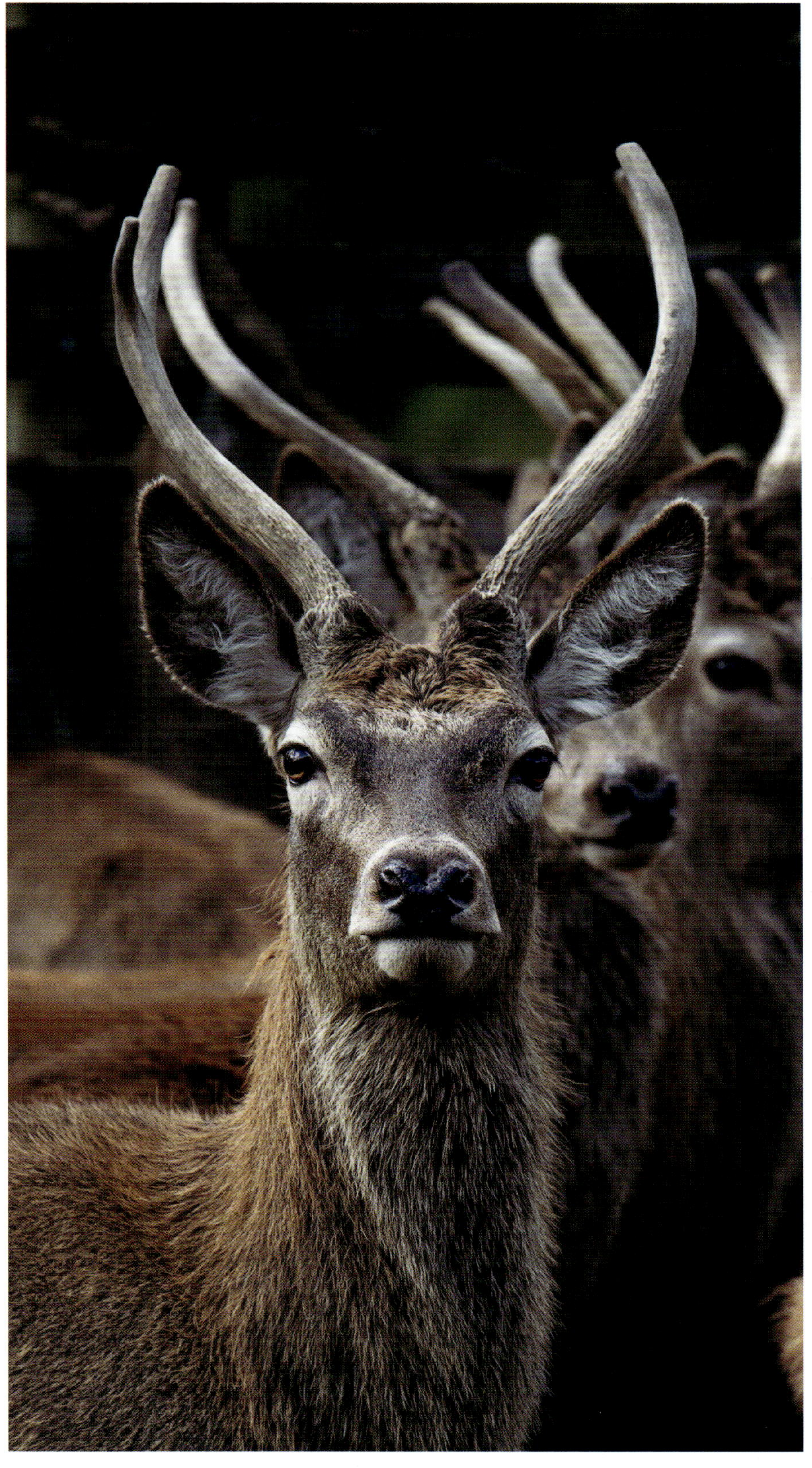

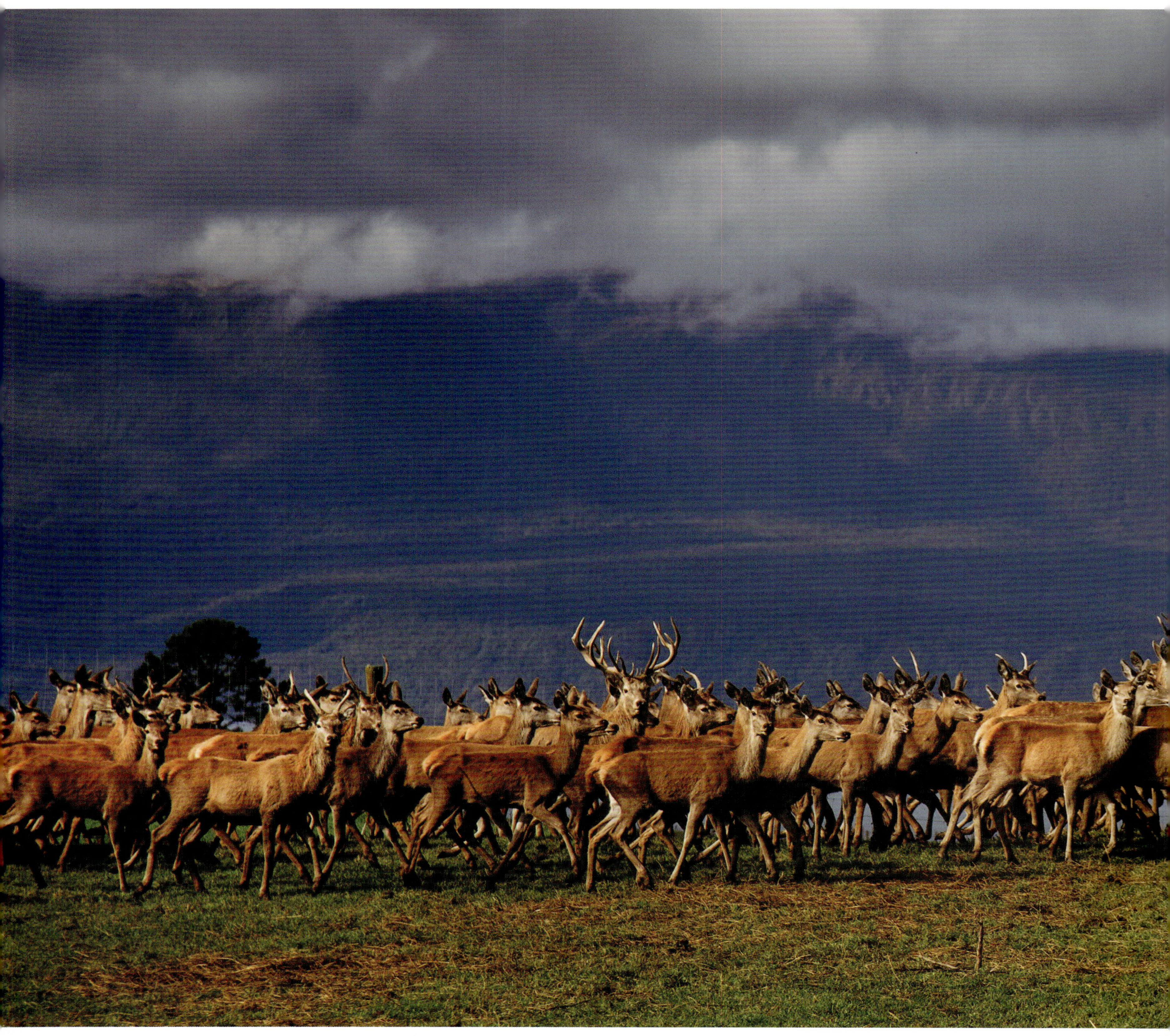

DEER FARMING

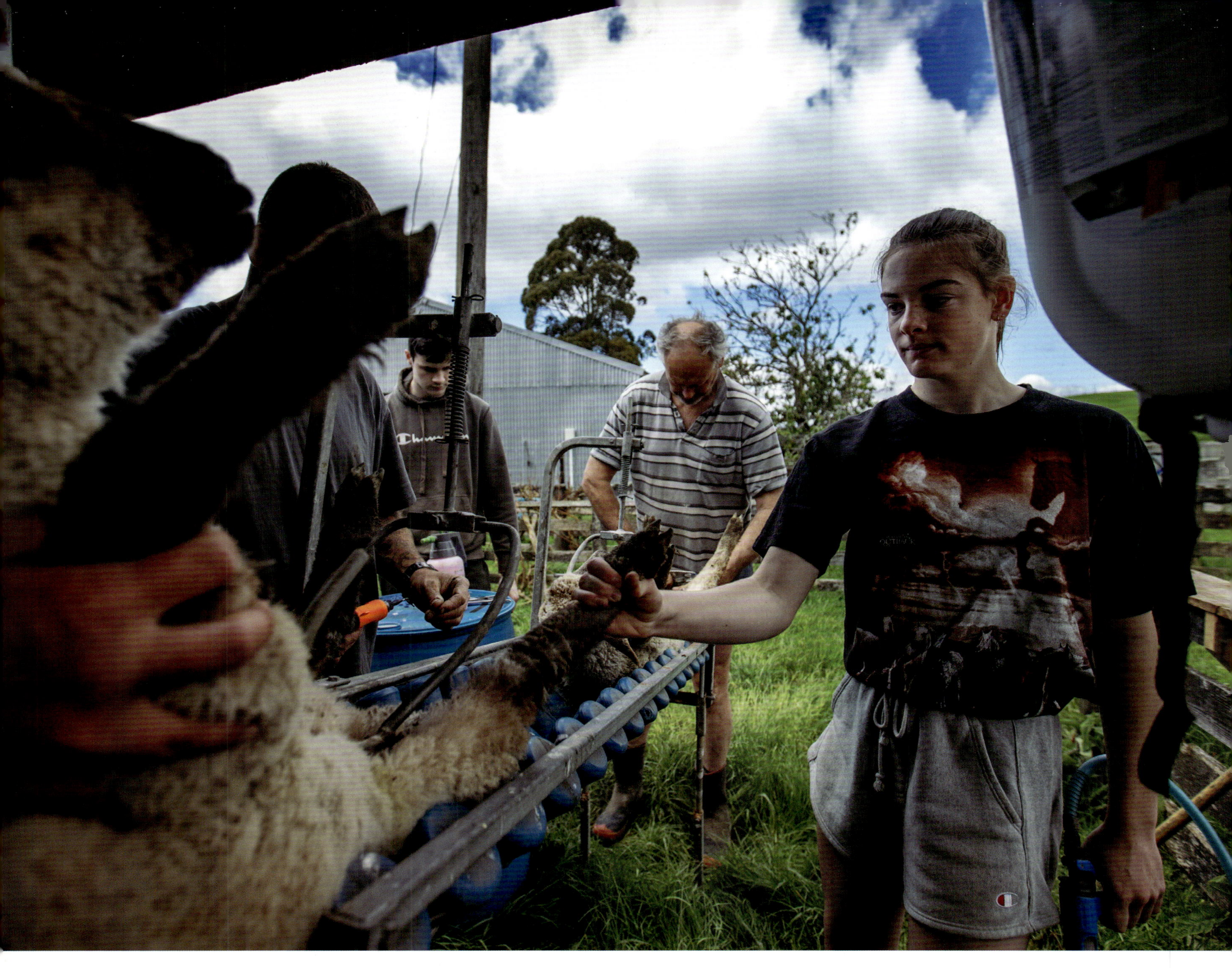

'The crater is unique; it's 97 acres, 400 feet deep. It's a big hole. I found out that I am one of the very few people in New Zealand to privately own a volcanic crater. It's hard case. The farm is one third venison, one third beef and one third sheep. We mainly focus on beef, mainly bulls, and I have been here for 10 years. Farming is everything really, isn't it? In the future there are government lake issues as I have three different lake catchments. There are concerns that I will be restricted to what I can run.

**Docking time means everyone has to help with the busy job of seeing to the property's lambs.**

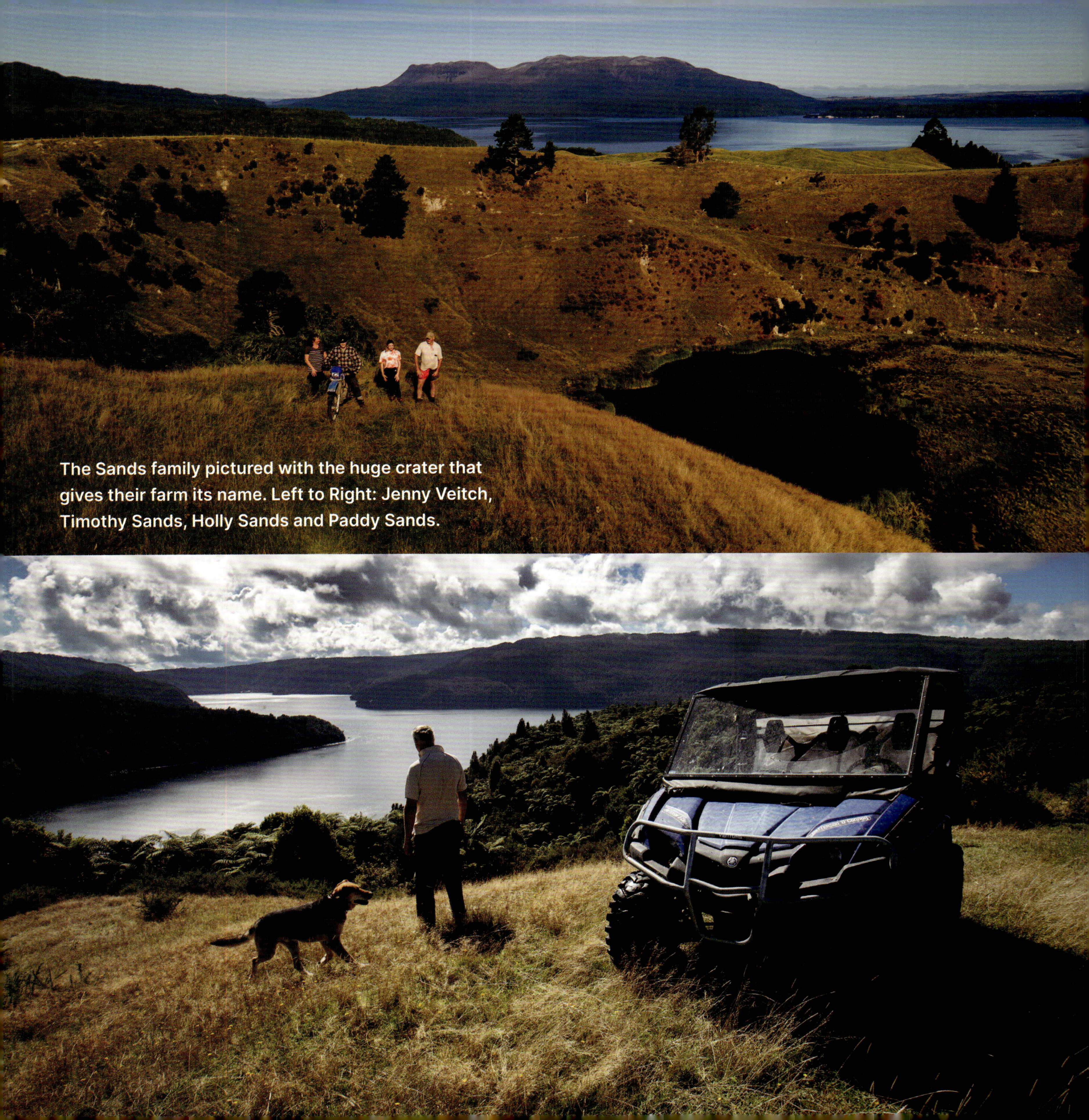

The Sands family pictured with the huge crater that gives their farm its name. Left to Right: Jenny Veitch, Timothy Sands, Holly Sands and Paddy Sands.

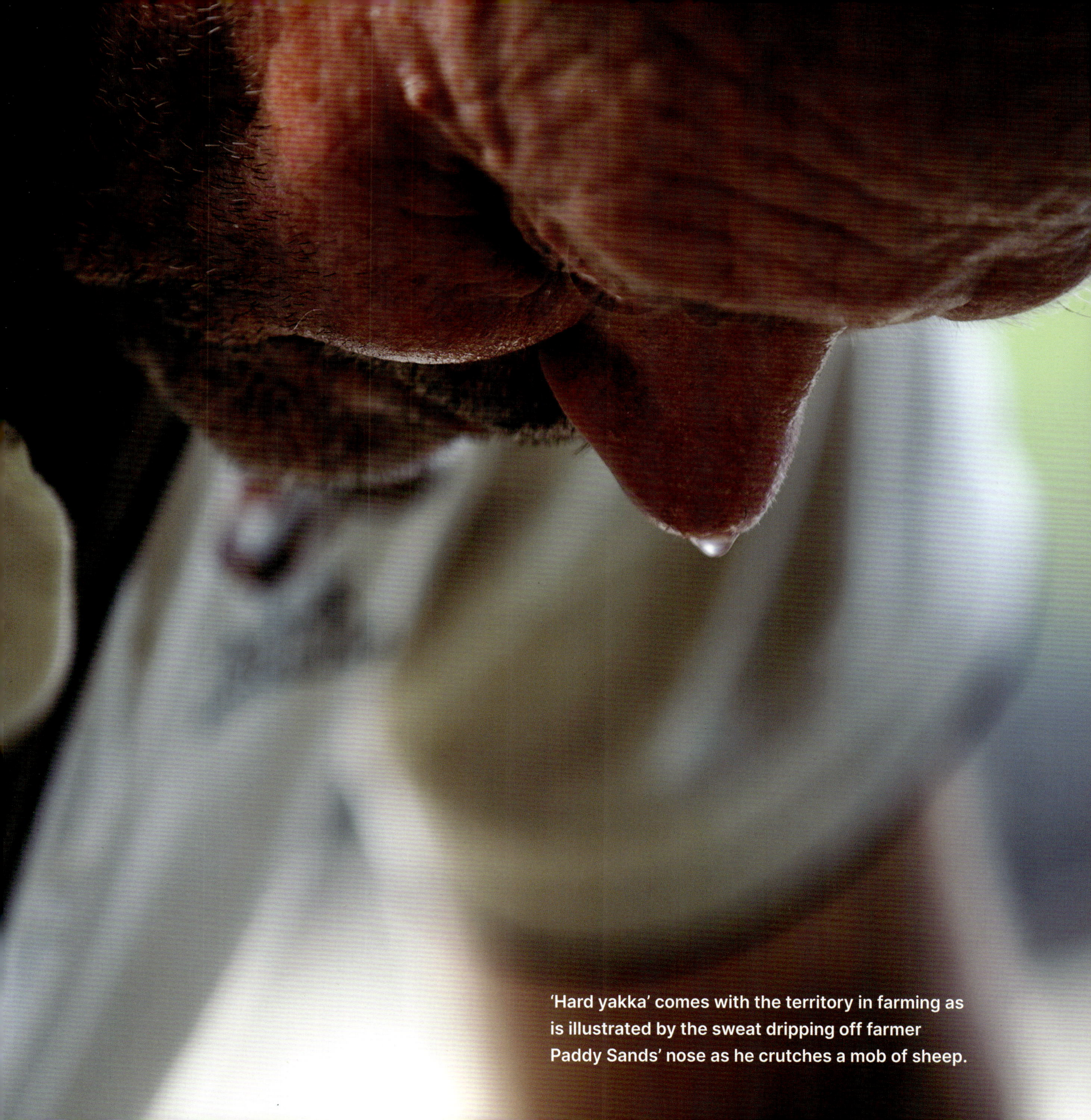

‘Hard yakka’ comes with the territory in farming as is illustrated by the sweat dripping off farmer Paddy Sands’ nose as he crutches a mob of sheep.

# KIWIFRUIT

In 2020, the New Zealand horticultural industry exceeded $10 billion of produce for the first time, with exports contributing two-thirds of that. Fresh fruit export earnings have increased significantly in recent years, led by kiwifruit, apples and avocados. Kiwifruit are originally from China and were first known here as 'Chinese gooseberries'. In 1904, Wanganui Girls' College headmistress Isabel Fraser brought seeds back from China and gave them to Alexander Allison, a Whanganui farmer with an interest in exotic plants. Little did they know what a thriving industry they were initiating. 'Chinese gooseberry' became 'kiwifruit' as a marketing ploy in 1959. Gold-fleshed kiwifruit were grown from imported seeds in the 1970s. Their smooth skins and more tropical flavour have made them very popular. Kiwifruit exports boomed in the 1970s, but prices crashed a decade later when other countries also began to grow and export the fruit. In 1988 the New Zealand Kiwifruit Marketing Board (now called Zespri) was set up to market and distribute kiwifruit internationally. Meanwhile, new varieties were being cultivated and vineyard practices researched. Most kiwifruit orchards are centred on Te Puke in the Bay of Plenty, with smaller plantings in Canterbury, Nelson and Auckland. The vines need fertile soil, shelter from the wind and protection from frost. Despite recent setbacks from viral pests, in 2020 some $2.5 billion worth of gold and green kiwifruit were exported, with key markets being Japan, Europe, China, South Korea, USA and Australia.

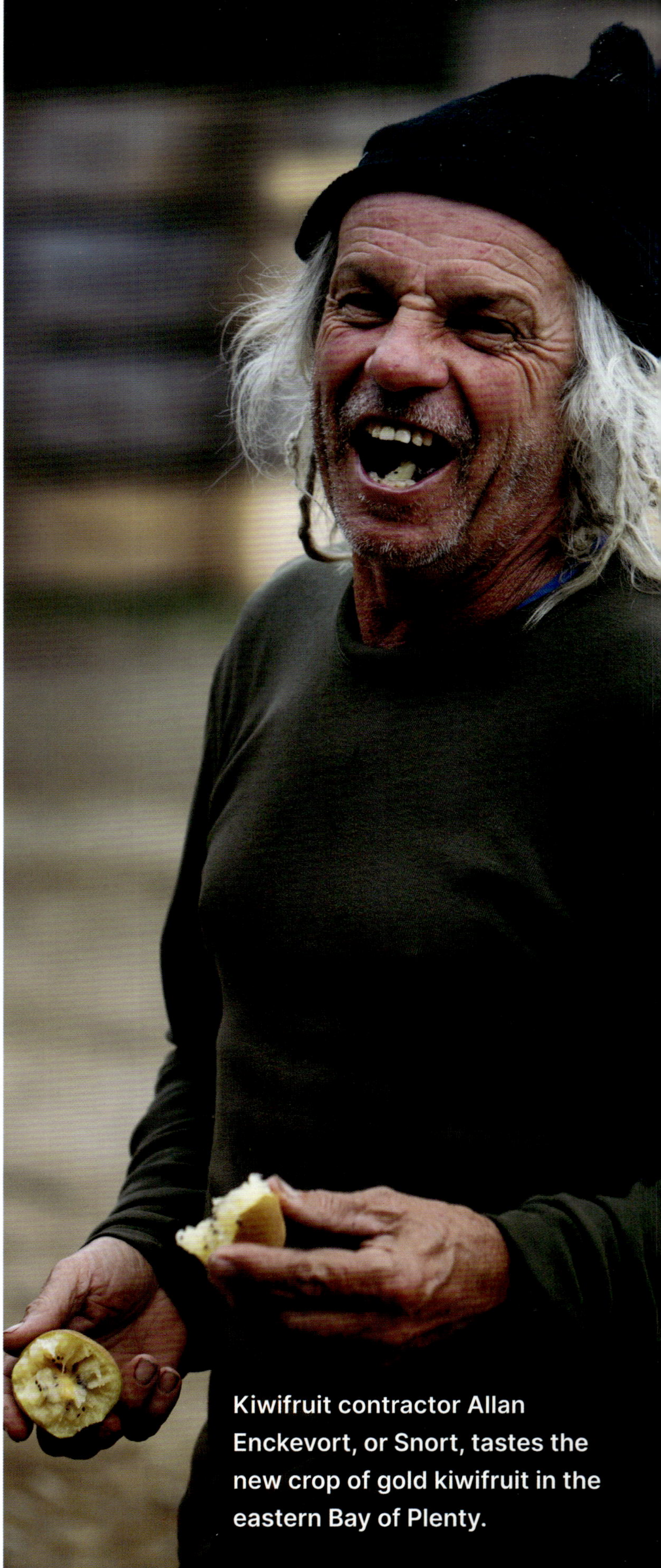

Kiwifruit contractor Allan Enckevort, or Snort, tastes the new crop of gold kiwifruit in the eastern Bay of Plenty.

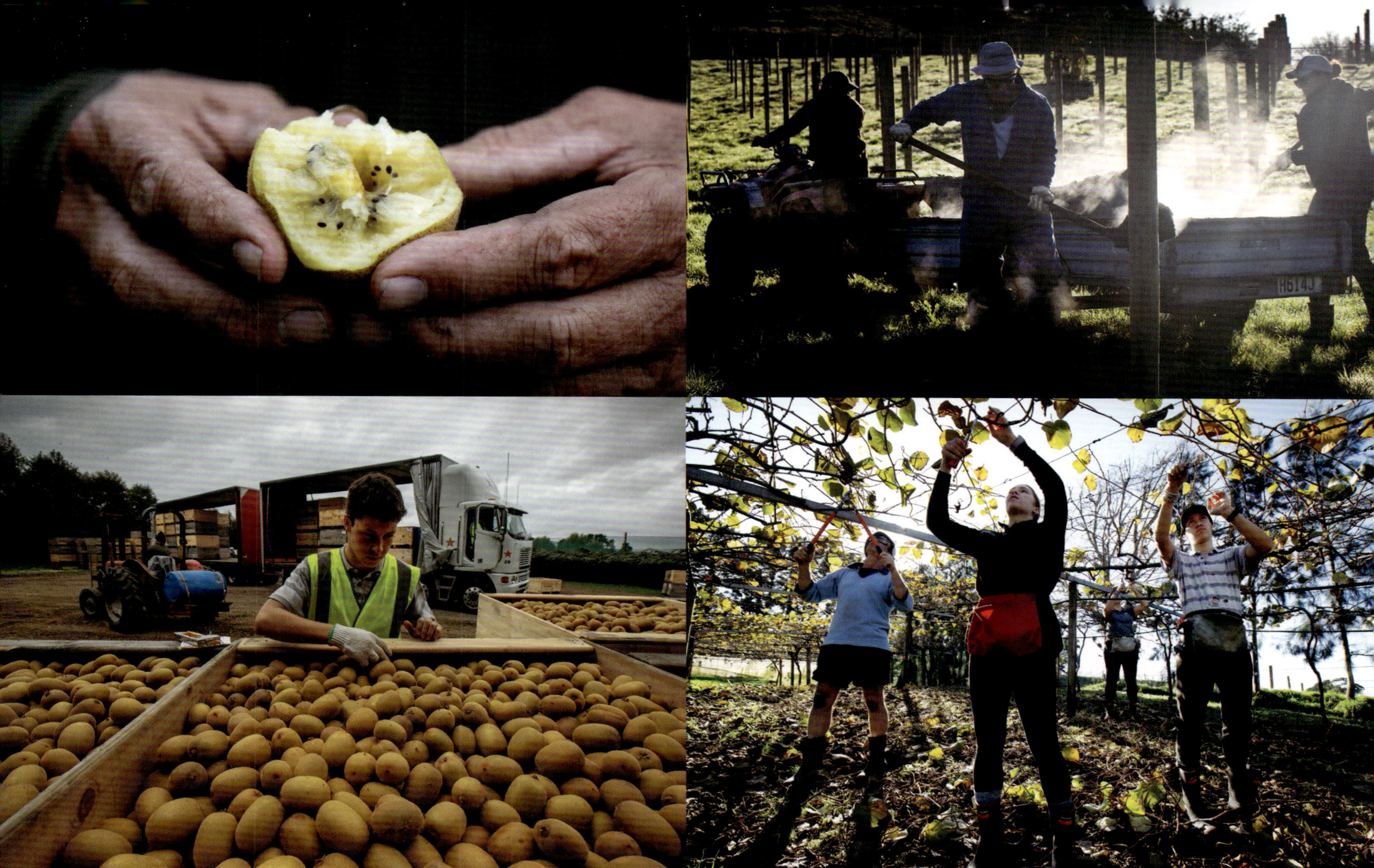


**MARK, CATRIONA (TRINA) and son Lochie White from Coast Kiwis Organic Orchard in Ōpōtiki grow organic kiwifruit and raise sheep using organic principles.**

**The White family work together to get the pruning done in the small block that Letisha (centre) and Lochie (right) manage for themselves on their parents' organic kiwifruit orchard near Ōpōtiki, Bay of Plenty.**

'Years ago, we looked into organic food, and we thought that this would be the way of the future and the way we will eat food. For a long time, Trina and I have had a philosophy that what we do or would expect to eat, or how we would expect to treat people, is how we would like to be treated, and that flowed through to what we would like to produce. — Mark White

'What I really love about farming is being about to work with Mark, and now we have the kids involved as well. Everything is changing throughout the year with the seasons. I like working outside on those nice days. I love it, really. — Trina White

'Farming with the family means quite a lot to me because I am part of fifth-generation orchardists in the same area. My grandad is working in the orchard next door and my great-grandad worked in the same orchard in the years before that.
— Lochie White

# APPLES

The missionary Samuel Marsden introduced the first apple and pear trees in 1819 to Kerikeri in Northland. Fruit was initially grown for domestic consumption, but pipfruit growers were quick to realise their export potential. The first apples were shipped from Christchurch to Chile in 1888, and exports to the UK began in the 1890s. Today, about two-thirds of New Zealand's pipfruit crop is exported. Domestic consumption accounts for most of the remainder of the annual crop, along with processing, mainly into juice. In 2020 around $898 million worth of apples were exported, with the staple varieties being Royal Gala, Braeburn, Envy, Jazz, Fuji and Pacific Queen. New varieties are being trialled all the time. Key export markets are Asia, Europe, UK and Ireland, North America and the Middle East.

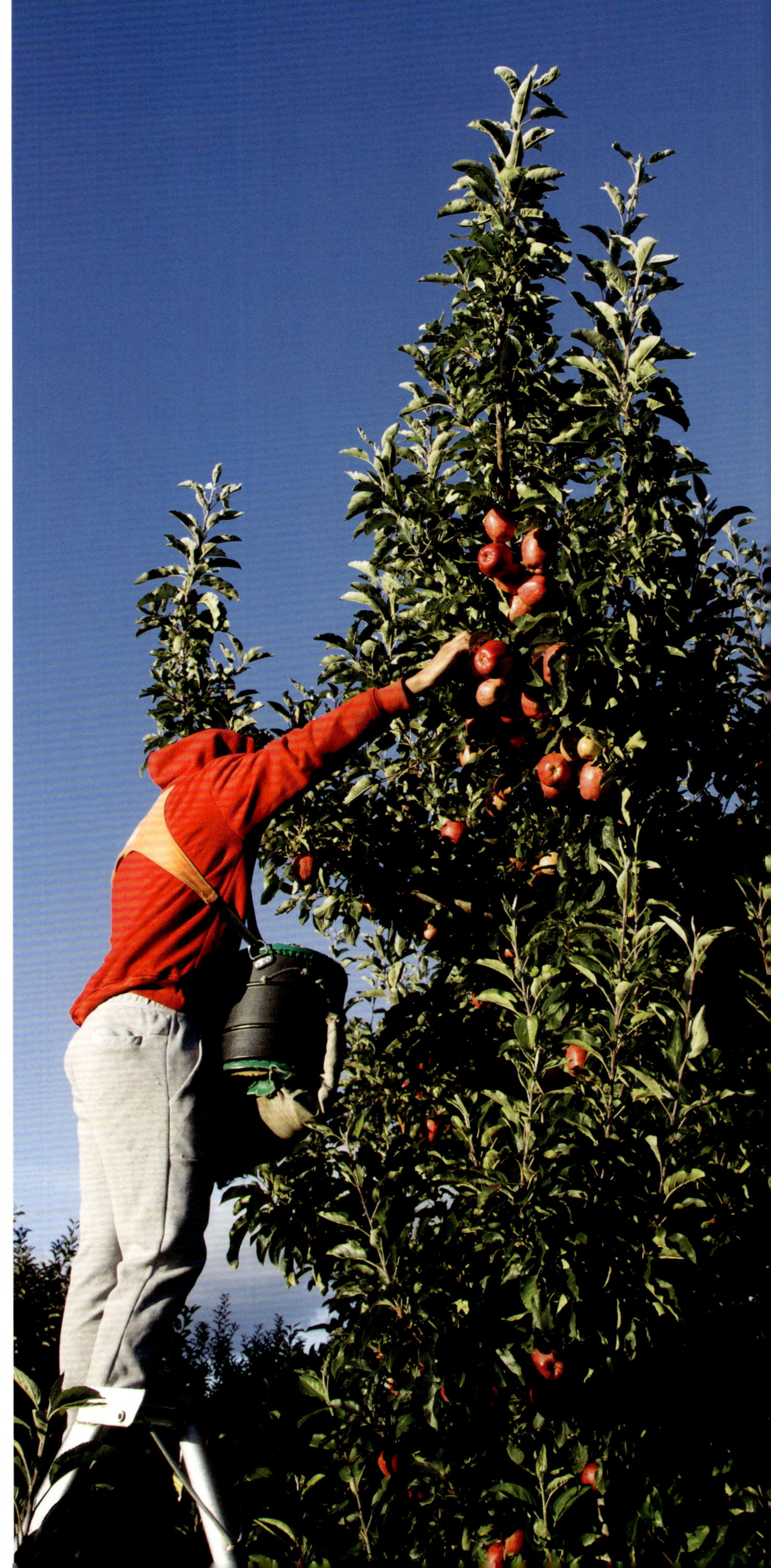

Pickers get to work in an apple orchard near Cromwell, Otago.

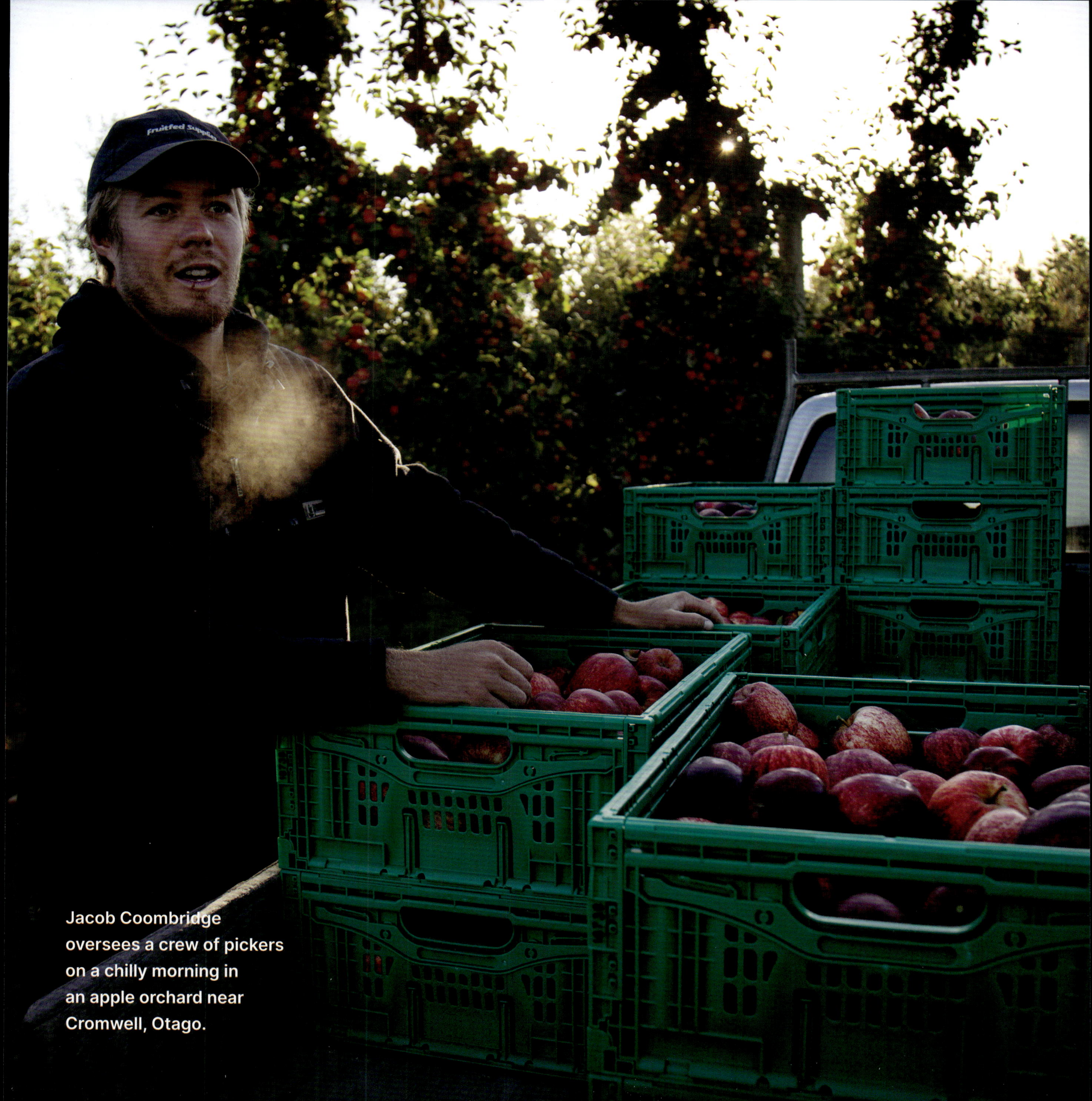

Jacob Coombridge oversees a crew of pickers on a chilly morning in an apple orchard near Cromwell, Otago.

# LAMBING

Lambing in New Zealand generally occurs in late winter and early spring, to take advantage of the plentiful grass feed available. The North Island season usually precedes that of the South. Good animal husbandry means consistently high lambing percentages are achieved, and most lambs are born outdoors. When feed quality begins to decline in early summer, young lambs are weaned and then grazed on the best pasture. Over summer, lambs are regularly selected for dispatch to the freezing works.

**Paddy Sands collects orphaned or abandoned lambs during the lambing beat he runs daily during lambing on Crater Lake Farm near Rotorua, Bay of Plenty.**

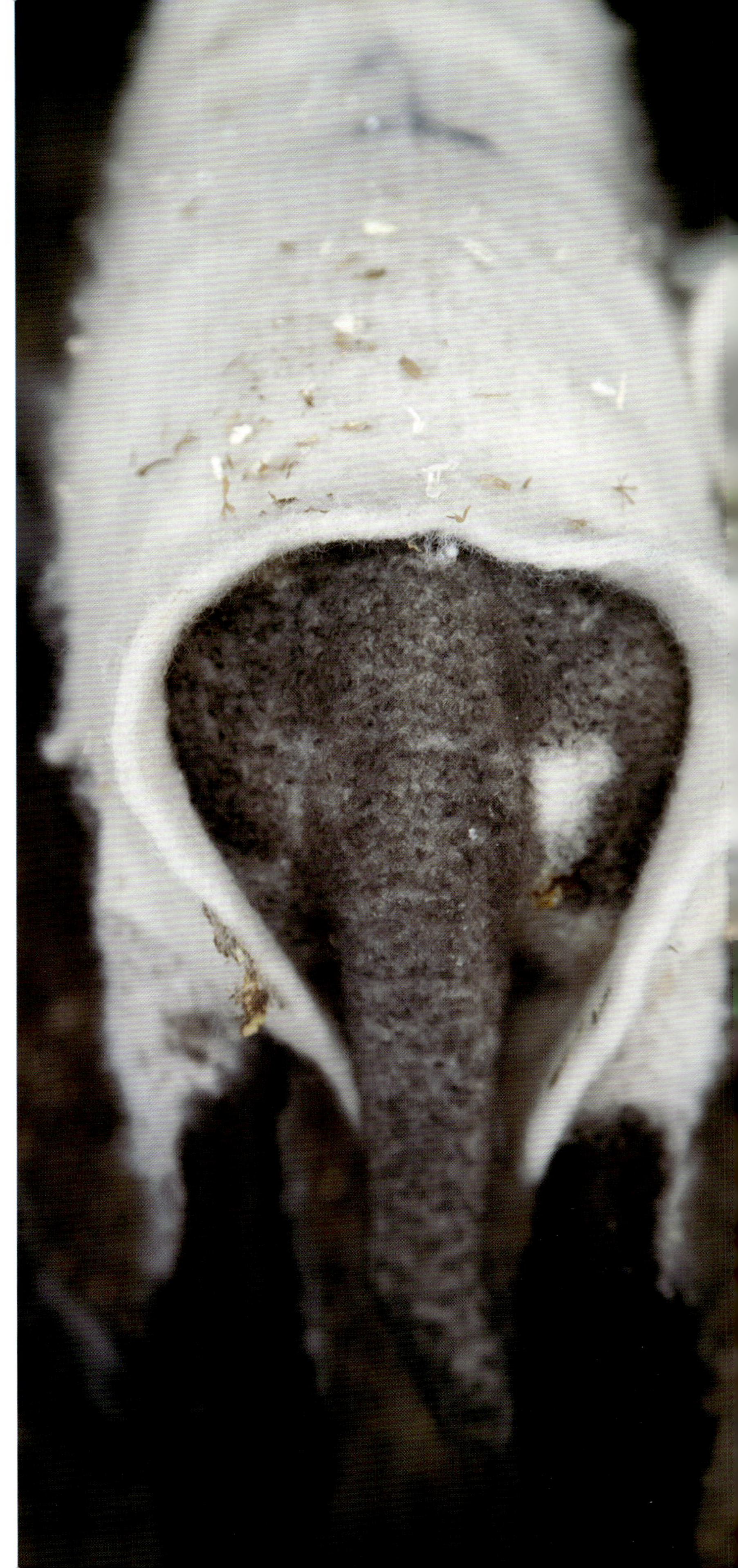

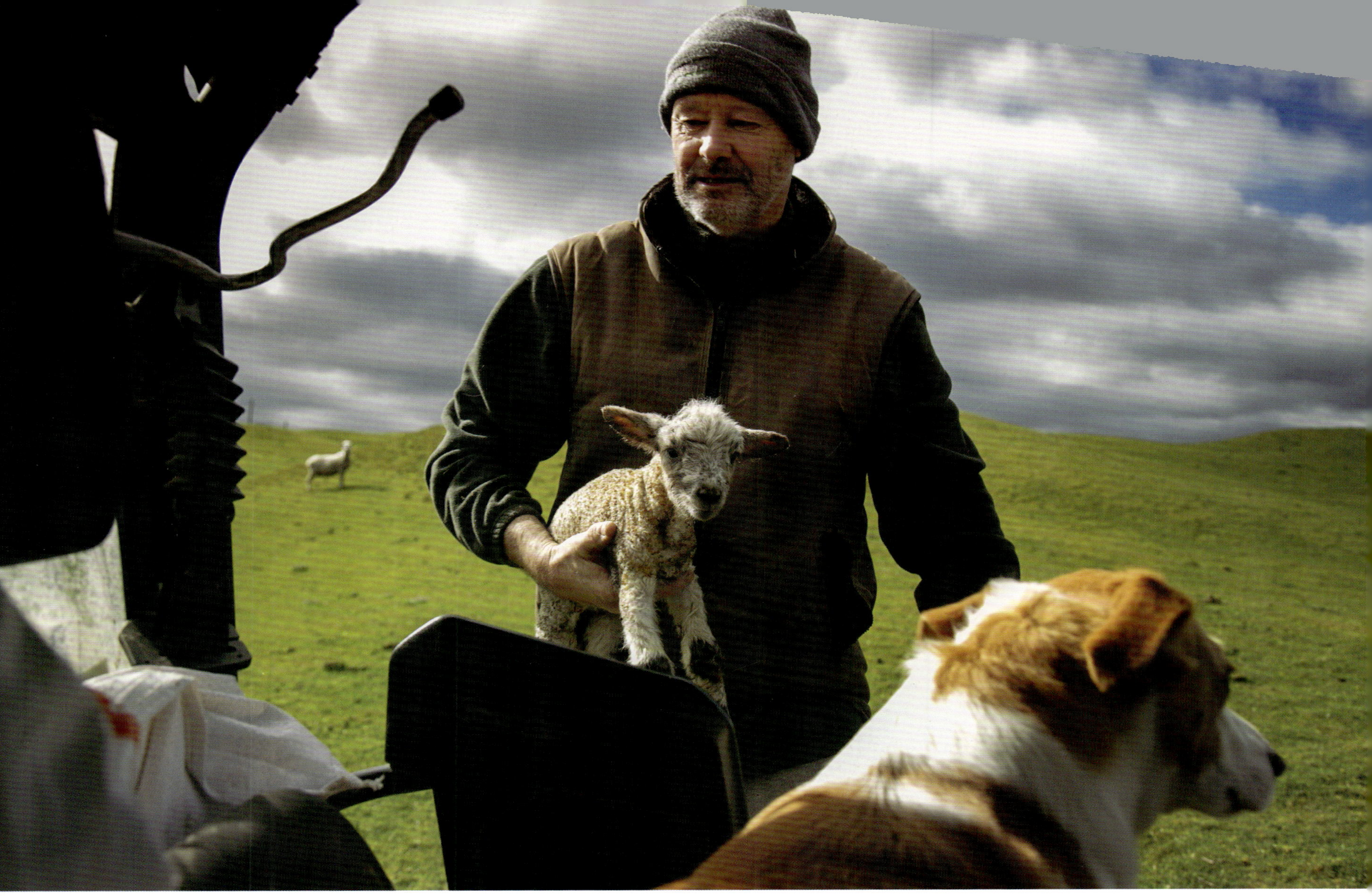

***❛ We lamb our own ewes, of which we have 400 to 500 depending on the year. During lambing we collect any lambs that are lost, left behind, are too cold or injured and we raise them. We buy colostrum for them from a dairy farmer to start them off. The colostrum is like liquid gold and so critical to their health. To add to those lambs while we were feeding them, we went to a farm that milks sheep for dairy milk and picked up the boy lambs that they don't want.***

— Jenny Veitch, Crater Lake Farm.

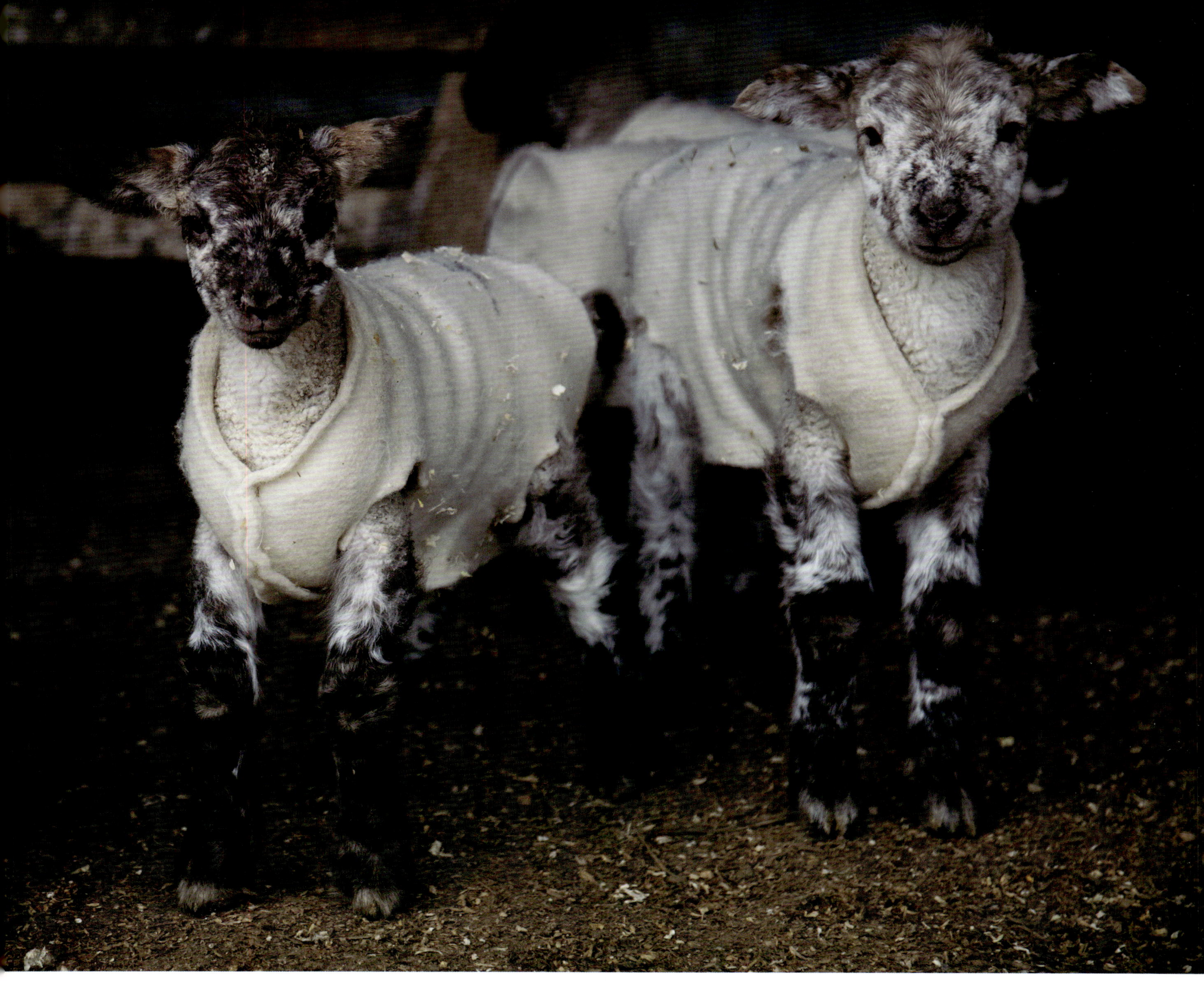

**❛ *We buy wool-over lamb covers from farm-supply stores and it helps to keep their body weight when they are really young or if they are sick.*** — Jenny Veitch

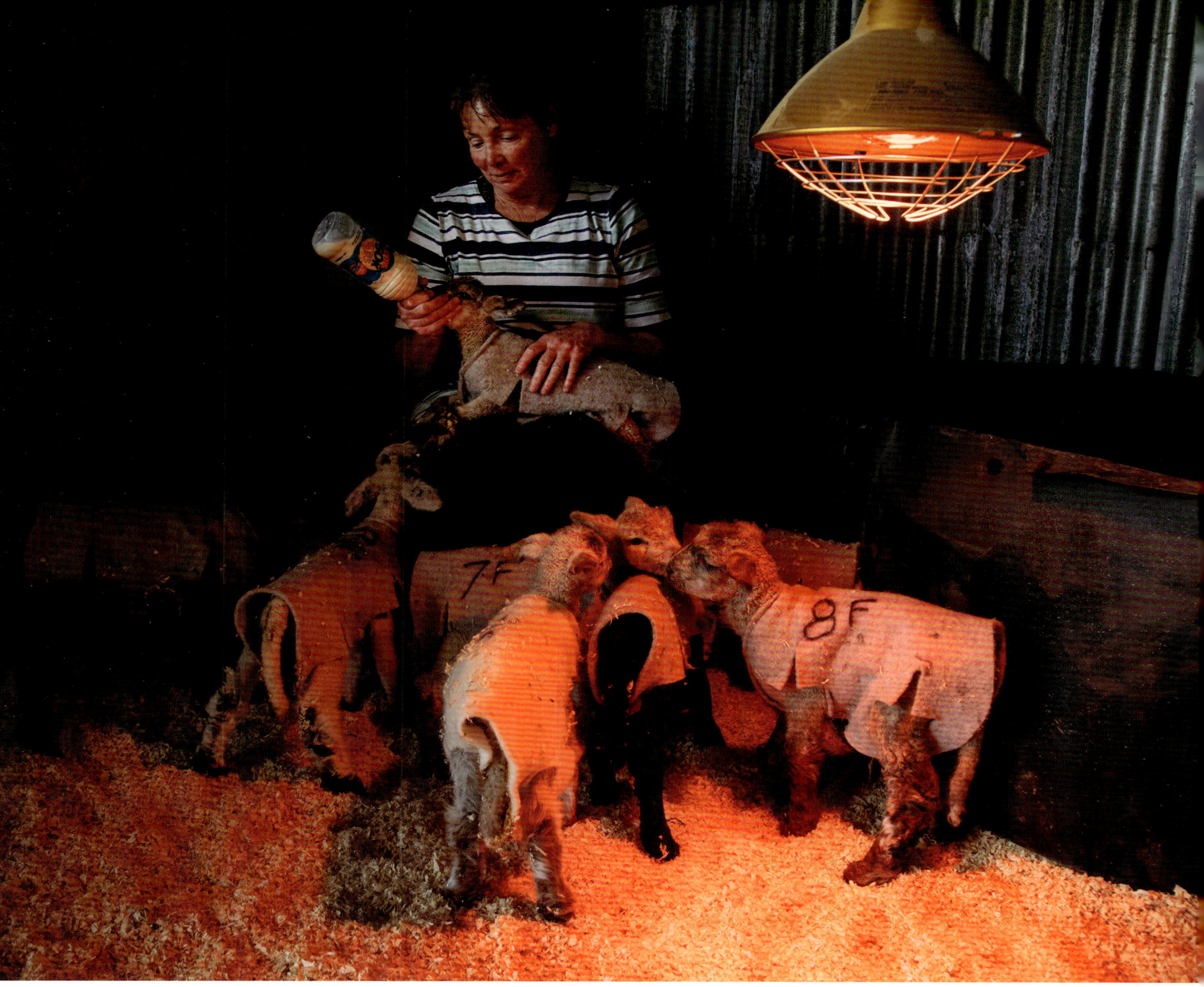


***‘When I first left school, I was a vet nurse for a few years and I love looking after animals.***

— Jenny Veitch

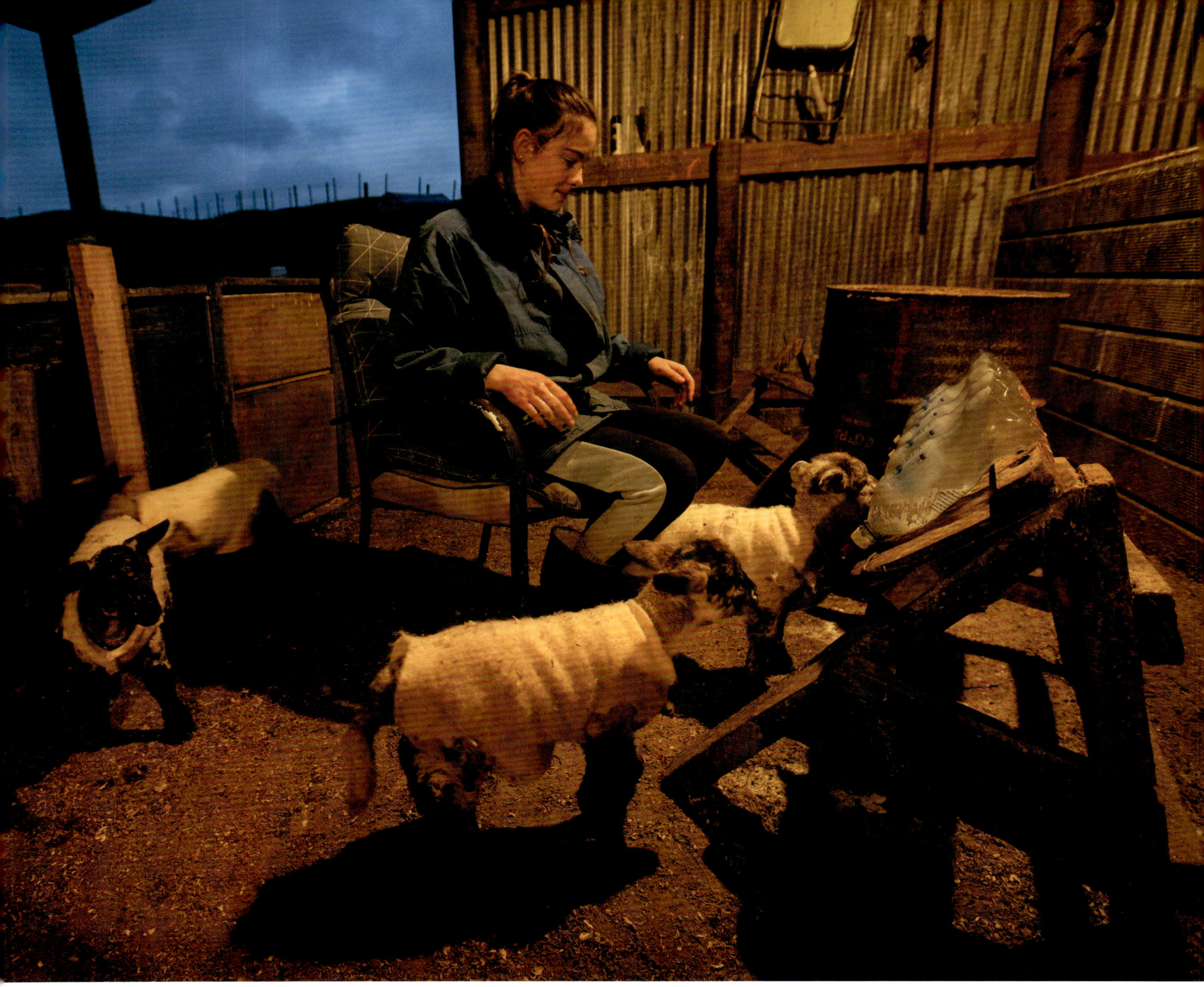

Holly Sands has her hands full trying to get lambs to feed in an orderly fashion in the shed at Crater Lake Farm.

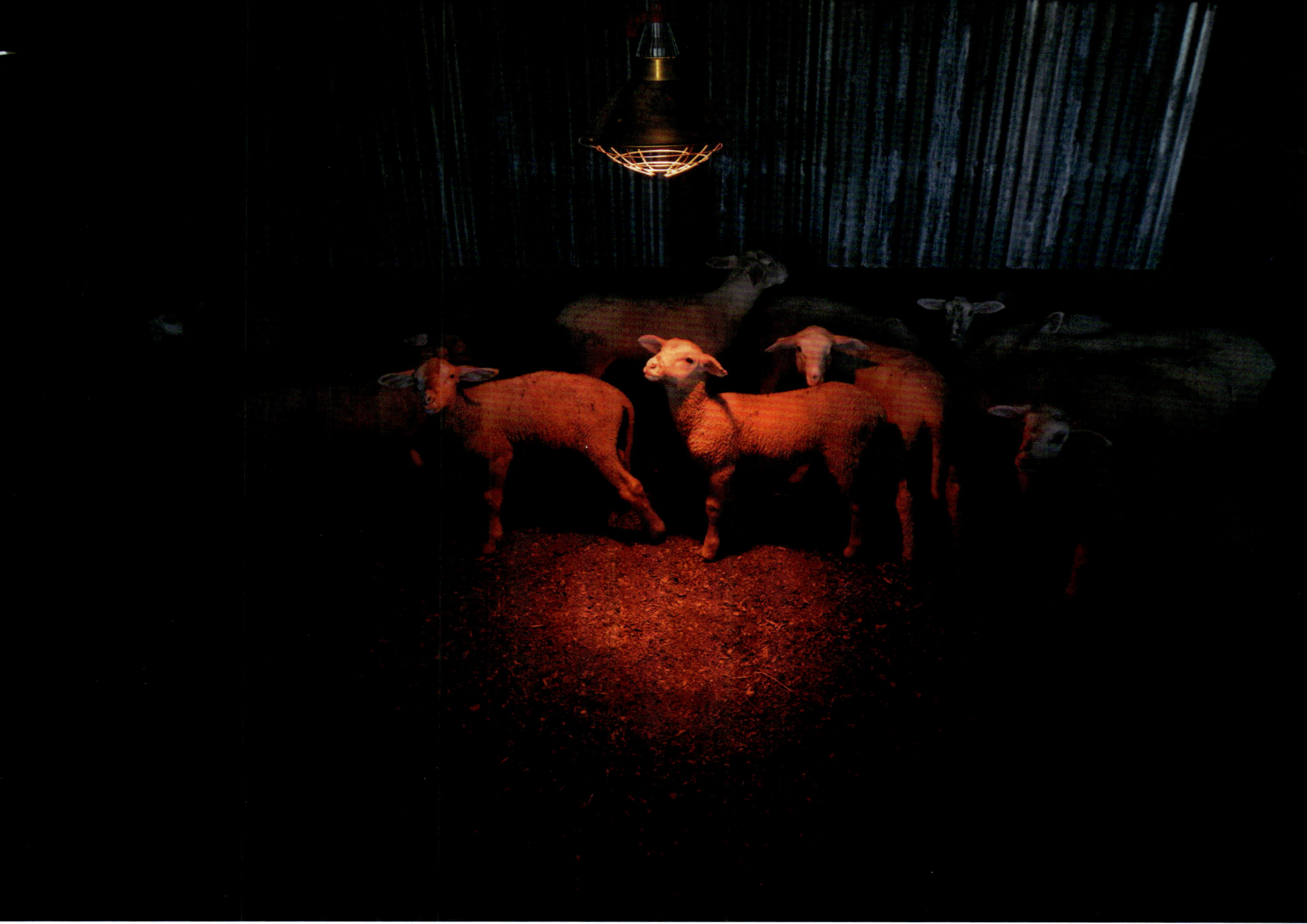

***❛ They go under heat lamps and that makes a big difference. There is a very high survival rate.***

— Jenny Veitch

# CHICKENS

In the early 1900s, half of New Zealanders kept hens for eggs in their backyard. Today, the country's hens produce 83 million dozen eggs — most of them eaten locally. The poultry industry is booming.

Richard and Jeannie Walker among their flock of chickens at their farm Happy Chicks near Mangawhai, Northland.

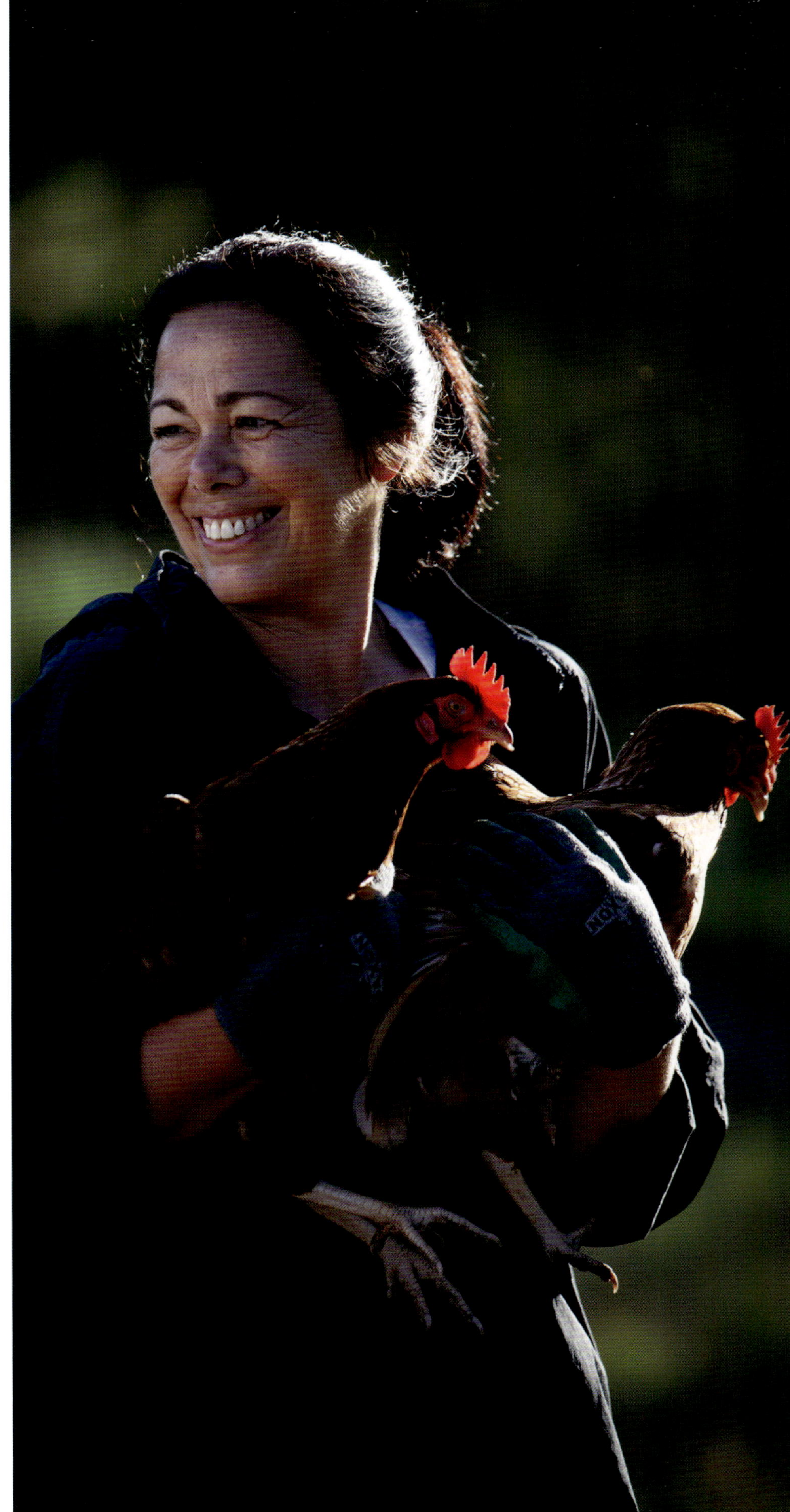

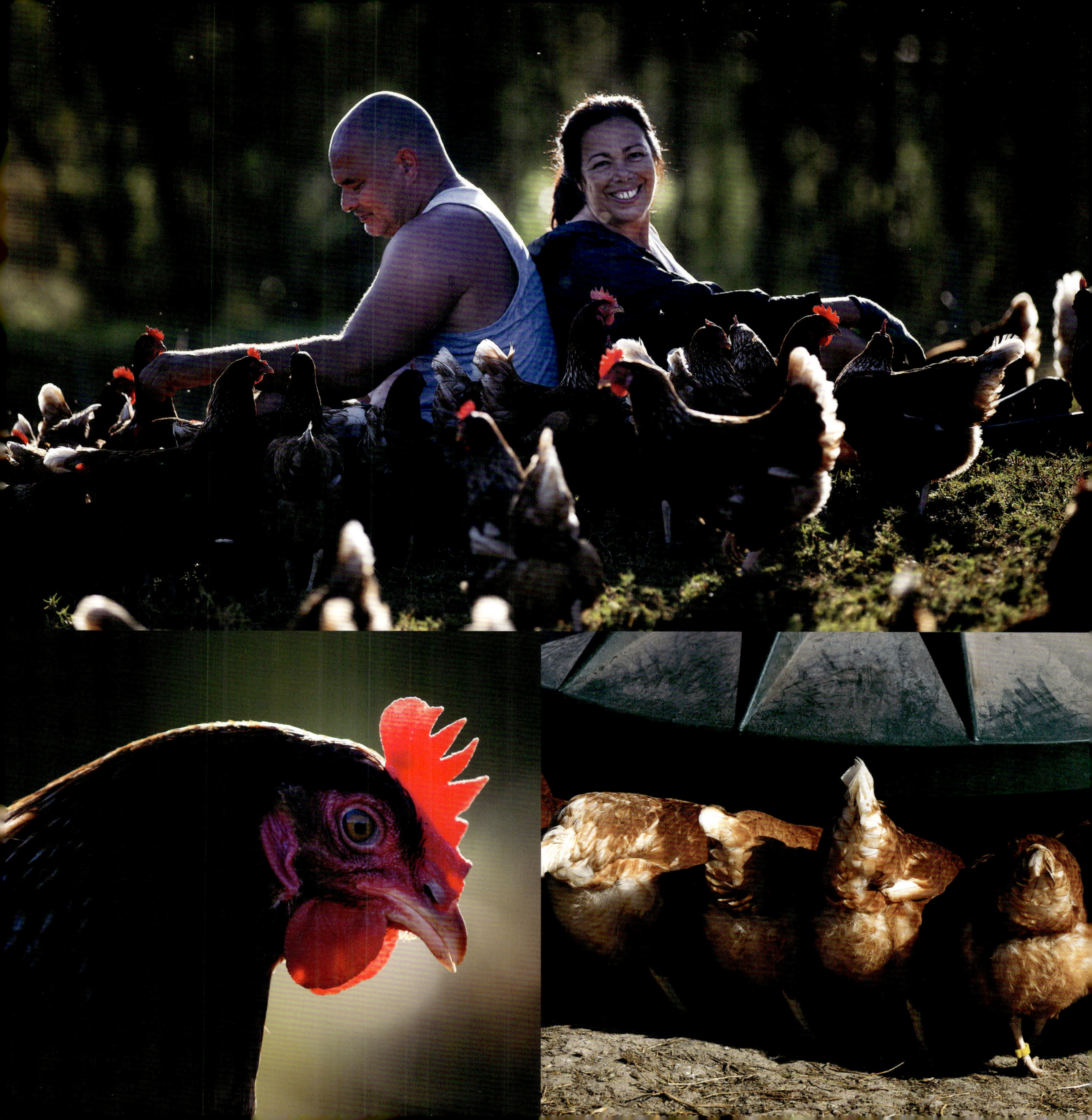

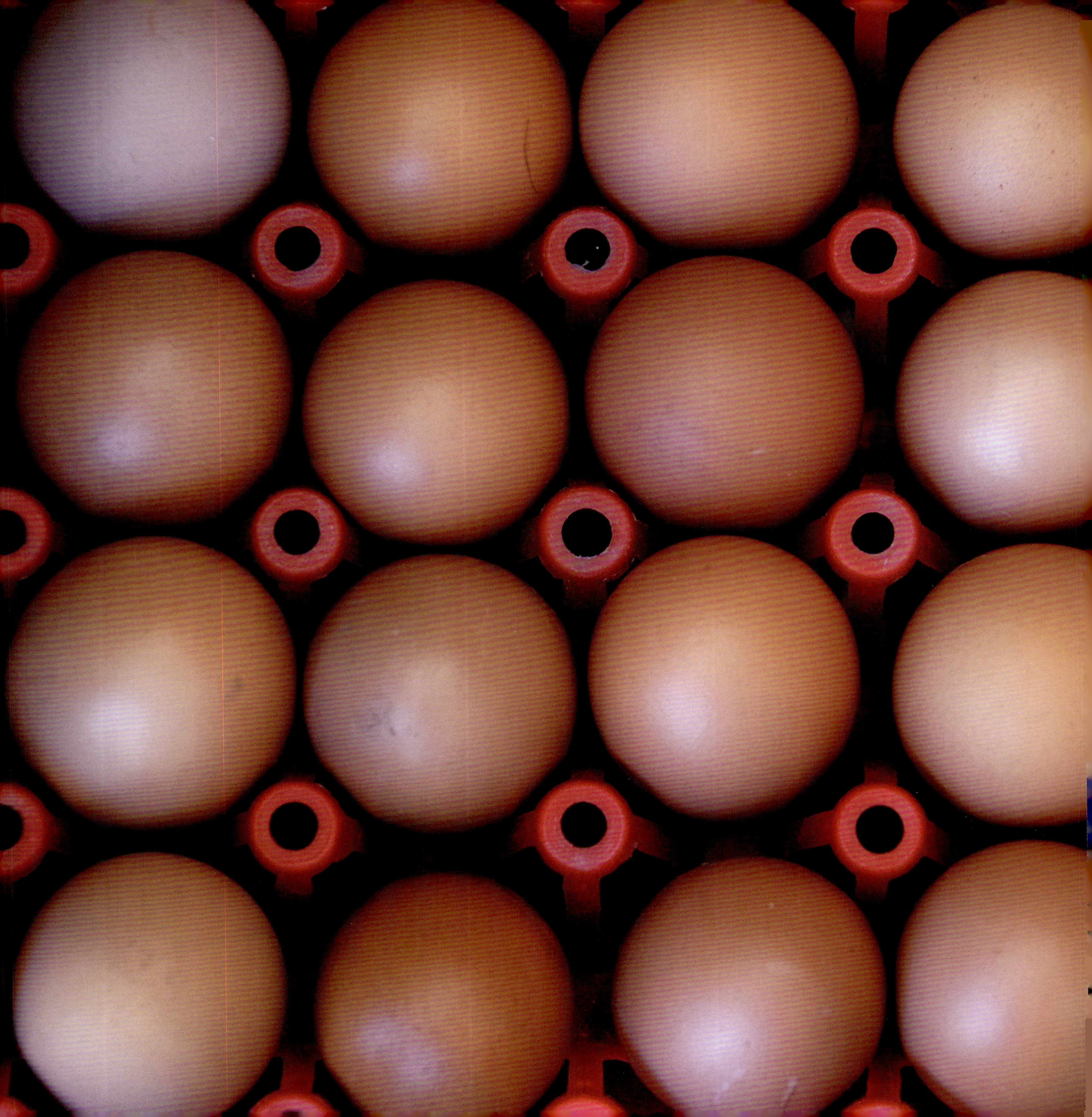

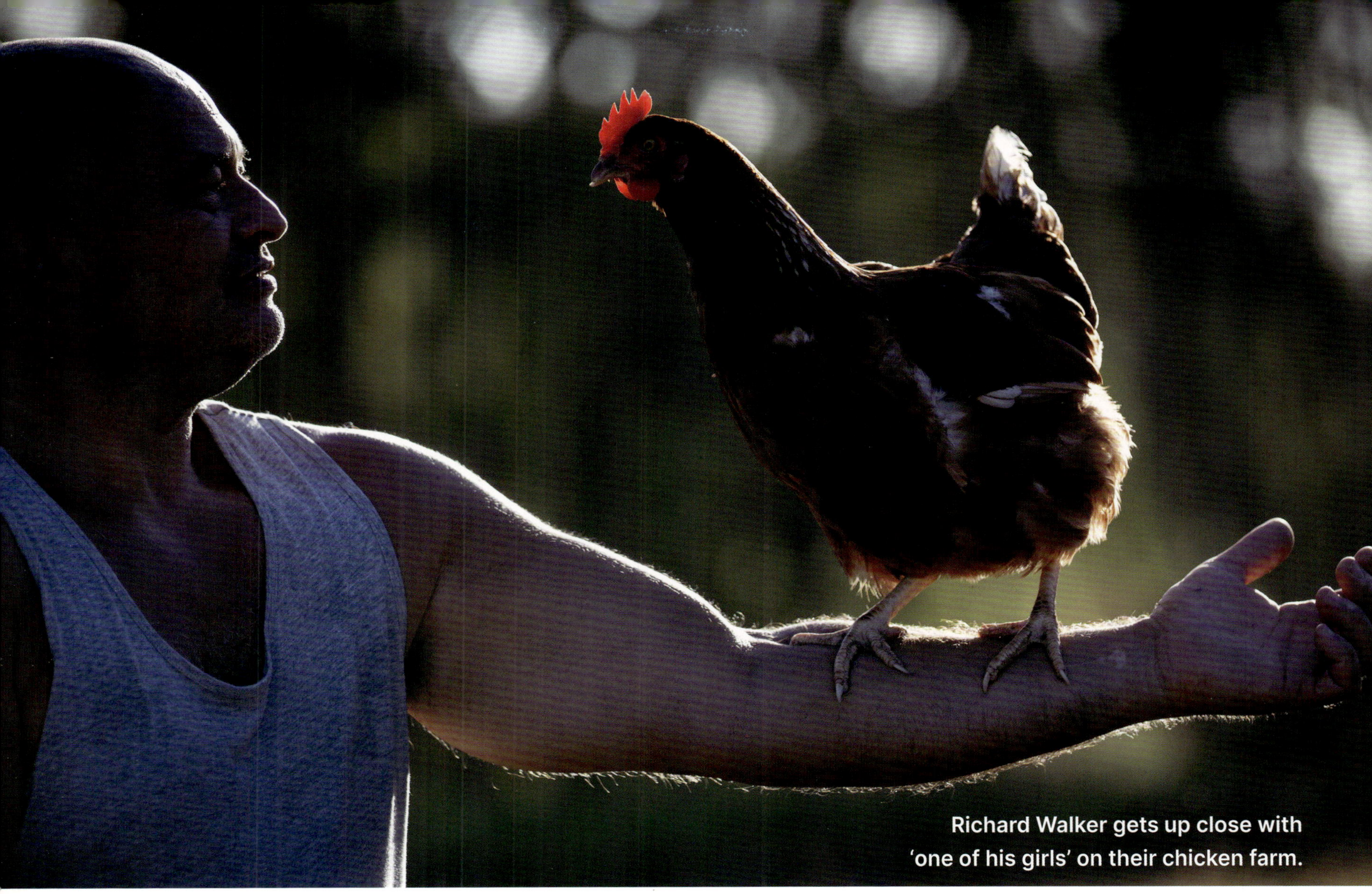

Richard Walker gets up close with 'one of his girls' on their chicken farm.

**Rich and Jeannie Walker are chicken farmers at Happy Chicks in Mangawhai, Northland:**

'We run 1350 hens at the moment — pasture grazed, free range with no cages or barns. We started in October 2020, when our first 500 hens turned up. We don't have a background in farming. It started for us when we were living in our Takapuna property and had six chickens and we discovered a really good fresh egg, and it got us thinking. We looked at a few properties and knew what we did like and what we didn't, and our dream was hatched from there.

It hasn't been a tough journey. We did a lot of research and thought we knew enough to deal with what we were going to face. You always get thrown curve balls, though. But you work around them and learn from your mistakes. We have learnt a lot.

We love the freedom of seeing the land being worked and being able to make money off our own land. We are proud of having good animal welfare practices — seeing hens doing what hens should do and not sitting in a cage.

It's been exciting getting our first customers and getting into more and more places.

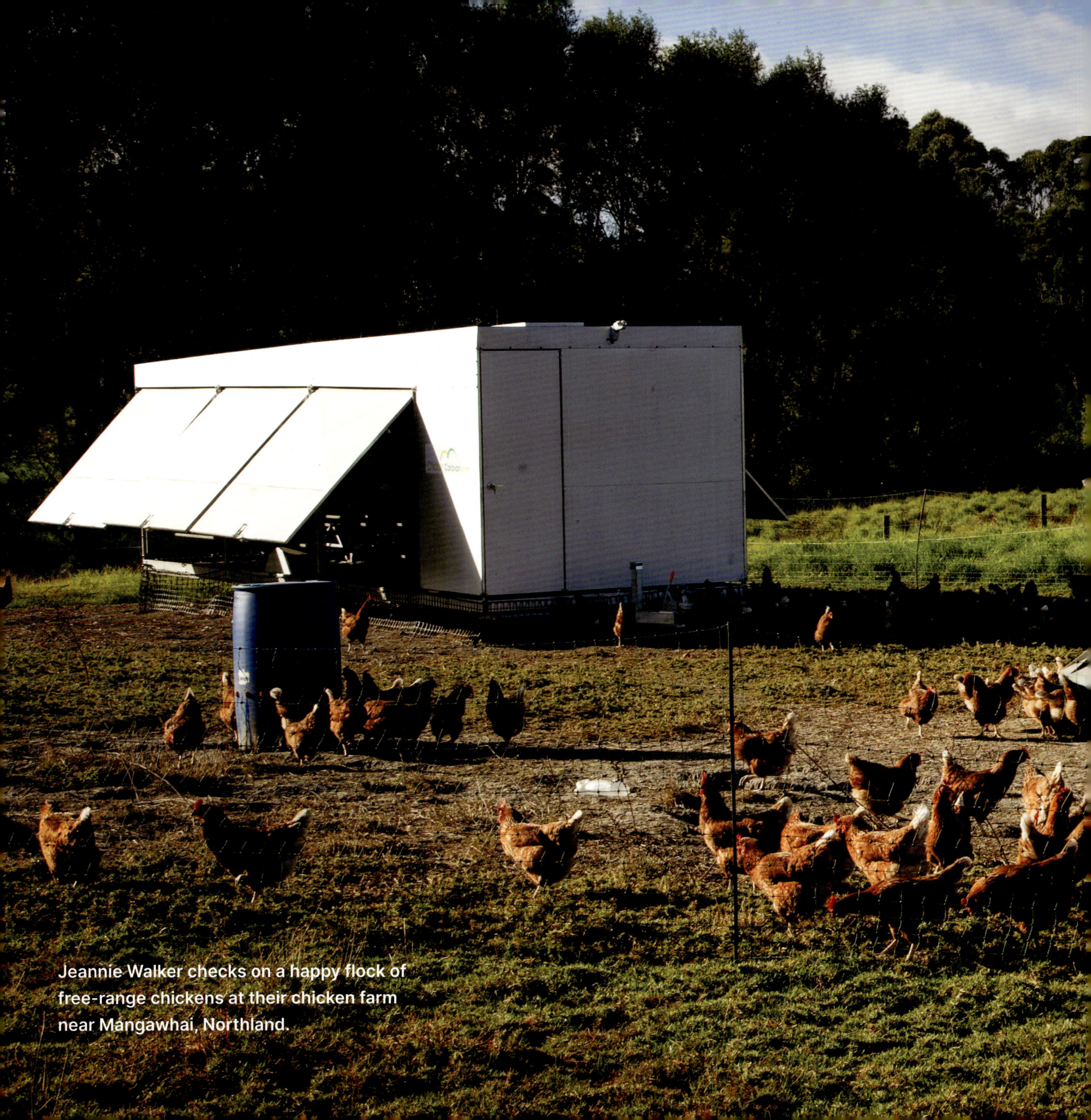

Jeannie Walker checks on a happy flock of free-range chickens at their chicken farm near Mangawhai, Northland.

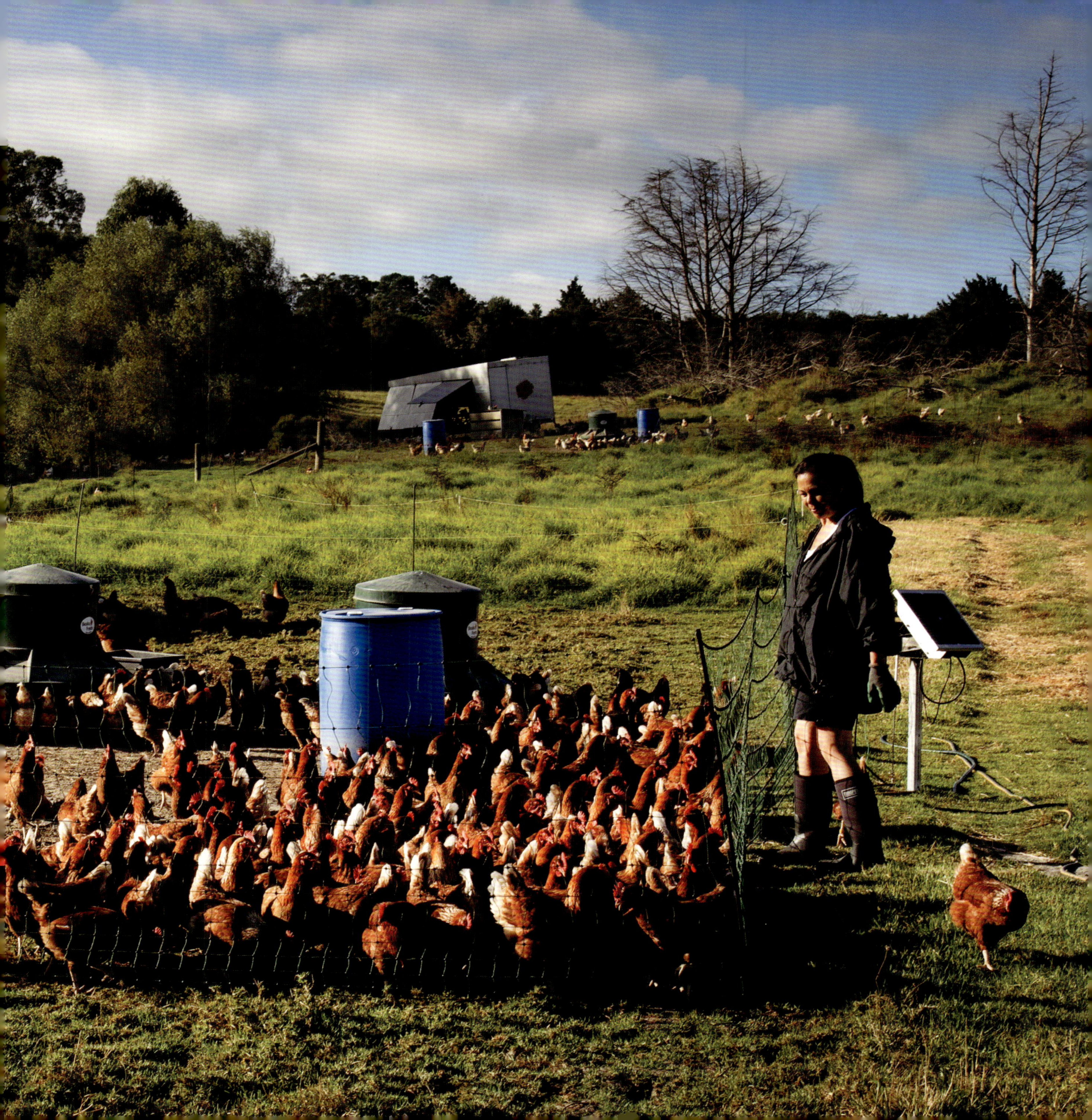

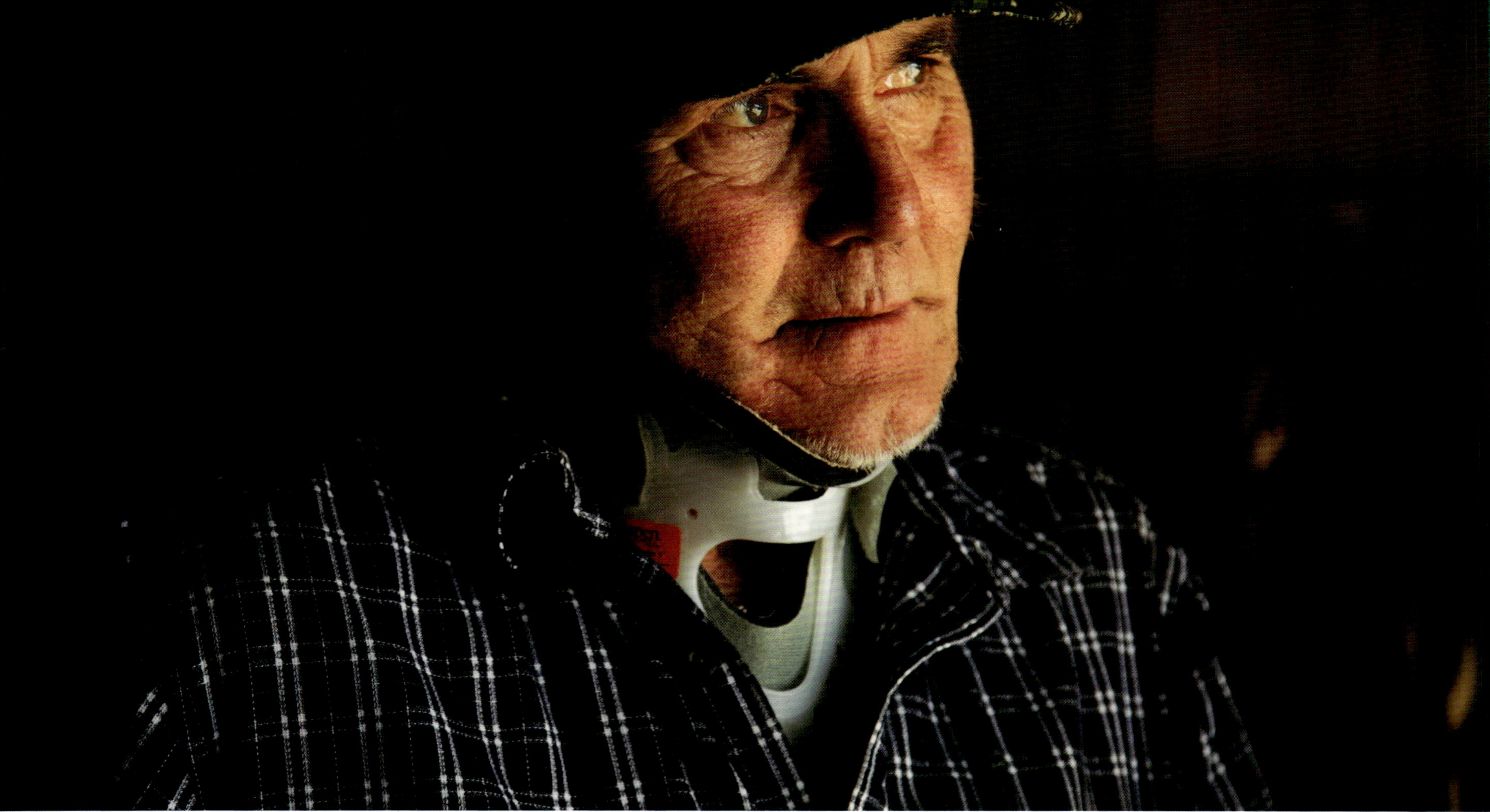

# CHARACTERS

It’s the worst nightmare for a farmer to have a bad accident on the farm and be injured. Young Willow Winters stepped up to run the family farm after his father’s accident in a farm vehicle. Often farming requires multi-generational commitment.

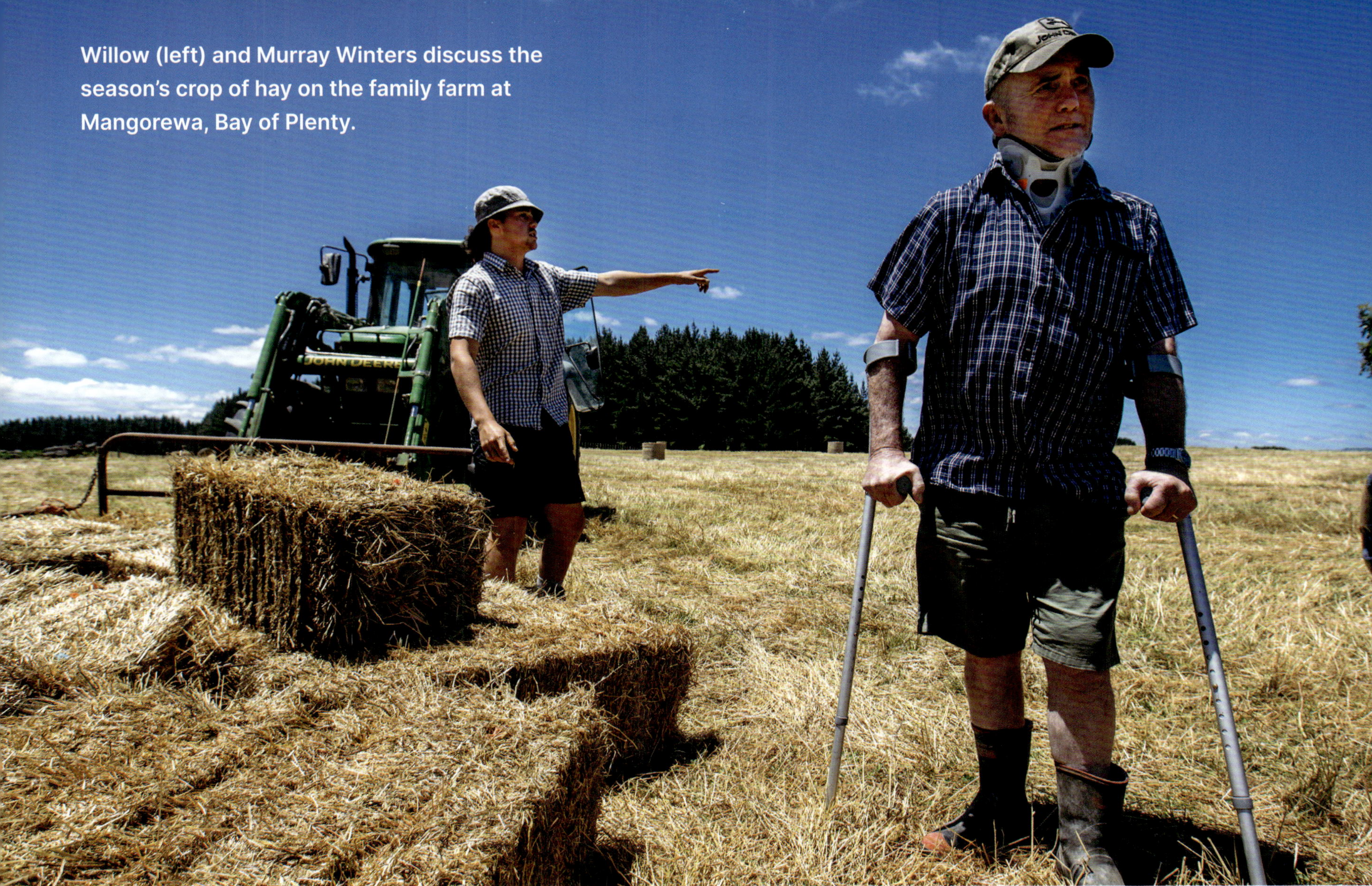


Willow (left) and Murray Winters discuss the season's crop of hay on the family farm at Mangorewa, Bay of Plenty.

## ‘I love working and caring for animals; it's who I am.

'This year has been a bit up and down. It's been rough and I have loved it at some points. It's stressful but I wouldn't change it. I have always loved farming and when they said they needed help I was happy to help. I have been helping my dad since I was five years old. Everything I know is from watching and observing. I learn a lot by watching and being hands on. I am always happy when I am outdoors farming. I have always loved it. I might try something else, but I will always come back to it.
— Willow Winters

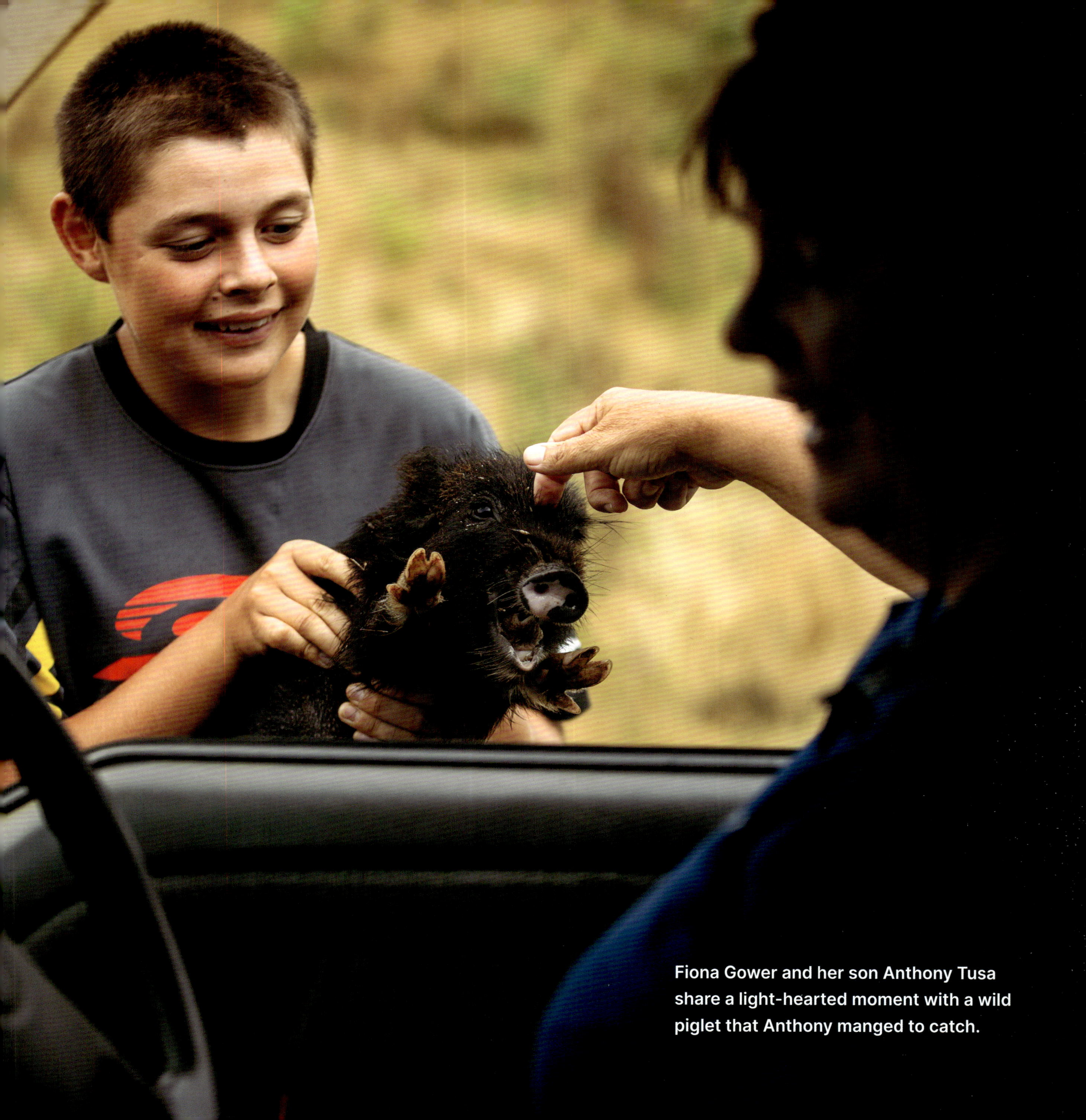

Fiona Gower and her son Anthony Tusa share a light-hearted moment with a wild piglet that Anthony manged to catch.

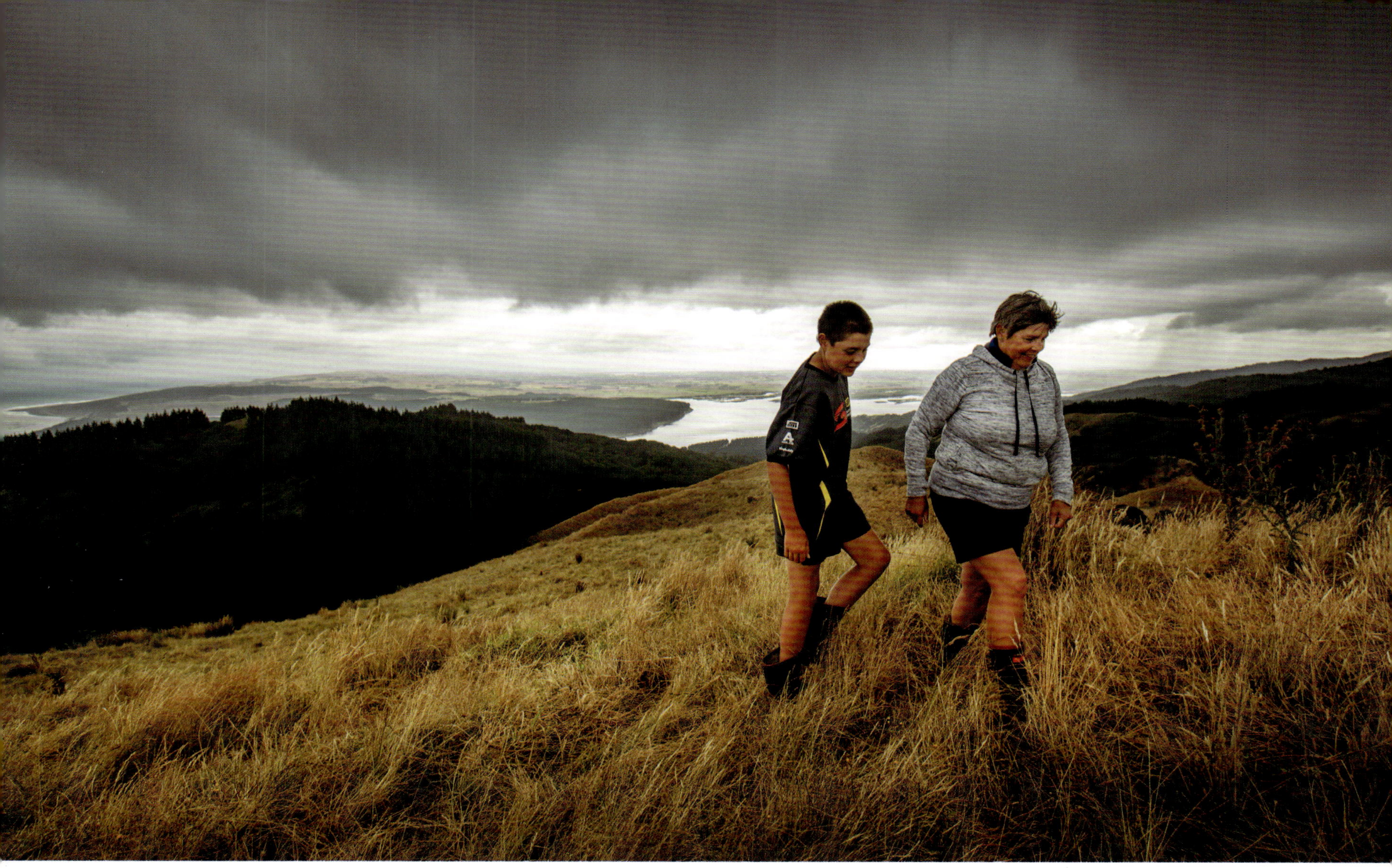

**Fiona Gower was formerly a president of Rural Women New Zealand. She had four years in the top job before returning home to the farm and to do local support work for the community.**

**Fiona Gower and her son Anthony walk the hills on the property they farm at Port Waikato.**

'We are living on a sheep and cattle property of 2500 hectares. It's a coastal property that surrounds the Port Waikato township with its own beautiful piece of coastline. It's hilly, and you can see bush, and we never get tired of the view.

It has been an amazing place to live. There is hunting, fishing and swimming all within easy reach. Our kids have learnt so many life skills living here. They have also learnt to use their initiative and be resilient and resourceful. They learn to not sit and wait for someone to do it, but to get up and do it themselves. They really love the rural life. I would encourage young people to think about taking up a role in the rural sector. Whatever it may be. They will learn so much and the people are amazing.

Women are the decision makers and the influencers right throughout the rural sector. Ignore them at your peril, because we are the ones that can make a huge difference because we see things so differently from our male counterparts. Not only are we doing the work in our rural businesses but we are also running our households, our families and our community.

# SALEYARDS

**CHRIS D'ARCY**, **farming veteran and saleyards manager at Rangiuru Saleyards, Paengaroa, Bay of Plenty:**

'I have always had a passion for farming. Ever since I was a kid. I have never wanted to do anything else.

Sale day is Tuesday. It's a very social thing. We have fabulous tea rooms. The saleyards are an integral part of a rural community. That's why it's so sad with the way things are going. Our stock numbers here are declining and they have been for a long time. With the development of horticulture and forestry.

At the Rangiuru Saleyards we cover a big area and get stock from the East Coast, from Cape Runaway, the odd bit out of Ruatōria, Taupō, all the Kaimai, some out of Coromandel and the odd load from Waikato. We cover a big area.

There will always be livestock sales. People want to see the stock in person, not in a photo. People need to see what the market is. Because the prices on sale day are the market. People need a guide, a barometer and that's what saleyards will do.

Most of my team are not here for the money. They are here for the interaction with the people. I've been lucky and had some interesting times.

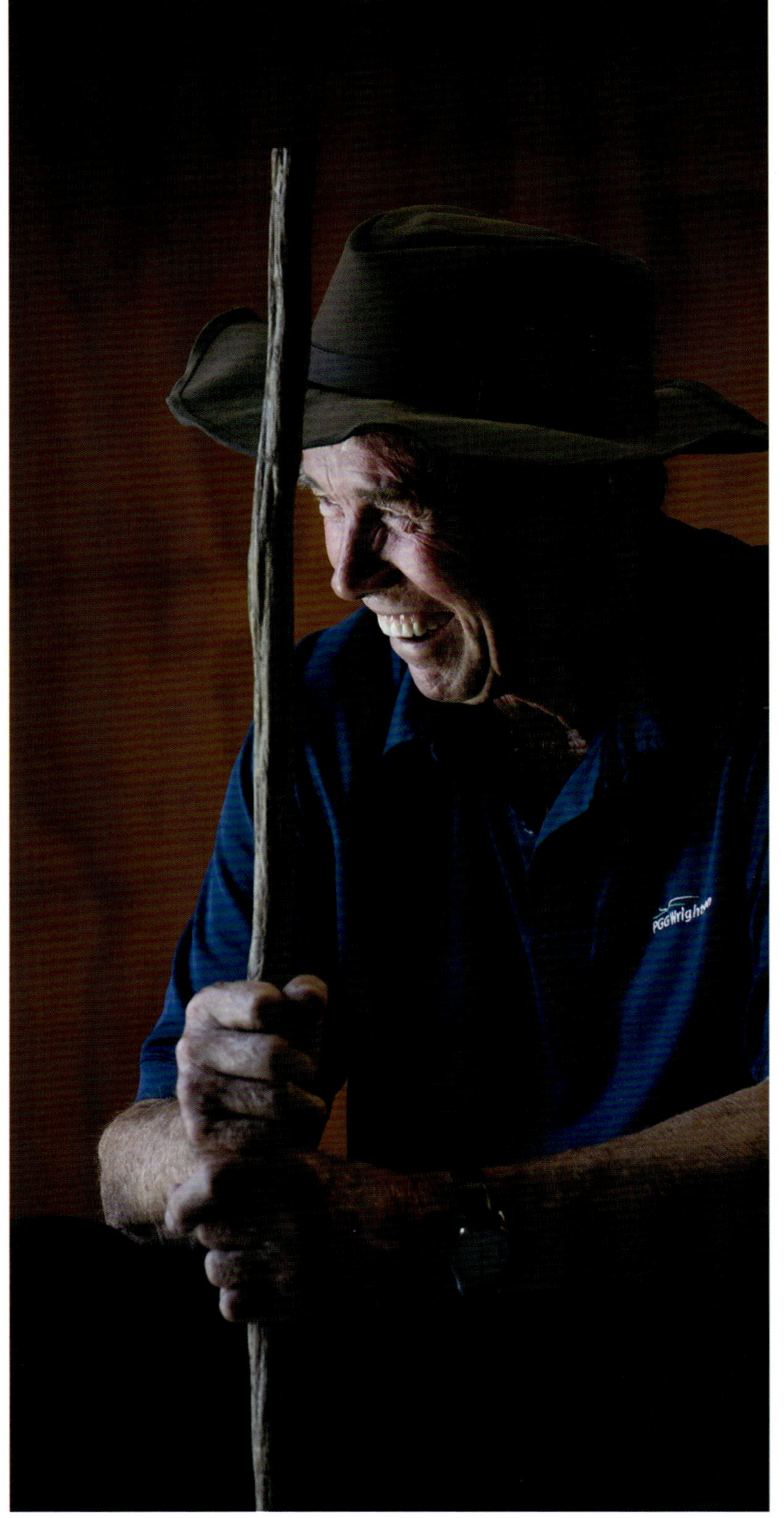

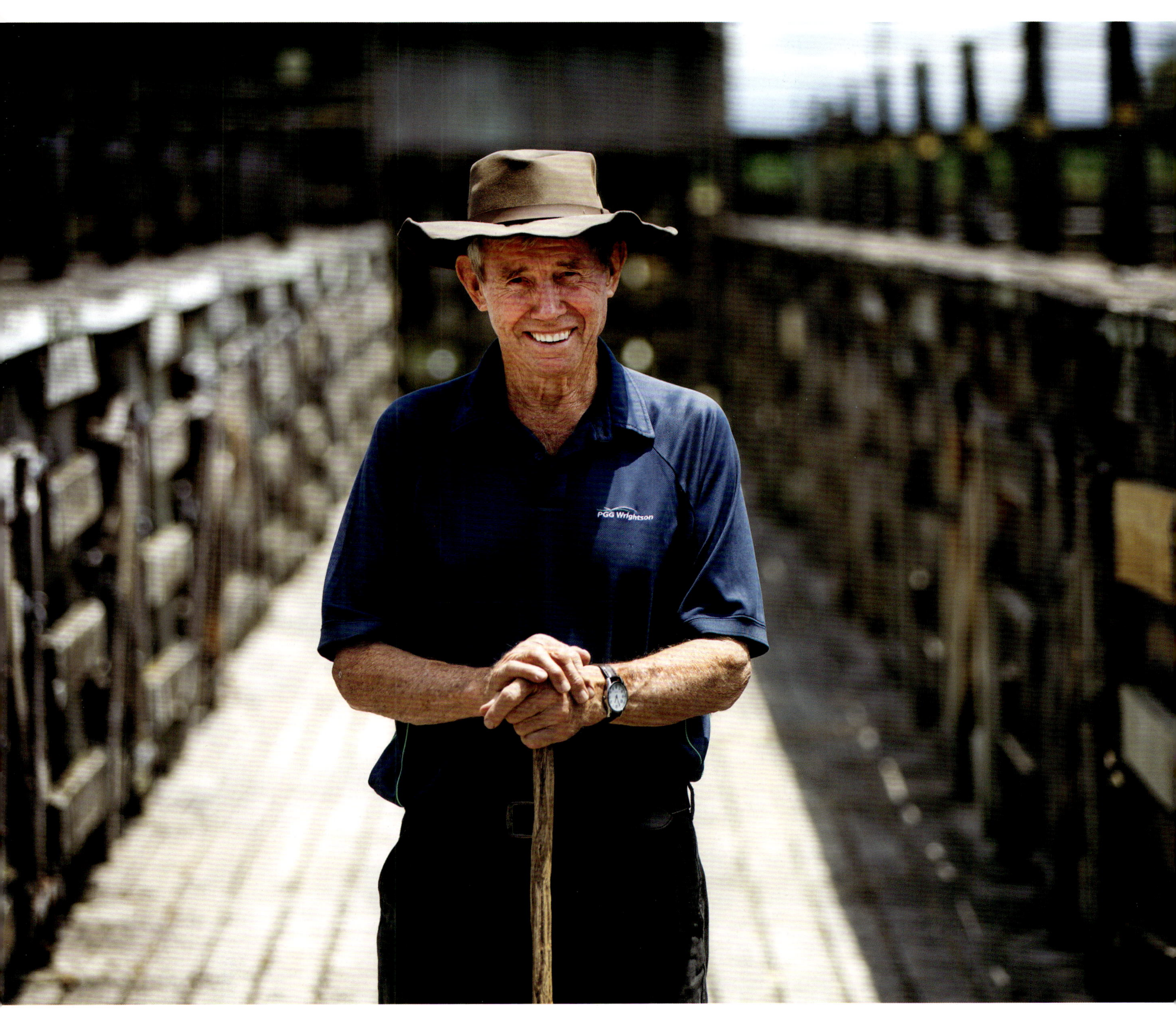


Chris D'Arcy at Rangiuru Saleyards, Bay of Plenty. As a veteran of farming in New Zealand, Chris has lived through the highs and the lows of the industry and has experienced everything from high-country mustering to managing a Hawaiian cattle ranch.

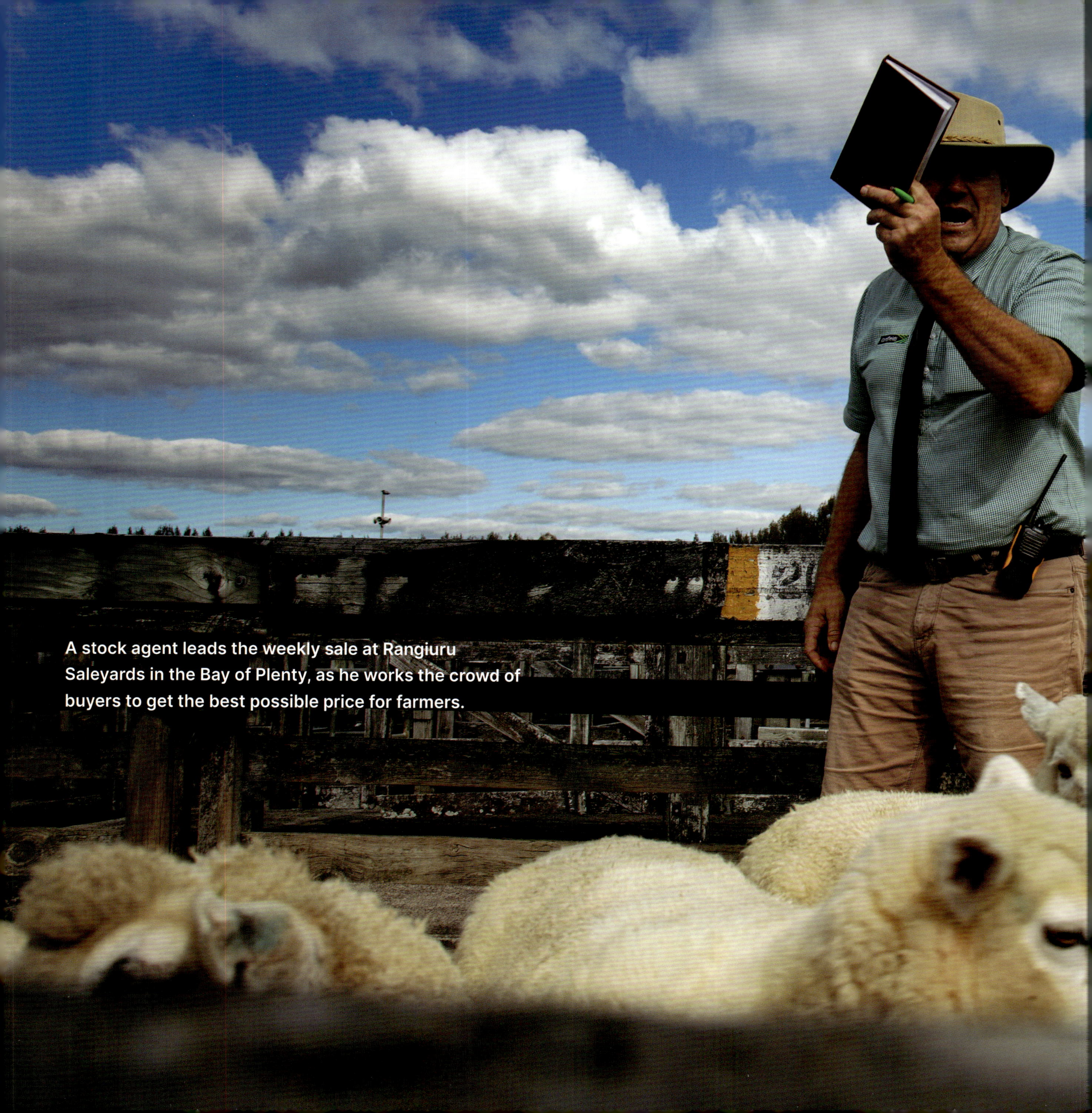

A stock agent leads the weekly sale at Rangiuru Saleyards in the Bay of Plenty, as he works the crowd of buyers to get the best possible price for farmers.

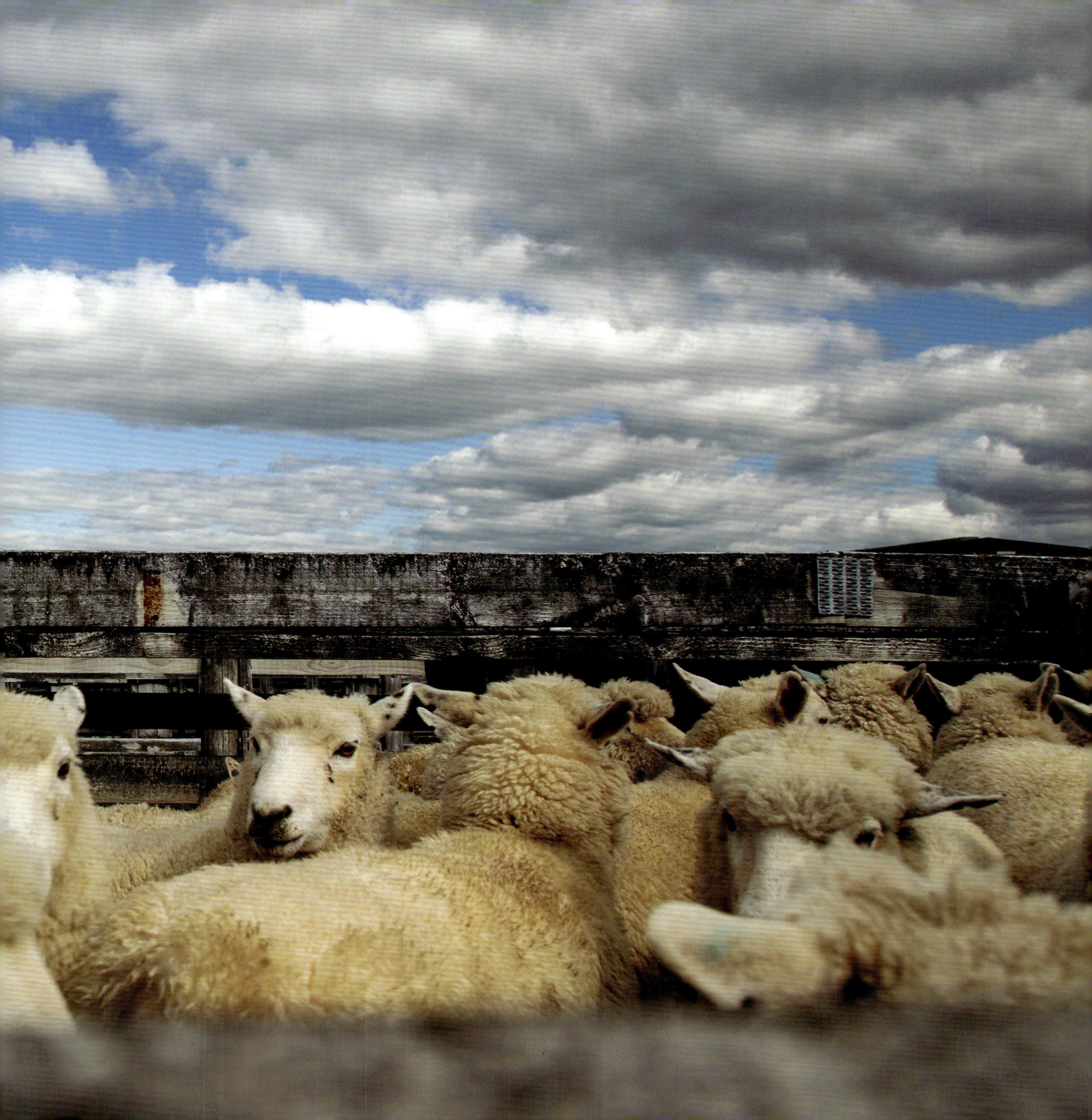

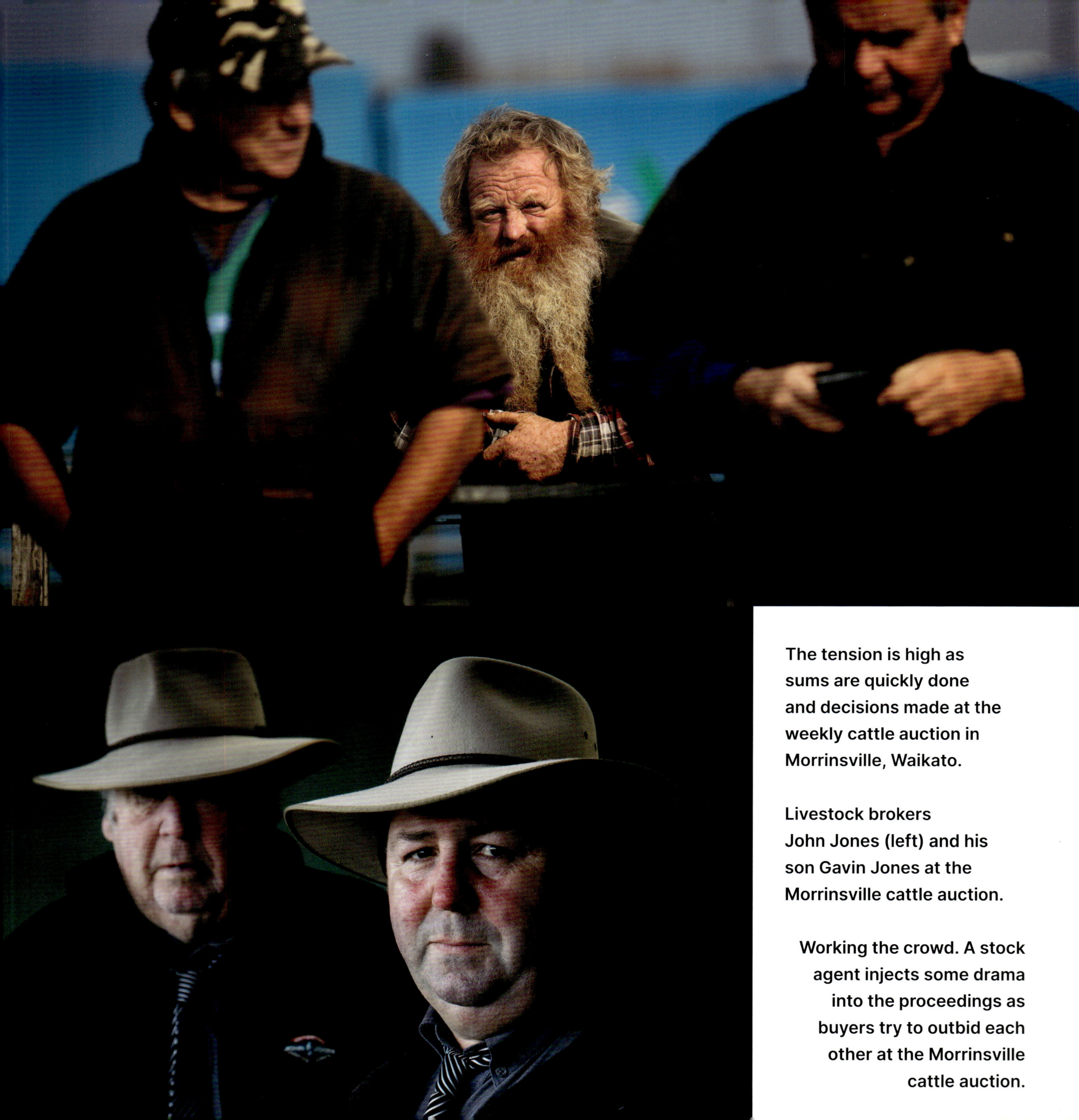

The tension is high as sums are quickly done and decisions made at the weekly cattle auction in Morrinsville, Waikato.

Livestock brokers John Jones (left) and his son Gavin Jones at the Morrinsville cattle auction.

Working the crowd. A stock agent injects some drama into the proceedings as buyers try to outbid each other at the Morrinsville cattle auction.

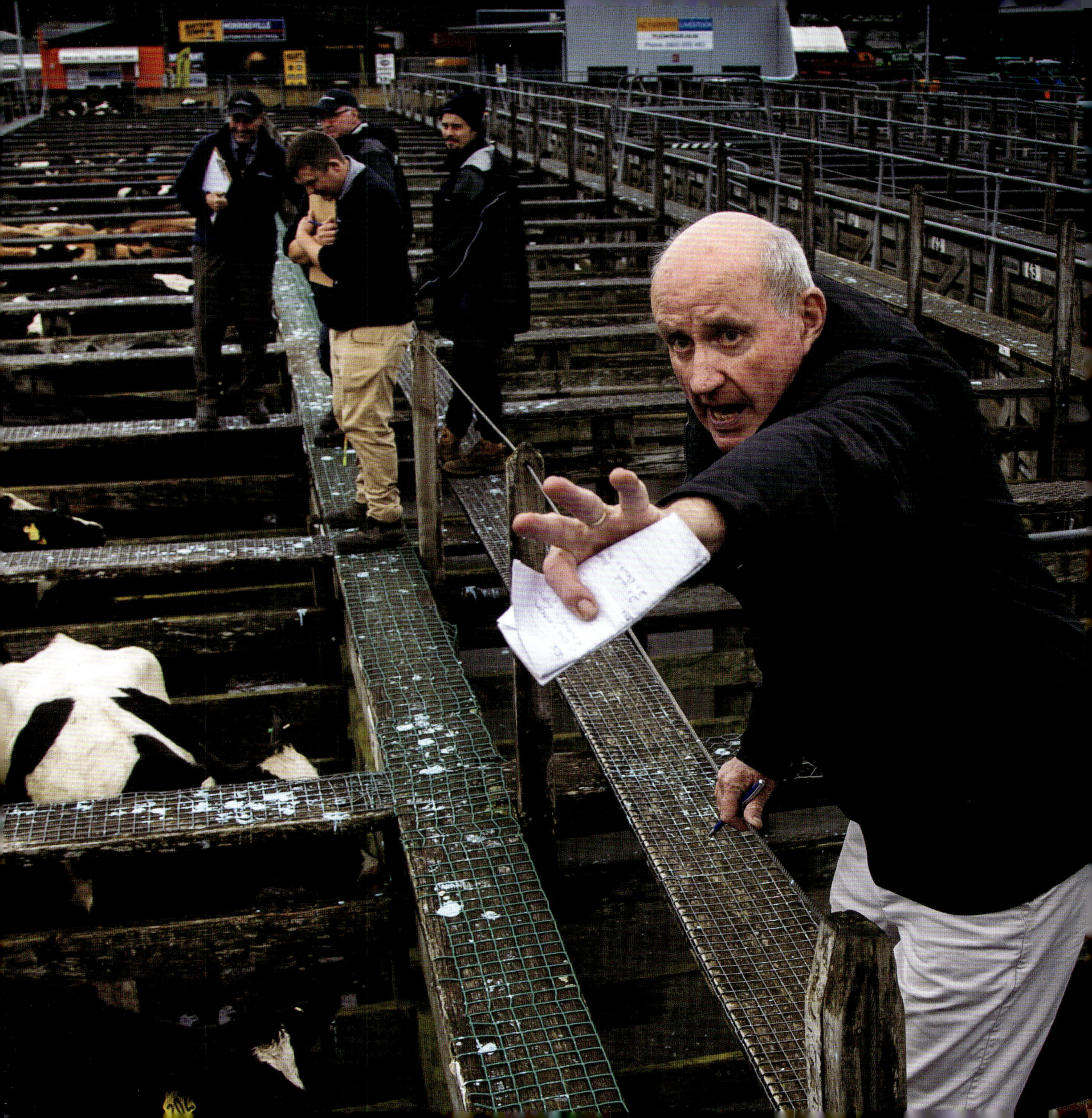
MORRINSVILLE

# A&P SHOW

Agricultural and pastoral (A&P) shows originated in Britain as a way to promote farming pursuits and development, and they were quickly adopted in New Zealand, with the first show held in the Bay of Islands in 1842. By the 1870s some local associations were holding annual shows, and they developed to be a celebrated feature on the rural calendar, drawing people from town and country nationwide. The early shows concentrated on competitions for butter, wool and other animal products as well as for crops such as grass seed, wheat, oats and hops, vegetables including turnips and potatoes, and fruit such as apples. Later, this was expanded to include the likes of shearing, wood chopping and horse riding; farm machinery displays, domestic crafts, sideshows and other entertainment.

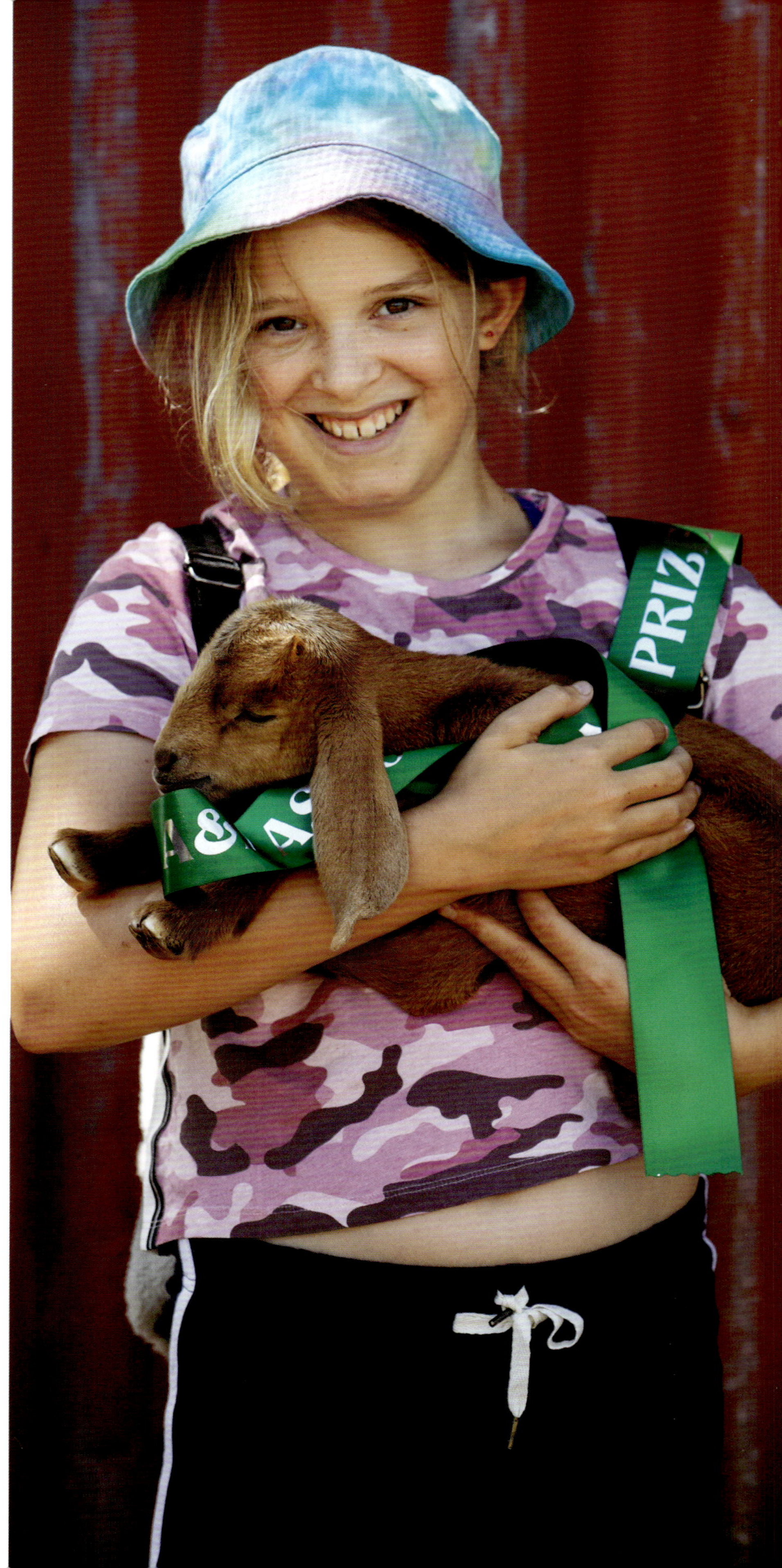

The annual Tākaka A&P Show, Golden Bay.

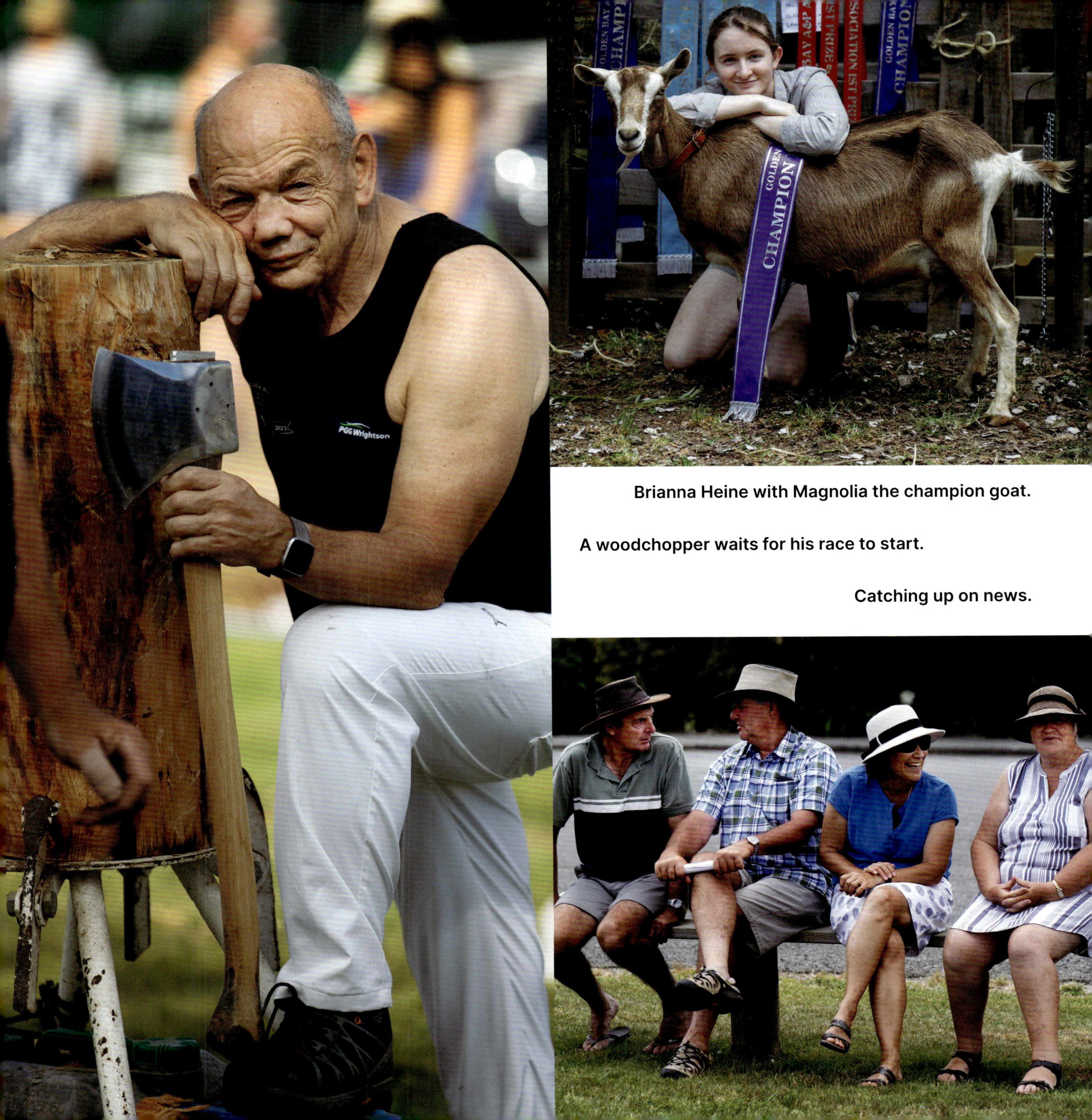


Brianna Heine with Magnolia the champion goat.

A woodchopper waits for his race to start.

Catching up on news.

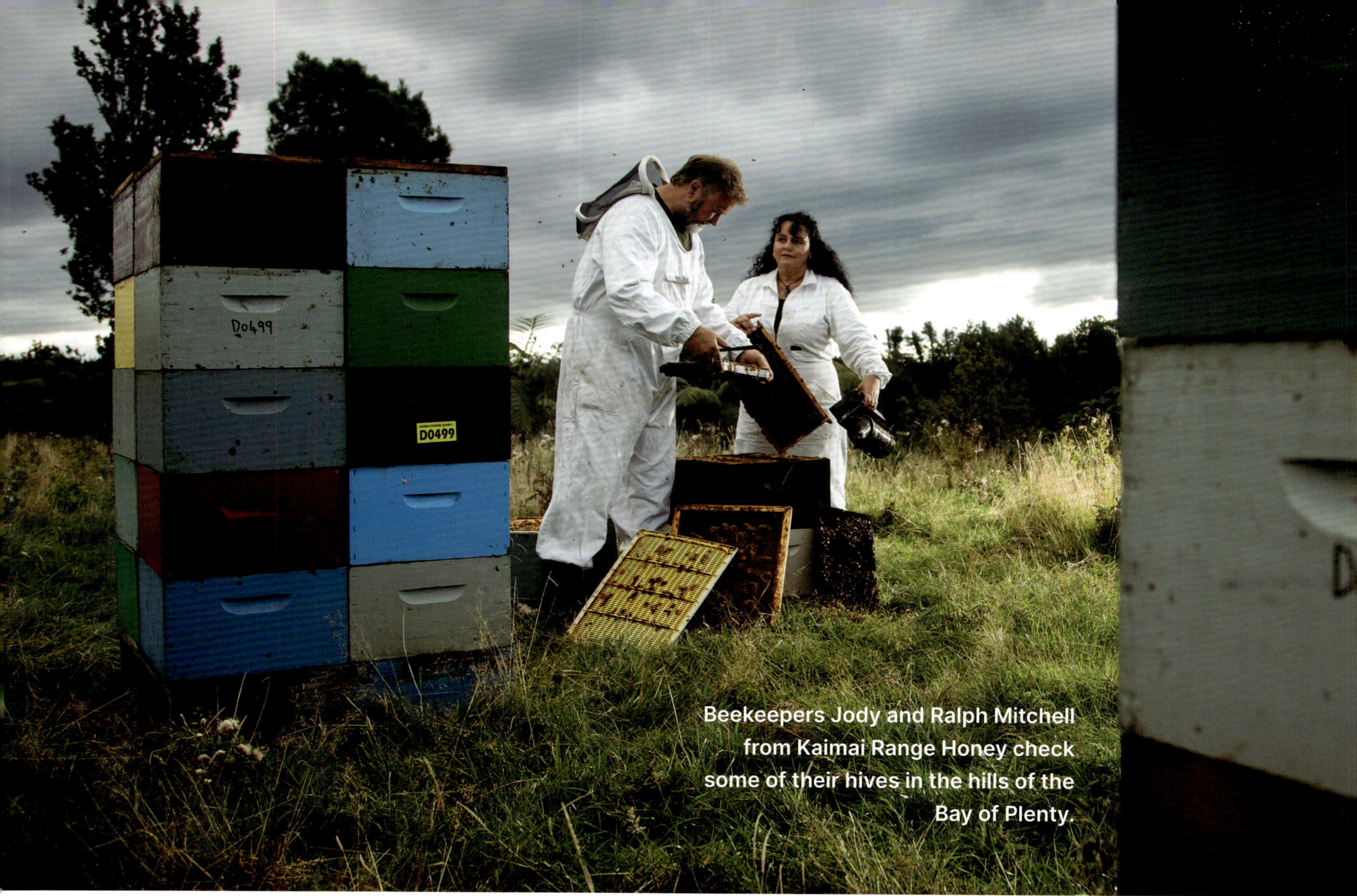


Beekeepers Jody and Ralph Mitchell from Kaimai Range Honey check some of their hives in the hills of the Bay of Plenty.

# BEES

New Zealand's over 20 species of native bees are solitary nesters and don't produce honey, although they are important pollinators. The European honey bee was reportedly first introduced in 1839 in Northland. By the 1860s, Māori were selling honey found in wild hives. The box-framed Langstroth beehive, still in use today, was introduced in the 1870s, facilitating commercial production. As well as providing honey, the bees were important pollinators of introduced fruit trees. Today New Zealand has a thriving beekeeping industry, with over 800,000 hives producing up to 20,000 tonnes of honey each year, with annual exports to over 40 countries earning more than $420 million.

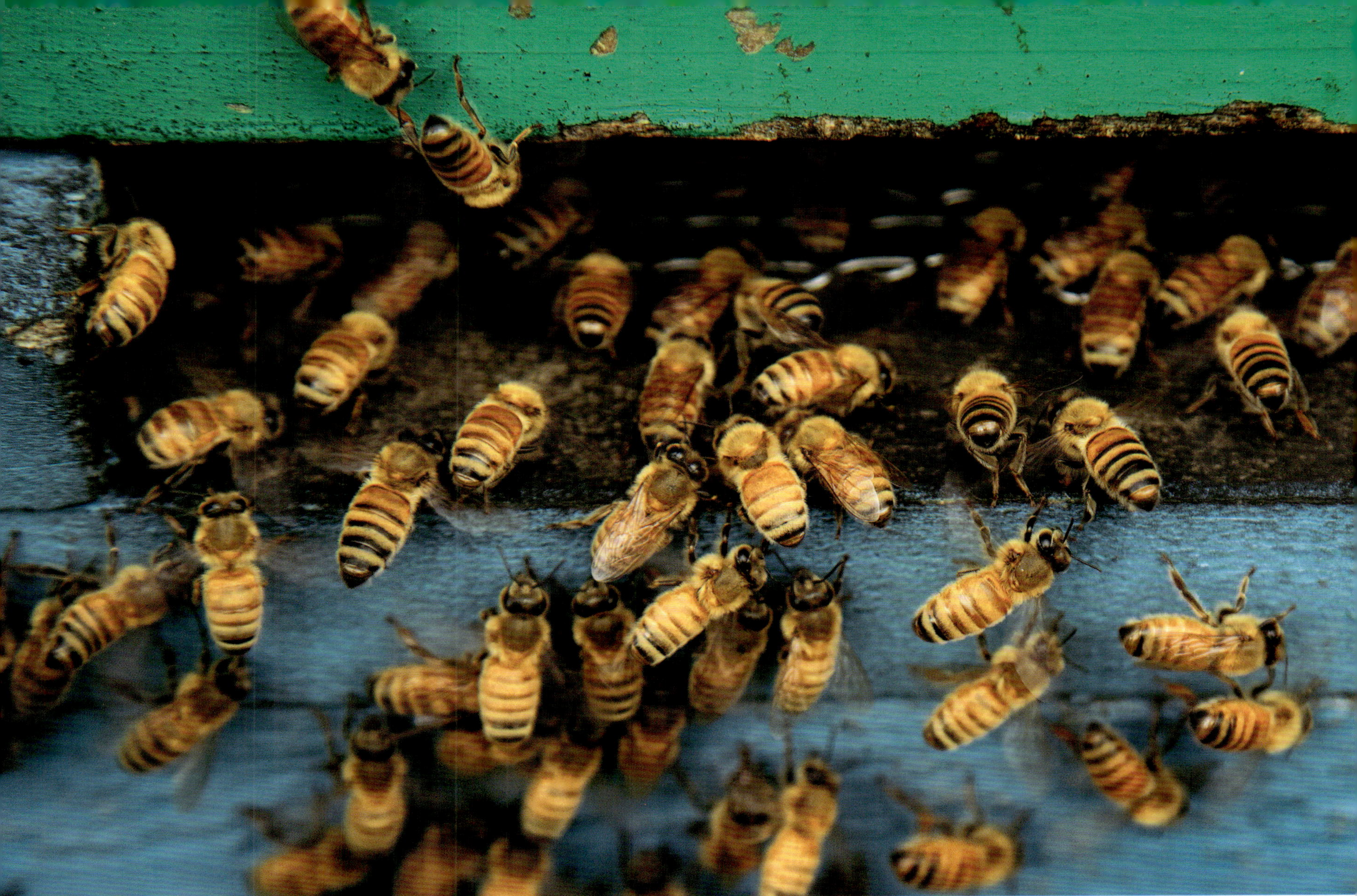

**Jody and Ralph Mitchell, from Kaimai Range Honey:**

'We are a small family business and New Zealand's most awarded honey company. We started in 2003 just with the two of us. Today we are running about 1200 hives. We love our bees.

Mānuka honey is amazing and it's a special honey for New Zealand. We are the guardians of that honey. It is exciting to hear that scientists are doing more studies to establish the many benefits of mānuka honey.

We make sure that the bees are cared for, and we won't have them in areas where there is spraying, this is really important. If we don't look after them, they can't look after us.

***' Without beekeepers there are no bees. This is a big deal when a third of the food that we eat is pollinated by bees.***

We have started to set up an organic part to our business and hope to do more of this in the future.

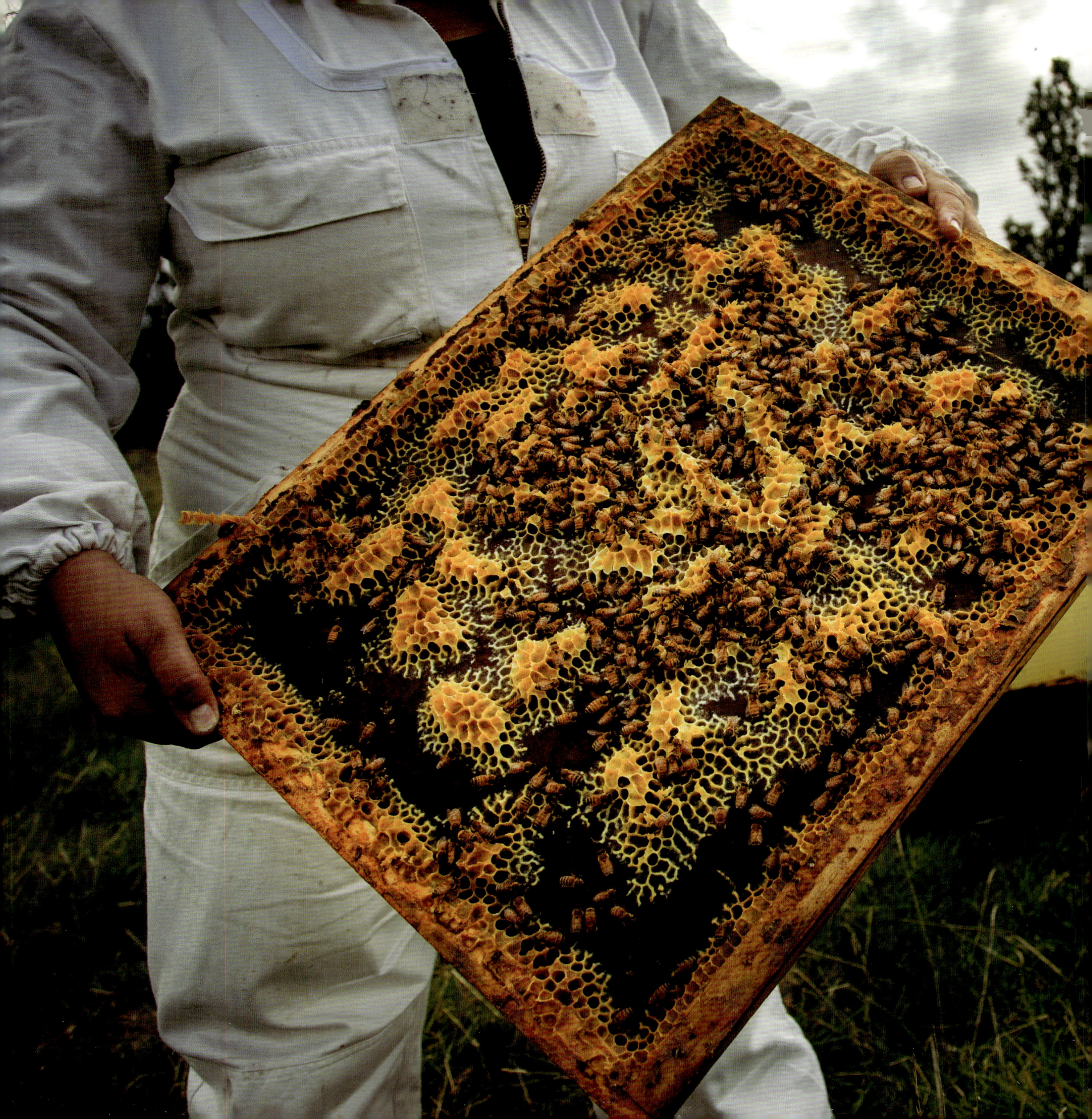

# INDEX


Alexandra 69
Anderson, Larisa and Daryl 49, 50
Auntsfield Estate 87–93

Bay of Plenty maize crops 43–45
Beattie, Rachel 34–35
Been, Tabokaai 93
Bourke, Zara 100
Burrell, Riley 83

Cambridge thoroughbred studs 30–33
Coast Kiwis Organic Orchard 121
Coombridge, Jacob 123
Cowley, Ben 88
Cowley, Luc 87, 88–89
Crater Lake Farm 4–5, 112–19, 124–29
Cromwell apple orchard 122–23

D'Arcy, Chris 5, 140–41

Enckevort, Allan 120
Ensor, Nick 102

Fitzgerald, Anna 101
Forster, Vanessa 32

Galatea 103
Gibbs, Brianna 49, 55
Gibbs, Killian 49, 52, 53
Gibbs, Loren 48–50, 52, 53, 54
Gibson, Bill viii, 1, 2, 3
Glen Lyon Station 2–3, 4, 8–15, 76–78, 110
Good Farm, The 48–57
Good, Michaela 48–50, 55
Gore Bay 101, 102
Gower, Fiona 5, 138–39
Gypsy Day 103

Happy Chicks 130–35
Harrison, Craig 43
Havelock 47

Hayes, Caro 4, 14, 110
Hector Mountains 67, 68
Heine, Brianna 147
Herbert, Skye 79
Herd, David 87

Jones, Gavin 144
Jones, John 144

Kaimai Range Honey 148–50
Keravos pellets 84–85
Kingston 68

Loch Linnhe Station 6–7, 56–67

Mangorewa 137
Matatā 70
McNamee, Chris 60, 67
Mitchell, Jody and Ralph 148–49
Morrinsville cattle auction 144, 145
Motatapu Station 82–83
Marlborough Sounds 4, 18, 19–25, 26
Mt Nicholas Station 16–17, 79

Ohiwa Oyster Farm 27–29
Ōpōtiki 6, 121

Phillips, Terence 74–75
Pooley, Simon 19, 20, 22, 23
Port Waikato 5, 139
Pukekohe 39

Ramaka, Rangi 82
Rangiuru Saleyards 140–43
Ranworth Farm 71
Rogers, Jonty 14
Rogers, Pippa 12–13
Rolleston 100

Sands, Holly 117, 118, 128
Sands, Paddy 5, 114–19, 124–25

Sands, Timothy 118
Scott, Karen 59, 62
Scott, Murray 59, 62
Scott, Sophie 59, 63, 64
Smith, Kelly 6–7, 61

Taieri Uplands 34–35
Tākaka A&P Show 146–47
Taranaki, Mt 102
Tarawera, Mt 112–13, 118
Te Ākau 2, 71–73, 75
Te Aroha dairy farm 4, 94–99
Turipa, Tip 76
Tusa, Anthony 5, 138, 139

Vaughan, Jessie 101
Veitch, Jenny 118, 125–27, 129

Waimai Valley 72–73, 75
Waiuku 36, 38, 40
Walker, Jeannie 130–31, 133, 134–35
Walker, Richard 131, 133
Webb, Bill 43, 45
Welch Shearing 75
White, Catriona (Trina) 6, 121
White, Lachlan (Lochie) 6, 121
White, Letisha 6, 121
White, Mark 6, 121
White, Ruby 6, 94, 96, 99
White, Tania 4, 6, 94, 95–99
Wigley, Johnny 4, 9, 14, 15
Williams, Logan 84–85
Winters, Murray 136–37
Winters, Willow 136–37

Yorke, Rick 27, 28, 29
Young, Jackie 36, 37, 38
Young, Jamie 37, 38

Zespri (formerly New Zealand Kiwifruit Marketing Board) 120

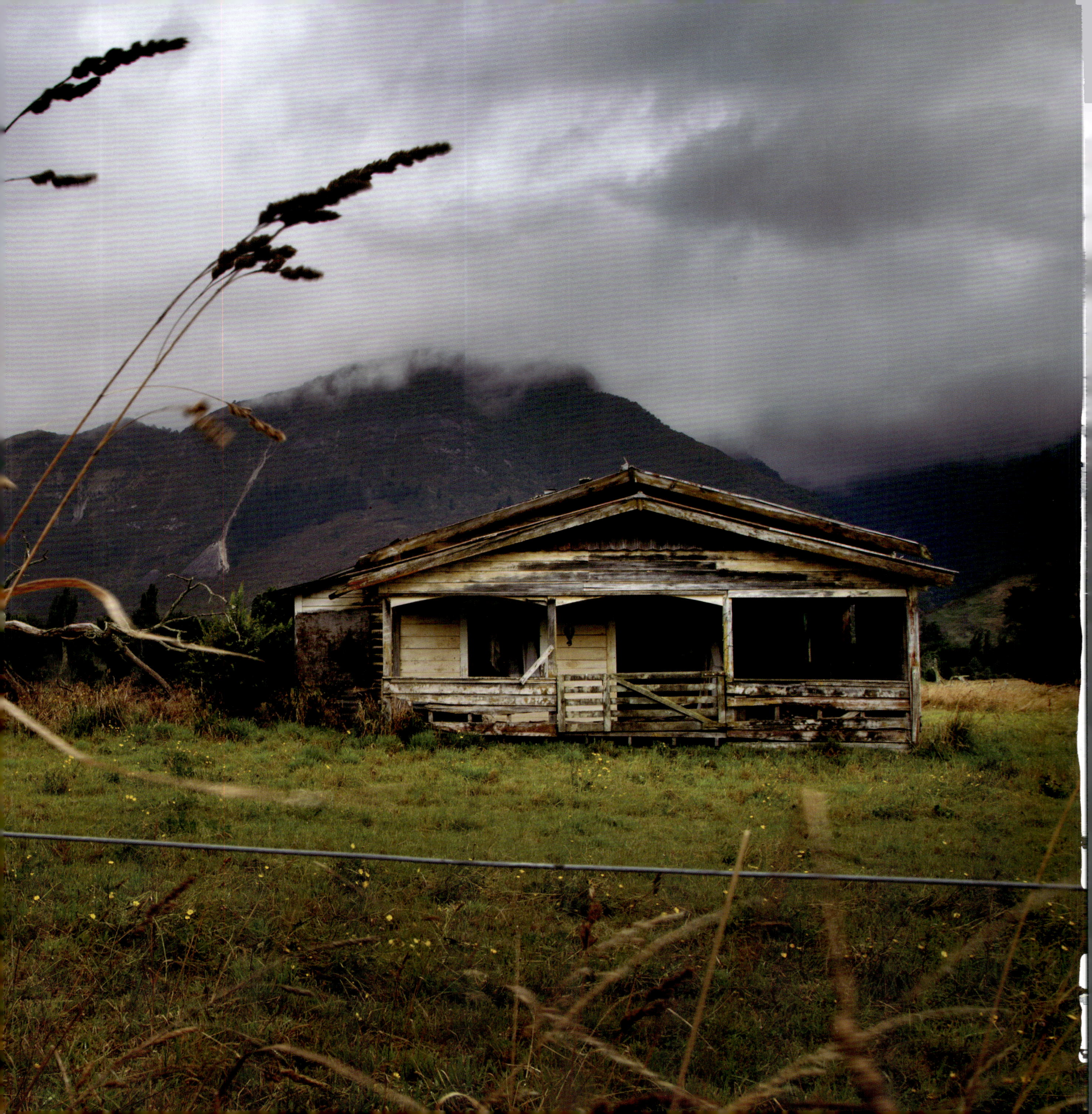

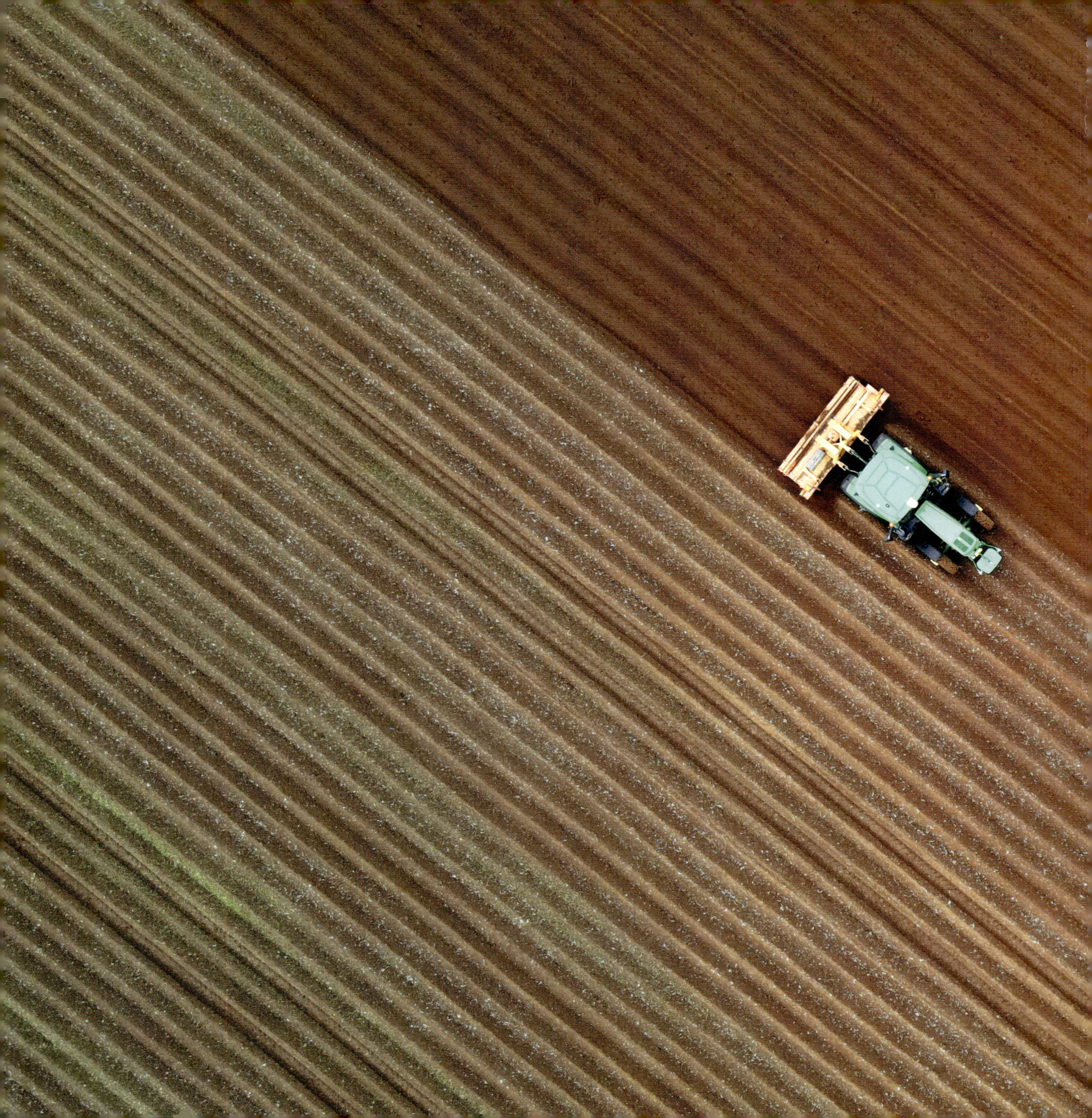